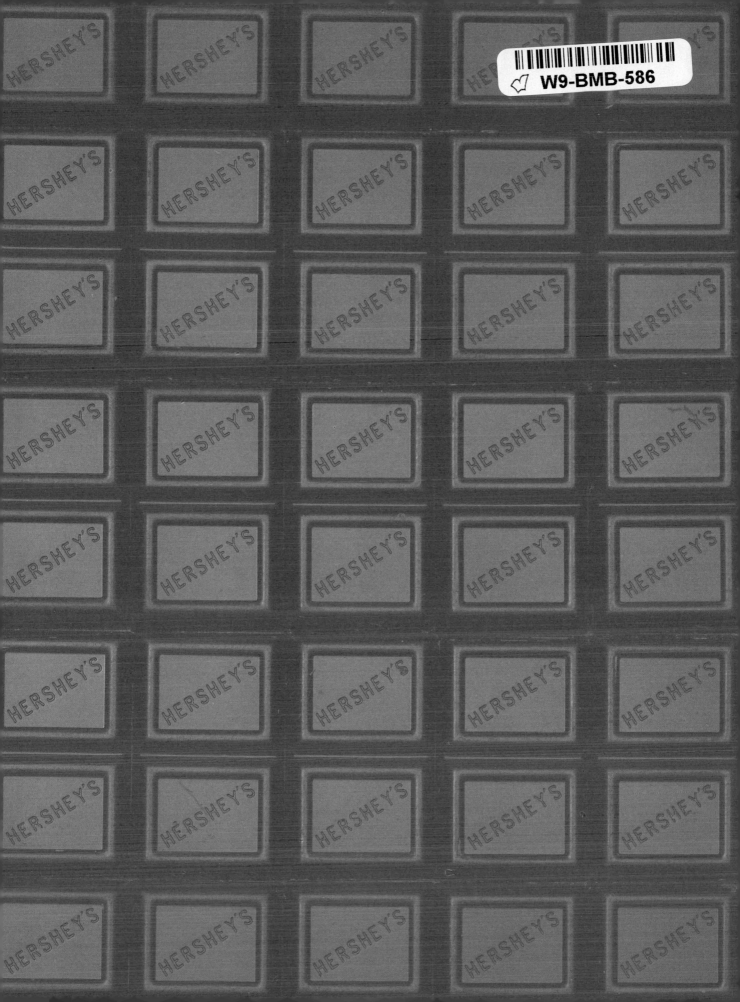

HERSHEY'S
Chocolate Treasury

GOLDEN PRESS • NEW YORK
Western Publishing Company, Inc.
Racine, Wisconsin

Art Director: Remo Cosentino
Designer: Diane Wagner
Photographer: Gordon E. Smith
(except pages 15, 55 and 179)
All recipes developed and tested in the HERSHEY Test Kitchens.

Produced in the U.S.A. by Western Publishing Company, Inc.
Published by Golden Press, New York, New York.
Library of Congress Catalog Card Number: 84-081439

Golden® and Golden Press® are trademarks of Western Publishing Company, Inc.
ISBN 0-307-49274-5

Contents

Preface

Say "chocolate." Inevitably, eyes brighten, hearts beat a little faster, mouths water in anticipation. Say "chocolate" and just as inevitably the word that next springs to mind is Hershey.

The connection is hardly recent. Chocolate and Hershey have been virtually synonymous since the turn of the century, when Milton Hershey built his chocolate factory amid the rich dairylands of Pennsylvania's Lebanon Valley. It's an association that's even stronger today, and one that we're very proud of.

Over the years, thousands upon thousands of chocolate recipes have been developed and tested in the Hershey Test Kitchens. The following pages feature more than 325 of the recipes that we deem to be the very best. Many of them will doubtless remind you of your favorite childhood chocolate treats; others will introduce you to imaginative new ways to enjoy chocolate and cocoa in all their delicious forms.

We hope you will enjoy browsing through the chapters, feasting on the photographs and sampling the wide variety of recipes offered for every taste and for every occasion.

Hershey's Chocolate Treasury was inspired by the ever-growing appreciation for chocolate among Americans of all ages—and it is to you, the American chocolate lover, that we dedicate this special collection.

The Hershey Story

What goes on in the big factory on Chocolate Avenue in Hershey, Pennsylvania, could never be kept a secret. Come anywhere near and the first thing a visitor notices is the sweet chocolate smell in the air. Even the parade of tall street lamps lining the avenue are shaped like giant *Hershey's Kisses™* — a light-hearted reminder that this is the town that chocolate built.

Could Milton Hershey, at 19, hand-wrapping "penny candy" with the help of his mother and aunt, possibly foresee that one day the company he founded would be the world's leading producer of chocolate and cocoa? Very possibly! Because even as a young man he had the vision, the energy and the entrepreneurial spirit to make things happen. His is the ultimate rags to riches story — the American Dream come true.

Born in 1857 in an old Pennsylvania farmhouse built by his great-grandfather, Milton Hershey was to spend most of his adult life within a few miles of his first home. His parents provided him with what education they could, but when Hershey was barely 14, it was decided that it was time he "learned a trade."

The young Hershey was apprenticed first to a nearby printer, then to a confectioner in Lancaster. Right from the start he enjoyed candy-making, so much so that after four years, and anxious to be his own boss, he started his own small candy business in Philadelphia. Despite his best efforts, he couldn't make a go of it. But he was determined. Again he struck out on his own: Chicago, New Orleans, New York. Although the public liked Hershey's candies — particularly the chewy caramels — his businesses failed. He was almost 30 years old when he returned to Lancaster and no closer to success than he was the day he'd left.

This time, in Lancaster, Hershey — and his caramels — made it. From peddling the candies door-to-door, to selling them from a pushcart, to mail order, to national distribution and even to international sales, Milton Hershey's caramel business prospered.

It wasn't until 1893 that Hershey's fascination with chocolate began. At the World's Exposition in Chicago he was intrigued by new German machinery that turned cocoa beans into chocolate candy — first roasting, hulling and grinding, then mixing and molding. Hershey bought the machines, shipped them to his Lancaster factory and began making candy from chocolate as well as caramel.

The real turning point in his life came at the start of the new century when Hershey, now 43 years old and married to the beautiful Catherine Sweeney, sold his thriving caramel business to his major competitor for $1 million. Significantly, he insisted on retaining his chocolate machinery and the right to make chocolate. Intuition told him that the future was in inexpensive, mass-produced chocolate candy. And he bet his entire million on it.

Hershey had already perfected his own formula for the milk chocolate bar in 1894. Now he could concentrate all his efforts on producing this candy at a low price so that it would be enjoyed by all. His success was swift and astounding.

Although the familiar *Hershey* Bar was the company's mainstay, it wasn't long before other chocolate products were developed — cocoa and baking chocolate among them. The still-growing family of specialty candies began in 1907, with the introduction of *Hershey's Kisses*.

Meanwhile, in 1903, Hershey broke ground for his new chocolate factory on a familiar site — the nearby Derry Church pastures of his boyhood. On adjacent fields he began to build not a typical "factory town," but a "people town" — broad, tree-lined avenues, quiet residential areas of individually designed homes, modern schools, churches, stores, a bank, park, theater and even a trolley line to transport workers and their families. Within a few short years, Hershey, Pennsylvania, was to become a thriving community and the Chocolate Capital of the World.

Milton Hershey's success in the chocolate business is, of course, legend. What is not as well known was his personal commitment to the community he had built and his desire to share his good fortune with that community. From the very beginning, the more he achieved, the more he gave back.

A notable example is the Milton Hershey School, founded by Hershey and his wife in 1909 for boys who had lost one or both parents. His purpose, as explained by his biographers, was to provide "the kind of good schooling and childhood security that he could never recover for himself."

Although Milton Hershey died in 1945 at the age of 88, he saw to it early on that his school would survive him. With no immediate heirs of his own, the boys at the school became Hershey's "sons," and nine years after its founding, the school actually became the owner of the Hershey Chocolate Company. Today, more than half the stock of the multi-billion dollar Hershey Foods Corporation is owned by the Milton Hershey School Trust, with the school its sole beneficiary.

The school's enrollment, which totaled four boys in its first year, has grown to more than 1200 and now includes both boys and girls, in grades from kindergarten through high school. Eligibility for admission still hinges on lack of "adequate care from one or both natural parents," and *all* costs are borne by the school: education, food, clothing, health services and lodging. Dotting the 10,000-acre campus are 86 comfortable homes, where groups of children live as a family with their house parents.

Success has come to many Hershey graduates, but three alumni in particular offer striking testimony to the excellence of the school's education: John M. Aichele, class of '39, is President of the Milton Hershey School, Kenneth V. Hatt, class of '41, is President and Chief Operating Officer of Hershey Entertainment and Resort Company and William E. C. Dearden, class of '40, is Chairman of the Board of Hershey Foods Corporation.

The company that Dearden oversees today has grown ten-fold since his student days. And although still primarily famous for chocolate, Hershey Foods Corporation has branched out into other areas, emerging as a major diversified food company.

A major force behind Hershey's growth has been the Hershey Foods Technical Center, which stands on its own seven-acre site near the factory. Its pilot plant and complete state-of-the-art laboratory facilities are devoted to product research and scientific studies in microbiology, chemistry and nutrition.

Here, too, are the Hershey Test Kitchens, staffed by experienced home economists. As important members of the researcher-scientist-technologist team, they help Hershey identify consumer needs and meet the ever-growing demand for new products to satisfy those needs. The recipes featured in *Hershey's Chocolate Treasury* attest to their fine work.

Without a doubt, the success of the Hershey Foods Corporation reflects the entire organization's commitment to research, to quality control and to the development of superior products at a fair price. And all these are just part of the legacy left by founder Milton S. Hershey, the rarest of men: both a dreamer and a builder.

All About Chocolate

Chocolate—The Beginnings

An "original American," the cacao bean was one of the treasures Columbus brought back from the New World. But neither he nor his patrons, Ferdinand and Isabella of Spain, understood its potential pleasures. It took Cortez, while conquering Mexico for Spain, to realize that there must be something very special about this *chocoatl* if Emperor Montezuma and his Aztec court sipped it from golden goblets.

Golden goblets notwithstanding, the rich chocolate liquid was not to Spanish tastes until someone added a bit of sugar, a drop or so of vanilla, heated the mixture and topped it with a cinnamon stick. With that, chocolate became the "in" drink of the day in Spain. Eventually chocolate fever spread to Italy, then to France and Holland and finally to England. There its popularity was so great that there were actually Chocolate Houses, where meeting, greeting and sipping were the order of the day.

Chocolate, however, was still considered exotic. It was also quite expensive, as the cacao beans were still grown, picked and processed much as they had been in Cortez's time. These lengthy and crude methods were put to rest by the Industrial Revolution. The chocolate itself also became finer and smoother. And, perhaps, the biggest step toward chocolate as we know it today was taken in Switzerland in the 1800's, when Daniel Peter added milk to basic chocolate. He also developed the formula for making the first solid chocolate. Chocolate finally sailed back across the Atlantic, and it was Milton S. Hershey who made it a true All-American. From then on, there was no stopping the Chocolate Revolution.

As you can see for yourself every day, from supermarket shelves to the smallest candy stand, chocolate is the world's most favored flavor . . . and with good reason.

Chocolate Is Chocolate…or Is It?

Purists would limit the use of the word "chocolate" to just two forms: solid unsweetened chocolate or its liquid form, chocolate liquor. They're right, of course. But the rest of the world is happily willing to accept a much broader definition. Here's a little background on chocolate in its various phases and forms:

Cacao (Cocoa) Beans are the starting point. They are the fruit of the cacao tree, which grows in a very limited climate zone—only 20 degrees north and south of the Equator—and mainly in West Africa and Latin America.

Cacao Nibs are the "meat" of the beans. The beans are cleaned and then roasted at carefully controlled temperatures to bring out their full flavor and aroma. When the outer shells are removed, the nibs are ready to go on to greater things. (They contain more than 50% cocoa butter, and that's rich treasure indeed.)

Chocolate Liquor is what makes all real chocolate products possible. The nibs are ground by a process that generates enough heat to liquefy the cocoa butter, thus creating the liquor. (The term "liquor" is used in its true sense, that of liquid essence—it has nothing to do with alcohol.)

Cocoa Butter is the vegetable fat that's extracted when the chocolate liquor is "pressed" under high pressure. This butter has a distinctive melting quality that gives chocolate products their unique texture.

Cocoa Powder made by the American process (such as *Hershey's Cocoa)* is the marvelous by-product that remains after most of the cocoa butter has been extracted from the liquor. It has no additives and no preservatives, so it's 100% pure. And because most of the cocoa butter has been removed, it has the lowest fat content of any chocolate product. Stored in a tightly closed container, cocoa will retain its freshness and quality almost indefinitely—and without refrigeration.

Dutch-Process Cocoa Powder is made from chocolate liquor that has been treated with an alkali agent. This makes a darker powder, with a flavor that differs from that of American-process cocoa.

Bitter Chocolate, commonly referred to as unsweetened, baking or cooking chocolate, is chocolate *au naturel.* It is pure chocolate liquor, cooled and molded, usually in blocks.

Semi-Sweet Chocolate is a combination of chocolate liquor with added cocoa butter and sugar. To qualify for this term, the product must contain at least 35% chocolate liquor. Available in bars, this form is more popularly available in chips.

Sweet (Dark) Chocolate combines the same ingredients as semi-sweet, but the balance is different. This form must contain at least 15% chocolate liquor, but it has a higher sugar level.

Milk Chocolate also uses the same ingredients but with the addition of milk or cream. At least 10% chocolate liquor is required in milk chocolate products.

White Chocolate, also called confectioners' chocolate, is known in the chocolate industry as compound chocolate. It isn't really chocolate at all. Most or all of the cocoa butter has been removed and replaced by another vegetable fat, and it contains no chocolate liquor. Also called confectioners' coating, it is available in a range of colors, from dark to white and even pastels.

Chocolate-Flavored is the term applied to food products that derive their flavor from cocoa and/or chocolate liquor but do not contain a sufficient quantity of these ingredients to meet the government's definition of "true" chocolate. Chocolate-flavored syrups, which combine chocolate liquor or cocoa, sugar, water, salt and sometimes other flavorings, are among the products in this category.

Artificial Chocolate is a product of the chemical industry, not chocolate-makers. Such products contain no ingredients derived from the cacao bean—and, at the extreme, contain no sugar or milk.

Storing Chocolate

Chocolate products will stay fresh for well over a year if stored in a cool, dry place (65°–70°F). It's a good idea to keep an eye on the temperature and humidity.

Temperatures above 78°F will cause chocolate to melt. The cocoa butter then rises to the surface and forms a grayish discoloration called "cocoa butter bloom." Condensation on milk or semi-sweet chocolate may cause the sugar to dissolve and rise to the surface as "sugar bloom." Neither "bloom" affects the quality or flavor of chocolate and, once melted, the chocolate will regain its original color. Thus, it's a good idea to keep chocolate (well wrapped, of course) in as cool a place as possible during prolonged periods of heat and high humidity.

Melting Chocolate

Using a Double Boiler: This is the preferred method for melting all types of chocolate, avoiding both scorching and the formation of steam droplets. Simply place the chocolate in the top of a double boiler over hot, not boiling, water.

Using Direct Heat: Because chocolate scorches so easily, this method is not strongly recommended. There are three "musts": very low heat; a heavy saucepan; constant stirring.

Using a Microwave Oven: See page 254 for detailed directions.

For Small Amounts: If melting less than 2 ounces, place in a small heatproof cup and place in a shallow pan with a small amount of warm water; stir until smooth. (Or use a microwave oven.)

Tips from the Experts
● Wash and dry the melting utensil thoroughly after each use. Any residue will affect the taste of chocolate.
● A wet utensil or the condensation of steam droplets can cause chocolate to get stiff and grainy. Don't panic. As an emergency measure, simply stir in 1 teaspoon solid vegetable shortening (not butter) for every 2 ounces of chocolate.
● Stir the melting chocolate periodically with a wire whisk to help blending and discourage scorching.
● Break chocolate into 1-inch pieces to speed the melting process.

Using Cocoa Instead of Chocolate

Cocoa is so convenient to use that many cooks use it as a substitute for chocolate in their favorite recipes. Here's an easy formula:

For unsweetened baking chocolate: 3 level tablespoons cocoa plus 1 tablespoon shortening (liquid or solid) equals 1 block (1 ounce).

For premelted unsweetened chocolate: 3 tablespoons cocoa plus 1 tablespoon oil or melted shortening equals 1 envelope (1 ounce).

For semi-sweet chocolate: 6 tablespoons cocoa plus 7 tablespoons sugar plus ¼ cup shortening equals one 6-ounce package (1 cup) semi-sweet chocolate chips or 6 blocks (1 ounce each) semi-sweet chocolate.

For sweet baking chocolate: 3 tablespoons cocoa plus 4½ tablespoons sugar plus 2⅔ tablespoons shortening equals 1 bar (4 ounces).

For Recipe Success

All of the recipes in this book were developed and tested in the Hershey Test Kitchens with Hershey products. A number of manufacturers, both foreign and domestic, make similar products. We cannot guarantee the same results if you substitute those of another manufacturer.

When the recipe calls for...	Use...
unsweetened cocoa	HERSHEY'S Cocoa
unsweetened baking chocolate	HERSHEY'S Unsweetened Baking Chocolate
semi-sweet baking chocolate	HERSHEY'S Semi-Sweet Baking Chocolate
semi-sweet chocolate chips	HERSHEY'S Semi-Sweet Chocolate Chips
semi-sweet chocolate Mini Chips	HERSHEY'S MINI CHIPS semi-sweet chocolate
milk chocolate chips	HERSHEY'S Milk Chocolate Chips
milk chocolate bar	HERSHEY'S Milk Chocolate
milk chocolate bar with almonds	HERSHEY'S Milk Chocolate with Almonds
Special Dark chocolate bar	HERSHEY'S SPECIAL DARK mildly sweet chocolate bar
Hershey's Kisses	HERSHEY'S KISSES milk chocolates
chocolate-flavored syrup	HERSHEY'S Chocolate Flavored Syrup
chocolate fudge topping	HERSHEY'S Chocolate Fudge Topping
peanut butter chips	REESE'S Naturally Flavored Peanut Butter Chips

HERSHEY'S, HERSHEY'S KISSES, KISSES, MINI CHIPS, SPECIAL DARK, REESE'S and CHOCOLATETOWN are Trademarks of Hershey Foods Corporation.

Showstoppers

Czar's Cake

This voluptuous double-chocolate dessert is lined with ladyfingers and crowned with brandied whipped cream.

14 ladyfingers, split
3 tablespoons brandy
⅔ cup semi-sweet chocolate chips
2 blocks (2 ounces) unsweetened baking chocolate
4 egg yolks, at room temperature
¼ cup sugar

¼ cup brandy
½ teaspoon vanilla
4 egg whites, at room temperature
⅛ teaspoon cream of tartar
1 cup heavy or whipping cream, well chilled
¼ cup sugar
Brandy Whipped Cream (below)

Line bottom of 9-inch springform pan with wax paper. Line bottom and side of pan with ladyfingers, with rounded sides touching pan. Brush cut sides of ladyfingers with 3 tablespoons brandy; set aside.

Melt chocolate chips and baking chocolate in top of double boiler over hot, not boiling, water, stirring until smooth; cool to lukewarm. Beat egg yolks and ¼ cup sugar in large mixer bowl until thick; add ¼ cup brandy and the vanilla. Blend in lukewarm chocolate.

Beat egg whites and cream of tartar in small mixer bowl until soft peaks form; fold into chocolate mixture. Beat cream and ¼ cup sugar in small mixer bowl until soft peaks form; fold into chocolate mixture. Spoon into ladyfinger-lined pan; cover. Chill 6 hours or until firm. Remove side of pan. Carefully invert onto serving plate; peel off wax paper. Prepare Brandy Whipped Cream; use to garnish cake. Serve immediately.

10 to 12 servings.

Brandy Whipped Cream
Beat 1 cup heavy or whipping cream, 2 tablespoons confectioners' sugar and 1 tablespoon brandy in small mixer bowl until stiff.

Crème de Cacao Torte

Three kinds of chocolate in a dazzling sky-high dessert.

⅔ cup butter or margarine, softened
1⅔ cups sugar
3 eggs
½ teaspoon vanilla
2 cups unsifted all-purpose flour
⅔ cup unsweetened cocoa
1¼ teaspoons baking soda
¼ teaspoon baking powder
1⅓ cups milk
2 tablespoons crème de cacao
Crème de Cacao Filling (below)
Chocolate Ganache Glaze (below)
Chocolate leaves (optional)

Cream butter or margarine, sugar, eggs and vanilla in large mixer bowl until light and fluffy. Combine flour, cocoa, baking soda and baking powder; add alternately with milk to creamed mixture, blending just until combined.

Pour into two greased and floured 9-inch layer pans. Bake at 350° for 30 to 35 minutes or until cake tester comes out clean. Cool 10 minutes; remove from pans. Sprinkle each layer with 1 tablespoon crème de cacao; cool completely.

Meanwhile, prepare Crème de Cacao Filling. Split each cake layer horizontally into 2 layers. Place one layer on serving plate; spread with a third of the filling. Repeat layering with remaining cake and filling, ending with cake layer. Cover tightly; chill at least 8 hours. Prepare Chocolate Ganache Glaze; spoon on top of chilled cake, allowing glaze to drizzle down side. Chill. Just before serving, garnish with chocolate leaves.

10 to 12 servings.

Crème de Cacao Filling

Beat 1 cup heavy or whipping cream, 2 tablespoons crème de cacao and 1 tablespoon unsweetened cocoa until stiff. Cover; chill.

Chocolate Ganache Glaze

1 Special Dark chocolate bar (8 ounces), broken into pieces
¼ cup heavy or whipping cream
1 tablespoon butter
1½ teaspoons crème de cacao

Combine chocolate bar pieces, cream and butter in medium saucepan. Cook over low heat, stirring constantly, until mixture is melted and smooth. Stir in crème de cacao. Cool to lukewarm (glaze will be slightly thickened).

Pears au Chocolat

4 fresh pears
½ cup sugar
1 cup water
1 teaspoon vanilla

Nut Filling (optional, below)
Chocolate Sauce (below)
Sweetened whipped cream

Core pears from bottom but leave stems intact; peel. Slice piece off bottom to make a flat base. Combine sugar and water in medium saucepan; add pears. Cover; simmer over low heat 10 to 20 minutes (depending on ripeness) or just until pears are soft. Remove from heat; add vanilla. Cool pears in syrup; chill. To serve, drain pears; spoon Nut Filling into cavities. Place pears on dessert plates. Prepare Chocolate Sauce; pour or spoon sauce onto each pear. Garnish with whipped cream. Serve with sauce.

4 servings.

Nut Filling

Combine 6 tablespoons finely chopped nuts, 2 tablespoons confectioners' sugar and 1 teaspoon milk in small bowl.

Chocolate Sauce

Combine 6 tablespoons water, 6 tablespoons sugar and ¼ cup butter in small saucepan; bring to full boil. Remove from heat; stir in 1⅓ cups semi-sweet chocolate Mini Chips. Stir until chocolate has completely melted; beat or whisk until smooth. Cool.

Chocolate-Filled Pecan Torte

A dense, devastatingly rich nut-based batter. The cake tiers are suspended with chocolate whipped cream.

7 egg whites, at room temperature
¼ teaspoon salt
1 cup sugar
7 egg yolks, at room temperature
1 teaspoon vanilla
2½ cups ground pecans
¼ cup packaged dry cracker crumbs
1 teaspoon baking powder
Filling (below)
Chocolate Glaze (below)

Line bottoms of three 8-inch layer pans with wax paper; set aside. Beat egg whites and salt in large mixer bowl until soft peaks form; gradually add ½ cup of the sugar, 2 tablespoons at a time, beating until stiff peaks form. With same beaters, beat egg yolks in small mixer bowl until thick and light; gradually add remaining ½ cup sugar, beating until thick, about 3 minutes. Add vanilla. Combine ground pecans, cracker crumbs and baking powder; fold into egg yolk mixture. Fold egg yolk mixture into egg whites just until combined.

Pour into prepared pans, dividing evenly; smooth surfaces. Bake at 375° for 20 to 25 minutes or until top springs back when touched lightly. To cool, hang each pan upside down between two other pans or containers for 1 hour. Meanwhile, prepare Filling.

With metal spatula, loosen sides of layers from pans. Turn out of pans; peel off wax paper. Place one layer on serving plate; spread with half the Filling. Top with second layer and spread with remaining Filling. Top with remaining layer. Prepare Chocolate Glaze. Spread glaze over top of torte, allowing glaze to run down side. Chill.

10 to 12 servings.

Filling

Combine 1 cup confectioners' sugar and 3 tablespoons unsweetened cocoa in small mixer bowl. Add 1 cup chilled heavy or whipping cream and 1 teaspoon vanilla. Beat until stiff. Chill.

Chocolate Glaze

2 tablespoons butter or margarine
¼ cup unsweetened cocoa
3 tablespoons water
½ teaspoon vanilla
1¼ cups confectioners' sugar

Melt butter or margarine in small saucepan over low heat. Stir in cocoa and water. Cook, stirring constantly, until mixture thickens; *do not boil.* Remove from heat. Stir in vanilla. Gradually add confectioners' sugar; beat until smooth.

Chocolate-Cherry Party Torte

¼ cup unsweetened cocoa
¼ cup boiling water
⅓ cup shortening
¾ cup sugar
½ teaspoon vanilla
1 egg
1 cup unsifted all-purpose flour

¾ teaspoon baking soda
¼ teaspoon salt
⅔ cup buttermilk or sour milk*
Cherry Filling (below)
Chocolate Whipped Cream
   Frosting (below)

Lightly grease 15½ x 10½ x 1-inch jelly roll pan; line with wax paper and lightly grease paper. Set aside. Combine cocoa and boiling water in small bowl. Stir until smooth; set aside. Cream shortening, sugar and vanilla in small mixer bowl; blend in egg. Combine flour, baking soda and salt; add alternately with buttermilk or sour milk to creamed mixture. Blend in reserved cocoa mixture.

Spread batter evenly in prepared pan. Bake at 350° for 16 to 18 minutes or until cake tester comes out clean. Cool 10 minutes; remove from pan. Remove wax paper; cool completely.

Cut cake crosswise into 4 equal pieces. Place one piece on serving plate; spread with a third of the Cherry Filling (about ⅔ cup). Repeat layering with remaining cake and filling, ending with cake layer. Frost top and sides of torte with Chocolate Whipped Cream Frosting; chill. Garnish as desired.

10 servings.

*To sour milk: Use 2 teaspoons vinegar plus milk to equal ⅔ cup.

Cherry Filling

1 cup heavy or whipping
   cream
¼ cup confectioners' sugar
1½ teaspoons kirsch or
   ⅛ teaspoon almond extract

⅓ cup chopped red candied
   cherries
¼ cup finely chopped slivered
   almonds

Beat cream, confectioners' sugar and kirsch or almond extract in small mixer bowl until stiff; carefully fold in candied cherries and almonds. Cover; chill about 1 hour.

Chocolate Whipped Cream Frosting

Combine 1 cup heavy or whipping cream, 2 tablespoons chocolate-flavored syrup, 1 tablespoon confectioners' sugar and 1 teaspoon unsweetened cocoa in small mixer bowl. Beat on low speed just until blended. Chill about 1 hour. Beat on high speed until stiff.

Deluxe Ice Cream Cocoa Roll

Think of this temptation as a hot fudge sundae wrapped in chocolate cake.

6 egg yolks, at room
　temperature
¾ cup sugar
1 teaspoon vanilla
6 egg whites, at room
　temperature

⅓ cup unsweetened cocoa
3 tablespoons flour
1 quart ice cream (any flavor)
　Hot Fudge Sauce (below) or
　confectioners' sugar

Grease 15½ x 10½ x 1-inch jelly roll pan; line with wax paper and lightly grease paper. Set aside. Beat egg yolks in small mixer bowl on high speed; gradually add ¼ cup of the sugar and the vanilla, beating until thick and lemon colored. Beat egg whites in large mixer bowl; gradually add ¼ cup of the sugar, beating until stiff but not dry. Carefully fold egg yolk mixture into beaten egg whites. Combine remaining ¼ cup sugar, the cocoa and flour; fold about 2 tablespoons at a time into egg mixture just until blended.

Spread batter evenly in prepared pan. Bake at 375° for 15 to 18 minutes or just until cake springs back when touched lightly in center. Invert onto slightly dampened towel; carefully peel off wax paper. Immediately roll cake and towel together starting from narrow end; place on wire rack to cool completely.

Carefully unroll cake; remove towel. Quickly spread with softened ice cream. Reroll; wrap and place in freezer. Freeze completely. At serving time, drizzle with Hot Fudge Sauce or sprinkle with confectioners' sugar; slice and serve with additional sauce, if desired.

8 to 10 servings.

Hot Fudge Sauce

¾ cup sugar
½ cup unsweetened cocoa
⅔ cup (5.3-ounce can)
　evaporated milk

⅓ cup light corn syrup
⅓ cup butter
1 teaspoon vanilla

Combine sugar and cocoa in saucepan; blend in evaporated milk and corn syrup. Cook over medium heat, stirring constantly, until mixture boils; boil and stir 1 minute. Remove from heat; stir in butter and vanilla. Serve warm.

Georgia Peach Shortcake

4 eggs, separated
½ cup sugar
½ cup unsifted all-purpose flour
⅓ cup unsweetened cocoa
¼ cup sugar
½ teaspoon baking soda
¼ teaspoon salt
⅓ cup water

1 teaspoon vanilla
2 tablespoons sugar
2 cups heavy or whipping
  cream
¾ cup confectioners' sugar
1 teaspoon vanilla
3 cups sliced peaches, well
  drained*

Grease bottom of two 9-inch square or layer pans; line with wax paper and grease paper. Set aside. Beat egg yolks 3 minutes on medium speed in small mixer bowl. Gradually add ½ cup sugar; continue beating 2 minutes. Combine flour, cocoa, ¼ cup sugar, the baking soda and salt; add alternately with water and 1 teaspoon vanilla on low speed just until batter is smooth. Beat egg whites in large mixer bowl until foamy; add 2 tablespoons sugar and beat until stiff peaks form. Carefully fold chocolate mixture into beaten egg whites.

Spread batter evenly in prepared pans. Bake at 375° for 14 to 16 minutes or until top springs back when touched lightly. Cool 10 minutes; remove cakes from pans. Peel off wax paper; cool completely.

Beat cream, confectioners' sugar and 1 teaspoon vanilla in large mixer bowl until stiff. Place one cake layer upside down on serving plate; frost with about 1 cup of the whipped cream. With pastry tube or spoon, make a border of whipped cream ½ inch high and 1 inch wide around edge of layer. Fill center with peach slices, reserving 12 peach slices for top of cake. Carefully place second layer, top side up, on filling. Gently spread all but 1 cup whipped cream on top of cake. With pastry tube or spoon, make a border of whipped cream around edge of top layer of cake. Arrange remaining peach slices in center. Chill about 1 hour before serving.

10 to 12 servings.

*Use fresh peaches or 16-ounce package frozen or 29-ounce can peach slices.

Royal Chocolate Nut Cake

A dense hazelnut batter spun with chocolate and no fewer than a dozen eggs.

1½ cups semi-sweet chocolate
    chips
12 egg yolks, at room
    temperature
½ cup sugar
2 cups ground hazelnuts
    (about 6 ounces whole)

1 teaspoon vanilla
12 egg whites, at room
    temperature
⅛ teaspoon cream of tartar
½ cup sugar
    Choco-Nut Cream Frosting
    (below)

Melt chocolate chips in top of double boiler over hot, not boiling, water; cool to lukewarm. Beat egg yolks with ½ cup sugar in large mixer bowl on high speed until thick. Reduce speed to low; blend in lukewarm chocolate. Stir in 1 cup of the ground hazelnuts and the vanilla. Beat egg whites with cream of tartar in large mixer bowl until foamy; add ½ cup sugar, 1 tablespoon at a time, beating until stiff peaks form. Gently fold egg whites into chocolate mixture; fold in remaining 1 cup hazelnuts.

Pour into ungreased 10-inch tube pan with removable bottom. Bake at 350° for 60 to 65 minutes or until top springs back when touched lightly. Invert cake over funnel or bottle until completely cool. Loosen cake from side and bottom of pan with knife; invert onto serving plate. Frost with Choco-Nut Cream Frosting. Chill.

12 to 14 servings.

Choco-Nut Cream Frosting

1 cup heavy or whipping cream
½ cup confectioners' sugar
2 tablespoons unsweetened
    cocoa

1 teaspoon vanilla
½ cup chopped toasted
    hazelnuts* (about 2 ounces
    whole)

Beat cream, confectioners' sugar, cocoa and vanilla in small mixer bowl until stiff. Stir in toasted hazelnuts.

*To toast hazelnuts: Combine the chopped nuts with 1½ tablespoons melted butter. Spread in shallow pan; bake at 375° for 5 to 7 minutes or until golden brown, stirring several times during toasting.

Peanut Butter Shells
with Chocolate-Almond Cream

Tip: You may prepare the shells weeks in advance of use, but for best results make the filling no earlier than a day ahead of serving time.

2 cups (12-ounce package) peanut butter chips
2 tablespoons shortening*

Chocolate-Almond Cream Filling (below)

Melt peanut butter chips and shortening in top of double boiler over hot, not boiling, water; stir until smooth. Remove from heat; cool slightly. Place 15 paper baking cups (2¾ inches in diameter) in muffin pans. Using a narrow, soft-bristled pastry brush, thickly and evenly coat the inside pleated surface and bottom of each cup with peanut butter mixture. (Reserve any remaining peanut butter mixture for touch-up.) Chill 10 minutes; coat any thin spots. (If peanut butter mixture thickens, stir over hot water until mixture becomes fluid again.) Cover; chill at least 1 hour or until firm.

Remove only a few peanut butter shells from refrigerator at a time; carefully peel paper from each cup. (Unfilled cups will keep for weeks in an airtight container in the refrigerator.) Fill each cup with Chocolate-Almond Cream Filling; chill several hours or overnight.

15 desserts.

*Do not use butter, margarine or oil.

Chocolate-Almond Cream Filling

1 milk chocolate bar with almonds (8 ounces)
1½ cups miniature or 15 large marshmallows
⅓ cup milk
1 cup heavy or whipping cream

Cut chocolate bar in pieces, chopping almonds into small pieces. Place in top of double boiler and melt with marshmallows and milk over hot, not boiling, water, stirring until chocolate and marshmallows are melted and mixture is smooth. Remove from heat; cool. Whip cream until stiff and fold into chocolate mixture. Cover; chill until ready to use.

Chocolate Dacquoise

Melt-in-your-mouth nut meringue layers afloat on richest chocolate-mocha buttercream. Like all meringue desserts, attempt only on a crisp nonhumid day.

3 egg whites, at room
   temperature
½ teaspoon cream of tartar
½ teaspoon vanilla
⅔ cup sugar

¾ cup finely chopped almonds
Chocolate-Mocha
   Buttercream (below)
Chocolate curls

Draw three 8-inch circles on parchment paper. Place paper on large cookie sheet; set aside. Beat egg whites, cream of tartar and vanilla in small mixer bowl until foamy. Beat in sugar, 1 tablespoon at a time, until stiff peaks form; *do not underbeat.* Fold in almonds.

Spread meringue evenly over circles on paper. Bake in a preheated 275° oven for 45 minutes. Without opening door, turn off oven; let meringues remain in oven for 45 minutes. Remove from oven; cool completely. Carefully peel off paper.

Prepare Chocolate-Mocha Buttercream. Place one meringue on serving plate; pipe on or spread with a third of the buttercream (about ¾ cup). Repeat layering with meringues and buttercream, ending with buttercream. Garnish with chocolate curls. Cover; chill no longer than 2 hours. (Meringue may soften if refrigerated for more than 2 hours.)

10 to 12 servings.

Note: If your cookie sheet is not large enough to hold the three meringues, you can put two cookie sheets together, overlapping slightly.

Chocolate-Mocha Buttercream

2 blocks (2 ounces)
   unsweetened baking
   chocolate
1 cup sugar
½ teaspoon cream of tartar
½ cup water

5 egg yolks, at room
   temperature
1 cup sweet butter, softened
¾ teaspoon instant coffee
   granules
1 tablespoon hot water

Melt baking chocolate in top of double boiler over hot, not boiling, water; set aside to cool slightly.

Combine sugar, cream of tartar and water in small heavy saucepan. Cook over medium heat, stirring constantly, until sugar dissolves and syrup is clear. Continue cooking over medium heat, *without stirring,* until syrup reaches 238°F (soft-ball stage) or until syrup, when dropped into very cold water, forms a soft ball that flattens when removed from water.

Meanwhile, beat egg yolks in small mixer bowl on high speed until thick and lemon colored, about 2 minutes. With mixer on high speed, slowly pour hot syrup in a thin stream over egg yolks, beating constantly until thick and cooled, about 5 minutes. Beat in butter, 1 tablespoon at a time. Dissolve instant coffee in hot water; add with melted chocolate to egg yolk mixture. Beat until well blended. Place in bowl of ice water; chill 15 to 20 minutes. Remove from water; beat on high speed until buttercream is thick enough to spread.

To make meringue layers, draw three 8-inch circles on parchment paper. Use a spatula to spread the meringue evenly over circles.

When making the buttercream, slowly add the hot syrup to the egg yolks in a thin, steady stream.

Almond Fudge Cake

Pastry Shell (below)
¾ cup semi-sweet chocolate chips
⅓ cup sugar
1 tablespoon shortening
2 eggs
6 tablespoons butter or margarine, softened

1 cup ground almonds (about 4½ ounces whole)
¼ teaspoon almond extract
Sweetened whipped cream
Maraschino cherries

Prepare Pastry Shell; set aside. Combine chocolate chips, sugar and shortening in top of double boiler over hot, not boiling, water; stir until chips are melted and mixture is smooth. Remove from heat; stir in eggs, blending well. Cream butter or margarine in small mixer bowl; blend in chocolate mixture, ground almonds and almond extract.

Spoon into Pastry Shell. Bake at 325° for 40 to 45 minutes or until crust is golden brown. (Center will not test done.) Cool completely; remove from pan. Garnish with dollops of sweetened whipped cream and maraschino cherries just before serving.

10 servings.

Pastry Shell

1½ cups unsifted all-purpose flour
⅓ cup sugar

1 teaspoon baking powder
½ cup butter or margarine
1 egg, slightly beaten

Combine flour, sugar and baking powder in medium mixing bowl. Cut in butter or margarine until mixture resembles coarse crumbs. Add egg and blend until flour is moistened. Press dough with lightly floured fingers evenly on bottom and up side of greased 9-inch layer pan with removable bottom or 9-inch spring-form pan.

Chocolate-Filled Boston Cream Pie

This chocolatey version of an American favorite might be rich enough to be banned in the city it's named for.

2 cups unsifted all-purpose flour
1½ cups sugar
3½ teaspoons baking powder
1 teaspoon salt
¼ cup butter or margarine, softened
¼ cup shortening
1 cup milk
3 eggs
1 teaspoon vanilla
Chocolate Cream Filling (below)
Chocolate Glaze (below)

Combine all ingredients except Chocolate Cream Filling and Chocolate Glaze in large mixer bowl. Blend 30 seconds on low speed; beat 3 minutes on high speed. Pour into two greased and floured 9-inch layer pans. Bake at 350° for 30 to 35 minutes. Cool 10 minutes; remove from pans. Cool completely.

Meanwhile, prepare Chocolate Cream Filling. Place one cake layer on serving plate; spread with filling. Top with second cake layer; refrigerate. Prepare Chocolate Glaze. Spoon hot glaze on top of cake, allowing glaze to drizzle down side. Chill before serving. Refrigerate any remaining glaze.

10 to 12 servings.

Chocolate Cream Filling

⅔ cup sugar
2 tablespoons cornstarch
⅛ teaspoon salt
1½ cups milk
2 egg yolks, slightly beaten
1 block (1 ounce) unsweetened baking chocolate, broken into pieces
2 teaspoons vanilla

Combine sugar, cornstarch and salt in medium saucepan; gradually add milk and egg yolks. Add baking chocolate. Cook over medium heat, stirring constantly, until mixture boils; boil and stir 1 minute or until chocolate flecks disappear. Remove from heat; add vanilla. Pour into bowl; press plastic wrap directly onto surface. Cool; chill.

Chocolate Glaze

¼ cup sugar
1 tablespoon cornstarch
Dash salt
⅓ cup water
1 block (1 ounce) unsweetened baking chocolate
1 tablespoon butter
½ teaspoon vanilla

Combine sugar, cornstarch, salt and water in small mixing bowl; set aside. Melt baking chocolate with butter in small saucepan over low heat. Add sugar-water mixture and bring to a boil, stirring constantly. Remove from heat; add vanilla.

Chocolate Baked Alaska

Unlike most meringue desserts, this can be completely assembled and popped into the freezer a full day ahead. (First, cover with a cake-saver lid; meringue will stick to foil or plastic wrap.) Just before serving, brown the Alaska in a preheated oven as directed.

Ice Cream Filling (below)
1½ cups unsifted all-purpose
    flour
  1 cup sugar
  ¼ cup unsweetened cocoa
  1 teaspoon baking soda
  ½ teaspoon salt
  1 cup water

¼ cup plus 2 tablespoons
    vegetable oil
  1 tablespoon vinegar
  1 teaspoon vanilla
    Marshmallow Meringue
    (below)
    Chocolate-flavored syrup
    (optional)

Prepare Ice Cream Filling. Combine flour, sugar, cocoa, baking soda and salt in large mixer bowl. Add water, oil, vinegar and vanilla; beat 3 minutes on medium speed until thoroughly blended. Pour into greased and floured 9-inch layer pan. Bake at 350° for 30 to 35 minutes or until cake tester comes out clean. Cool 10 minutes; remove from pan. Cool completely. Cut 12-inch square of brown paper or wax paper; place on top of wooden board or cookie sheet. Center cake layer on paper; top with unmolded Ice Cream Filling, rounded side up. Cover; freeze until cake is firm.

When ready to serve dessert, prepare Marshmallow Meringue. Remove dessert from freezer. Spread meringue evenly about 1 inch thick over entire surface, covering any holes and sealing down to paper. Bake in preheated 450° oven for 3 to 5 minutes or until lightly browned. Remove from oven; slice in wedges. Serve immediately with syrup. Cover and refreeze any leftovers; serve within several days.

10 to 12 servings.

Ice Cream Filling
Soften ½ gallon mint chocolate chip ice cream (or your favorite flavor). Line 2½-quart mixing bowl with aluminum foil; spread ice cream evenly in bowl. Cover; freeze until hard.

Marshmallow Meringue
Bring 6 egg whites to room temperature. Beat with ⅛ teaspoon salt in large mixer bowl until soft peaks form. Gradually add 1¾ cups (7-ounce jar) marshmallow creme, beating until stiff peaks form.

Chocolate Rainbow Dessert

1½ cups chocolate wafer crumbs or graham cracker crumbs
⅓ cup butter or margarine, melted
1 envelope unflavored gelatine
3 tablespoons cold water
¾ cup milk, scalded
1 package (8 ounces) cream cheese, softened
½ cup sugar
1 cup chocolate-flavored syrup
1 teaspoon vanilla
1 package (3 ounces) strawberry-flavored gelatine
1 cup boiling water
1 package (10 ounces) frozen sliced strawberries, partially thawed
1 cup vanilla ice cream
Sweetened whipped cream (optional)
Fresh strawberries (optional)

Combine crumbs and butter or margarine in small mixing bowl; blend well. Press mixture evenly onto bottom and halfway up side of 9-inch springform pan; chill.

Sprinkle unflavored gelatine onto cold water in small mixing bowl; let stand 3 to 4 minutes to soften. Add to hot milk; stir to dissolve gelatine. Combine cream cheese and sugar in large mixer bowl; blend in syrup and vanilla. Gradually add gelatine-milk mixture. Chill until mixture mounds when dropped from spoon.

Remove from refrigerator and let stand at room temperature while preparing strawberry layer. Dissolve strawberry-flavored gelatine in boiling water. Add strawberries with syrup; stir until completely thawed. Strain mixture; reserve strawberry halves for garnish, if desired. Add ice cream to strawberry-gelatine mixture; if necessary, chill until mixture mounds when dropped from spoon.

Spoon 1½ cups chocolate mixture into prepared crust; chill a few minutes until set but not firm. Gently spoon strawberry mixture over chocolate; chill a few minutes until set. Spoon remaining chocolate over strawberry mixture. Chill until firm. When ready to serve, remove side of pan. Garnish with sweetened whipped cream and fresh or reserved frozen strawberry halves.

10 to 12 servings.

Mexican Cocoa Torte

In many Mexican recipes, cinnamon and chocolate are a popular flavor match.

1 cup sugar
½ cup unsweetened cocoa
¼ teaspoon cinnamon
⅓ cup shortening
½ cup strong coffee

1 package (11 ounces) pie crust mix
2 cups heavy or whipping cream
Semi-sweet chocolate Mini Chips (optional)

Combine sugar, cocoa, cinnamon, shortening and coffee in small saucepan. Cook over very low heat, stirring constantly, until smooth and creamy. Cool to room temperature. Place pie crust mix in medium mixing bowl; stir in ¾ cup of the cocoa mixture, blending thoroughly. Shape into smooth ball; chill 1 hour.

Divide dough into 4 pieces. Line two cookie sheets with aluminum foil; mark two 8-inch circles on each. Place balls of dough on foil; press with fingers into marked circles. Bake at 375° for 10 to 12 minutes or until almost set; cool on cookie sheets.

Add remaining cocoa mixture to cream in small mixer bowl; beat until stiff. Place one pastry round on serving plate; spread with a fourth of the whipped cream mixture. Repeat layering with remaining three rounds and whipped cream mixture, ending with whipped cream. Chill several hours. Garnish with Mini Chips.

8 to 10 servings.

Hershey Bar-Cookie Torte

¾ cup sugar
½ cup packed light brown sugar
⅓ cup butter or margarine, softened
1 egg
1 teaspoon vanilla
2½ cups unsifted all-purpose flour

1 teaspoon baking soda
½ teaspoon baking powder
½ teaspoon salt
7 tablespoons buttermilk or sour milk*
Hershey Bar Cream Filling (below)
Glossy Hershey Bar Glaze (below)

Combine sugar, brown sugar and butter or margarine in large mixer bowl on medium speed. Add egg and vanilla; blend well. Combine flour, baking soda, baking powder and salt; add alternately with buttermilk or sour milk to creamed mixture. Pour batter by level ½ cupfuls onto lightly greased cookie sheet (2 cookies per sheet). With spatula, spread evenly into 6-inch circles, 3 inches apart. Bake at 375° for 7 to 8 minutes or until lightly browned. Remove from cookie sheet; cool completely on wire rack. Chill.

Prepare Hershey Bar Cream Filling. Place one cookie on serving plate; spread with ½ cup Hershey Bar Cream Filling. Repeat layering with remaining cookies and filling, ending with a cookie. Spoon Glossy Hershey Bar Glaze over top of torte. Refrigerate.

8 to 10 servings.

*To sour milk: Use 1½ teaspoons vinegar plus milk to equal 7 tablespoons.

Hershey Bar Cream Filling
Sprinkle 1 teaspoon unflavored gelatine onto 5 tablespoons cold water in saucepan; let stand a few minutes to soften. Cook over medium heat, stirring constantly, until gelatine is dissolved. Remove from heat; add 1½ eight-ounce milk chocolate bars, broken into pieces (reserve remaining half for glaze). Stir until chocolate is completely melted. (If necessary, melt over low heat.) Cool to lukewarm, about 10 minutes. Whip 1 cup heavy or whipping cream until stiff; gradually add whipped cream to chocolate mixture, blending carefully. Chill about 1 hour or until filling begins to set.

Glossy Hershey Bar Glaze
Melt ½ milk chocolate bar (reserved from filling) with 1 tablespoon water in top of double boiler over warm water; stir to blend well. Add teaspoonfuls of water as needed until glaze is of spreading consistency.

Chocolate English Trifle

Chocolate Filling (below)
½ cup apricot preserves
3 tablespoons light rum
16 to 18 ladyfingers, split

Sweetened whipped cream
¼ cup toasted slivered almonds
  or chocolate curls
  (optional)

Prepare Chocolate Filling; set aside. Combine apricot preserves and rum; spread flat side of each ladyfinger with mixture. Put 6 to 8 ladyfingers together sandwich style; arrange on bottom of 1½-quart glass serving bowl. Arrange single ladyfingers around sides of bowl, rounded sides touching bowl. Spoon half the cooled Chocolate Filling into ladyfinger-lined bowl. Arrange single layer of ladyfingers on filling. Top with remaining Chocolate Filling. Cover; refrigerate several hours. Garnish with sweetened whipped cream and almonds or chocolate curls.

10 to 12 servings.

Chocolate Filling

⅓ cup sugar
3 tablespoons cornstarch
¼ teaspoon salt
2¼ cups milk
⅔ cup chocolate-flavored syrup

1 egg, well beaten
1 tablespoon butter or
  margarine
1 teaspoon vanilla

Combine sugar, cornstarch and salt in medium saucepan; gradually stir in milk, syrup and egg. Cook over medium heat, stirring constantly, until mixture boils; boil and stir 1 minute. Remove from heat; blend in butter or margarine and vanilla. Pour into bowl; press plastic wrap directly onto surface. Cool to room temperature.

Choco-Coconut Cake Roll

4 egg whites, at room temperature
½ cup sugar
4 egg yolks, at room temperature
⅓ cup sugar
1 teaspoon vanilla
½ cup unsifted all-purpose flour
⅓ cup unsweetened cocoa
½ teaspoon baking powder
¼ teaspoon baking soda
⅛ teaspoon salt
⅓ cup water
Cherry-Coconut Filling (below)
Confectioners' sugar

Line 15½ x 10½ x 1-inch jelly roll pan with aluminum foil; generously grease foil. Set aside. Beat egg whites in large mixer bowl until foamy; gradually add ½ cup sugar and beat until stiff peaks form. Set aside.

Beat egg yolks in small mixer bowl 3 minutes on high speed. Gradually add ⅓ cup sugar and the vanilla; continue beating 2 additional minutes. Combine flour, cocoa, baking powder, baking soda and salt; add alternately with water to egg yolk mixture on low speed, beating just until batter is smooth. Gradually fold chocolate mixture into beaten egg whites until mixture is well blended.

Spread batter evenly in prepared pan. Bake at 375° for 12 to 15 minutes or until top springs back when touched lightly. Invert onto towel sprinkled with confectioners' sugar; carefully peel off foil. Immediately roll cake and towel together starting from narrow end; place on wire rack to cool completely.

Prepare Cherry-Coconut Filling. Carefully unroll cake; remove towel. Spread cake with filling; reroll and refrigerate. Sprinkle with confectioners' sugar just before serving.

8 to 10 servings.

Cherry-Coconut Filling

1 cup heavy or whipping cream
3 tablespoons confectioners' sugar
Few drops red food color (optional)
⅓ cup chopped maraschino cherries, well drained
½ cup flaked coconut

Beat cream until slightly thickened. Add confectioners' sugar and food color; beat until stiff. Fold in chopped cherries and coconut.

Chocolate Cream Crepes

Chocolate Cream (below)
Apricot Sauce (below)
½ cup milk
2 eggs
½ teaspoon vanilla

½ cup plus 2 tablespoons
  unsifted all-purpose flour
1 tablespoon sugar
⅛ teaspoon salt
2 tablespoons butter, melted

Prepare Chocolate Cream and Apricot Sauce. Combine milk, eggs and vanilla in small mixer bowl; beat slightly. Combine flour, sugar and salt in small bowl; add to egg mixture, beating until smooth. Blend in butter. Heat crepe pan or small omelet pan over medium heat; brush lightly with oil. Pour about 2 tablespoons batter into pan for each crepe; quickly tilt and spread batter evenly over bottom. Cook about 1 minute or until underside is golden brown. Loosen edges; turn and cook until lightly browned. Remove from pan. Place 3 tablespoons Chocolate Cream on each crepe; fold. Top with Apricot Sauce. Refrigerate leftovers.

About 10 crepes.

Chocolate Cream

⅓ cup unsweetened cocoa
¼ teaspoon salt
1⅓ cups (14-ounce can)
  sweetened condensed
  milk*

¼ cup hot water
2 tablespoons butter
½ teaspoon vanilla
1 cup heavy or whipping cream

Combine cocoa and salt in top of double boiler; gradually stir in sweetened condensed milk. Place over boiling water and cook, stirring constantly, until mixture is very thick. Gradually stir in hot water. Continue cooking 5 minutes, stirring frequently, until mixture thickens again. Remove from heat; stir in butter and vanilla. Cool to room temperature. Whip cream; fold into chocolate mixture. Chill thoroughly.

*Do not use evaporated milk.

Apricot Sauce

1½ cups (17-ounce can) apricot
  halves
¼ cup sugar
4 teaspoons cornstarch

¼ cup water
½ teaspoon lemon juice
1 tablespoon orange-flavored
  liqueur

Drain and slice apricots (reserve ½ cup syrup). Combine sugar and cornstarch in 2-quart saucepan; gradually stir in reserved syrup and the water. Cook over low heat, stirring constantly, until mixture thickens and just begins to boil. Add apricots and lemon juice; heat until fruit is warm. Remove from heat; stir in liqueur. Serve warm. (Sauce can be reheated over low heat.)

Mandarin Orange-Cocoa Torte

1 package (8 ounces) cream
    cheese, softened
½ cup sugar
5 eggs, at room temperature
½ cup butter or margarine,
    softened

1 cup sugar
1 teaspoon vanilla
½ cup unsifted all-purpose flour
⅓ cup unsweetened cocoa
½ cup chopped nuts
    Orange Glaze (below)

Grease two 8-inch layer pans; line with wax paper and set aside. Beat cream cheese and ½ cup sugar in small mixer bowl 2 minutes on medium speed. Add 3 eggs, one at a time, beating well after each addition. Beat 5 minutes on medium speed; set aside. Cream butter or margarine, 1 cup sugar and the vanilla in small mixer bowl. Add 2 eggs; beat 3 minutes on medium speed. Combine flour and cocoa; gradually blend into creamed butter mixture until smooth. Stir in nuts.

Spread cocoa mixture evenly in prepared pans; pour cheese mixture evenly over cocoa mixture. Bake at 350° for 30 to 35 minutes or until cake tester comes out clean; *do not overbake.* Cool 10 minutes; remove from pans.

Arrange one layer, cheese side up, on serving plate; spread with ⅓ cup of the Orange Glaze. Top with second layer, cheese side up, and spread with ⅓ cup glaze. Place well-drained mandarin oranges (reserved from glaze recipe) on top of torte; brush side with remaining glaze. Let stand 30 minutes at room temperature to blend flavors. Chill thoroughly.

10 to 12 servings.

Orange Glaze

1 cup (11-ounce can)
    mandarin oranges
2 tablespoons cornstarch

1½ tablespoons sugar
½ cup water

Drain oranges, reserving ½ cup syrup; set oranges aside for top of torte. Combine cornstarch and sugar in small saucepan; gradually stir in water and reserved syrup. Cook over medium heat, stirring constantly, until mixture boils. Simmer 2 to 3 minutes, stirring frequently.

Elegant Chocolate Torte

If the filling is a little too soft to spread, refrigerate for a short time. And the torte will stack up more successfully if each layer is spread with filling, then chilled until the filling sets.

6 eggs, at room temperature
1 cup sugar
1 teaspoon vanilla
½ cup unsifted all-purpose flour
½ cup unsweetened cocoa
½ cup butter or margarine, melted and slightly cooled
Peanut Butter Cream Filling (below)

6 tablespoons strained apricot preserves
Sliced peaches, brushed with lemon juice
Sliced peeled kiwifruit
Fresh strawberries

Beat eggs in large mixer bowl until foamy. Gradually add sugar; continue beating until thick and lemon colored, about 5 minutes. Blend in vanilla. Thoroughly combine flour and cocoa; gradually fold into egg mixture with rubber scraper. Fold in slightly cooled butter or margarine with rubber scraper until well blended.

Divide batter evenly between three greased and floured 8-inch layer pans. Bake at 350° for 15 minutes or until cake springs back when touched lightly. Cool 5 minutes; remove from pans. Cool completely.

Meanwhile, prepare Peanut Butter Cream Filling. Spread top surface of each layer with 2 tablespoons apricot preserves. Place one cake layer, apricot side up, on serving plate. Spread a third of the Peanut Butter Cream Filling over preserves. Set second layer, apricot side up, on top of first layer; spread with a third of the filling. Top with third layer; spread top with remaining filling. Refrigerate until serving time. Just before serving, arrange fruits decoratively on top and around base of cake.

10 to 12 servings.

Peanut Butter Cream Filling

1½ cups miniature marshmallows
1 cup peanut butter chips

⅓ cup milk
1 cup heavy or whipping cream
½ teaspoon vanilla

Place marshmallows, peanut butter chips and milk in top of double boiler over hot, not boiling, water. Stir until marshmallows and chips are melted and mixture is smooth; cool to lukewarm. Whip cream in chilled bowl until stiff; fold in vanilla and lukewarm peanut butter mixture. Chill thoroughly.

Paradise Chocolate Tarts

¾ cup butter, softened
1 cup sugar
2 eggs, slightly beaten
1½ teaspoons vanilla
3½ cups unsifted all-purpose flour
1 teaspoon baking powder
½ teaspoon salt
¼ teaspoon nutmeg
Chocolate Filling (below)
Sweetened whipped cream

Cream butter and sugar in large mixer bowl until light and fluffy. Add eggs and vanilla; blend well. Combine flour, baking powder, salt and nutmeg; gradually add to butter mixture, beating until dough forms. Cover; chill about 1 hour or until stiff. Form dough into 4 balls; roll each ball between wax paper to ⅛-inch thickness. Cut into 3-inch circles. Gently press circles into buttered muffin pans (2¾ inches in diameter).

Prepare Chocolate Filling; spoon into shells. Bake at 400° for 25 to 30 minutes or until crust is golden brown. Cool 15 minutes; carefully remove from pan onto wire rack. Cool completely; chill. Serve topped with dollop of sweetened whipped cream. Store leftover tarts, covered, in refrigerator.

About 3 dozen tarts.

Chocolate Filling
Combine 3 cups (1½ pounds) ricotta cheese, ¾ cup sugar, ¼ cup unsweetened cocoa, ¼ teaspoon cinnamon and 2 eggs, beaten, in large mixer bowl; blend well.

Cakes, Frostings & Fillings

Cocoa Medallion Cake

One of our most revered and requested recipes. A velvety, old-fashioned favorite.

¾ cup unsweetened cocoa
¾ cup boiling water
¼ cup butter or margarine, softened
¼ cup shortening
2 cups sugar
1 teaspoon vanilla

⅛ teaspoon salt
2 eggs
1½ teaspoons baking soda
1 cup buttermilk or sour milk*
1¾ cups unsifted all-purpose flour

Stir together cocoa and boiling water until smooth; set aside. Cream butter or margarine, shortening, sugar, vanilla and salt in large mixer bowl until light and fluffy. Add eggs; beat well. Stir baking soda into buttermilk or sour milk; add alternately with flour to creamed mixture. Blend in cocoa mixture.

Pour into two greased and wax-paper-lined 9-inch layer pans or 8-inch square pans. Bake at 350° for 30 to 35 minutes for 9-inch pans or 40 to 45 minutes for 8-inch pans, or until cake tester comes out clean. Cool 10 minutes; remove from pans. Cool completely; frost as desired (see pages 68–74).

8 to 10 servings.

*To sour milk: Use 1 tablespoon vinegar plus milk to equal 1 cup.

Variation
Picnic Medallion Cake: Prepare batter as directed above; pour into greased and floured 13 x 9-inch pan. Bake at 350° for 40 to 45 minutes or until cake tester comes out clean. Cool completely; frost as desired.

Chocolatetown Special Cake

½ cup unsweetened cocoa
½ cup boiling water
⅔ cup shortening
1¾ cups sugar
1 teaspoon vanilla
2 eggs
2¼ cups unsifted all-purpose flour
1½ teaspoons baking soda
½ teaspoon salt
1⅓ cups buttermilk or sour milk*

Stir together cocoa and boiling water in small bowl until smooth; set aside. Cream shortening, sugar and vanilla in large mixer bowl until light and fluffy. Add eggs; beat well. Combine flour, baking soda and salt; add alternately with buttermilk or sour milk to creamed mixture. Blend in cocoa mixture.

Pour into three greased and floured 8-inch or two 9-inch layer pans. Bake at 350° for 25 to 30 minutes for 8-inch pans or 35 to 40 minutes for 9-inch pans, or until cake tester comes out clean. Cool 10 minutes; remove from pans. Cool completely; frost as desired (see pages 68–74).

8 to 10 servings.

*To sour milk: Use 4 teaspoons vinegar plus milk to equal 1⅓ cups.

Hershey Bar Cake

1 milk chocolate bar (8 ounces), broken into pieces
¼ cup butter or margarine
1⅔ cups boiling water
2⅓ cups unsifted all-purpose flour
2 cups packed light brown sugar
2 teaspoons baking soda
1 teaspoon salt
2 eggs
½ cup sour cream
1 teaspoon vanilla

Combine chocolate bar pieces, butter or margarine and boiling water in medium mixing bowl; stir until chocolate is melted. Combine flour, brown sugar, baking soda and salt in large mixer bowl; gradually add chocolate mixture, beating until thoroughly blended. Blend in eggs, sour cream and vanilla; beat 1 minute on medium speed.

Pour into greased and floured 13 x 9-inch pan. Bake at 350° for 35 to 40 minutes or until cake tester comes out clean. Cool completely; frost as desired (see pages 68–74).

8 to 10 servings.

On facing page—Chocolatetown Special Cake (this page) with Chocolate Fudge Frosting (page 68)

Sour Cream Chocolate Cake

2 teaspoons baking soda
1 cup buttermilk
¾ cup butter or margarine, softened
1⅔ cups sugar
1 egg

1 teaspoon vanilla
½ teaspoon salt
2 cups unsifted all-purpose flour
⅔ cup unsweetened cocoa
¾ cup sour cream

Stir baking soda into buttermilk; set aside. Cream butter or margarine and sugar in large mixer bowl until light and fluffy; blend in egg, vanilla and salt. Combine flour and cocoa; add alternately with buttermilk mixture and sour cream to creamed mixture. Beat 2 minutes on medium speed.

Pour into two greased and floured 9-inch layer pans. Bake at 350° for 30 to 35 minutes or until cake tester comes out clean. Cool 10 minutes; remove from pans. Cool completely; frost as desired (see pages 68–74).

8 to 10 servings.

Devil's Food Cake

¾ cup butter or margarine, softened
1½ cups sugar
1½ teaspoons vanilla
2 eggs
1¾ cups unsifted all-purpose flour

½ cup unsweetened cocoa
1 teaspoon baking soda
¼ teaspoon salt
½ cup buttermilk or sour milk*
½ cup boiling water

Cream butter or margarine, sugar and vanilla in large mixer bowl until light and fluffy. Add eggs; beat well. Combine flour, cocoa, baking soda and salt; add alternately with buttermilk or sour milk to creamed mixture. Add boiling water; beat until smooth.

Pour into wax-paper-lined 13 x 9-inch pan. Bake at 350° for 35 to 40 minutes or until cake tester comes out clean. Cool 10 minutes; remove from pan. Cool completely; frost as desired (see pages 68–74).

8 to 10 servings.

*To sour milk: Use 1½ teaspoons vinegar plus milk to equal ½ cup.

Black Magic Cake

Mouthwateringly moist, with mysterious dark depths of flavor, this is our most requested cake recipe.

1¾ cups unsifted all-purpose
    flour
2 cups sugar
¾ cup unsweetened cocoa
2 teaspoons baking soda
1 teaspoon baking powder
1 teaspoon salt
2 eggs
1 cup strong black coffee*
1 cup buttermilk or sour milk**
½ cup vegetable oil
1 teaspoon vanilla

Combine flour, sugar, cocoa, baking soda, baking powder and salt in large mixer bowl. Add eggs, coffee, buttermilk or sour milk, oil and vanilla; beat 2 minutes on medium speed (batter will be thin).

Pour into greased and floured 13 x 9-inch pan or two 9-inch layer pans. Bake at 350° for 35 to 40 minutes for oblong pan or 30 to 35 minutes for layer pans, or until cake tester comes out clean. Cool 10 minutes; remove from pans. Cool completely; frost as desired (see pages 68–74).

8 to 10 servings.

*Or 2 teaspoons instant coffee granules plus 1 cup boiling water.

**To sour milk: Use 1 tablespoon vinegar plus milk to equal 1 cup.

Cocoa Party Cake

1 cup butter or margarine,
    softened
2¼ cups sugar
2 eggs
1 teaspoon vanilla
2¾ cups unsifted cake flour
½ cup unsweetened cocoa
2 teaspoons baking soda
1 teaspoon salt
2 cups buttermilk or sour milk*

Cream butter or margarine and sugar in large mixer bowl until light and fluffy. Add eggs and vanilla; beat well. Combine cake flour, cocoa, baking soda and salt; add alternately with buttermilk or sour milk to creamed mixture.

Pour into greased and floured 13 x 9-inch pan or three 8- or 9-inch layer pans. Bake at 350° for 55 to 60 minutes for oblong cake or 30 to 35 minutes for layers, or until cake tester comes out clean. Cool 10 minutes; remove from pans. Cool completely; frost as desired (see pages 68–74).

10 to 12 servings.

*To sour milk: Use 2 tablespoons vinegar plus milk to equal 2 cups.

Orange Cocoa Cake

½ cup unsweetened cocoa
½ cup boiling water
¼ cup butter or margarine, softened
¼ cup shortening
2 cups sugar
⅛ teaspoon salt
1 teaspoon vanilla
2 eggs
1½ teaspoons baking soda

1 cup buttermilk or sour milk*
1¾ cups unsifted all-purpose flour
3 tablespoons buttermilk or sour milk*
⅛ teaspoon baking soda
¾ teaspoon grated orange peel
¼ teaspoon orange extract
Orange Buttercream Frosting (below)

Grease three 8- or 9-inch layer pans and line with wax paper; set aside. Stir together cocoa and boiling water until smooth; set aside. Cream butter or margarine, shortening, sugar, salt and vanilla in large mixer bowl until light and fluffy. Add eggs; beat well. Stir 1½ teaspoons baking soda into 1 cup buttermilk or sour milk; add alternately with flour to creamed mixture.

Measure 1⅔ cups batter into small bowl. Stir in 3 tablespoons buttermilk or sour milk, ⅛ teaspoon baking soda, the orange peel and orange extract; pour into one prepared pan. Blend cocoa mixture into remaining batter; divide evenly among remaining two prepared pans. Bake at 350° for 25 to 30 minutes or until cake tester comes out clean. Cool 10 minutes; remove from pans. Cool completely. Place one chocolate layer on serving plate; spread with some of the Orange Buttercream Frosting. Top with orange layer and spread with frosting. Top with remaining chocolate layer and frost entire cake.

10 to 12 servings.

*To sour milk: Use 1 tablespoon vinegar plus milk to equal 1 cup; use ½ teaspoon vinegar plus milk to equal 3 tablespoons.

Orange Buttercream Frosting

⅔ cup butter or margarine, softened
6 cups confectioners' sugar

2 teaspoons grated orange peel
1½ teaspoons vanilla
4 to 6 tablespoons milk

Cream butter or margarine, 1 cup confectioners' sugar, the orange peel and vanilla in large mixer bowl. Add remaining confectioners' sugar alternately with milk, beating to spreading consistency.

Lickity-Split Cocoa Cake

Perfect for small families. And when you need a homemade chocolate cake—in a hurry.

1½ cups unsifted all-purpose
    flour
1 cup sugar
¼ cup unsweetened cocoa
1 teaspoon baking soda
½ teaspoon salt
1 cup water
¼ cup plus 2 tablespoons
    vegetable oil
1 tablespoon vinegar
1 teaspoon vanilla

Combine flour, sugar, cocoa, baking soda and salt in large mixing bowl. Add water, oil, vinegar and vanilla; stir with spoon or wire whisk just until batter is smooth and ingredients are well blended.

Pour into greased and floured 9-inch layer pan or 8-inch square pan. Bake at 350° for 35 to 40 minutes or until cake tester comes out clean. Cool in pan; frost as desired (see pages 68–74).

6 to 8 servings.

Hershey Bar Swirl Cake

1 cup butter or margarine,
    softened
2 cups sugar
1 teaspoon vanilla
5 eggs
2½ cups unsifted all-purpose
    flour
¾ teaspoon baking soda
¼ teaspoon salt
1½ cups sour cream
¼ cup honey or light corn
    syrup
¾ cup chopped pecans
1 milk chocolate bar
    (8 ounces), broken
    into pieces
½ cup (5.5-ounce can)
    chocolate-flavored syrup

Cream butter or margarine, sugar and vanilla in large mixer bowl until light and fluffy. Add eggs; beat well. Combine flour, baking soda and salt; add alternately with sour cream to creamed mixture. Measure 2 cups batter; stir in honey or corn syrup and pecans. Set aside.

Melt chocolate bar pieces in chocolate-flavored syrup in top of double boiler over hot, not boiling, water; blend into remaining batter. Pour into greased and floured 10-inch tube pan (do not use Bundt pan). Spoon reserved pecan batter evenly over chocolate batter; *do not mix*. Bake on lowest rack of oven at 350° for 45 minutes; without opening oven door, decrease temperature to 325° and continue to bake for 50 to 55 minutes or until cake tester comes out clean. Cool 1 hour; remove from pan. Cool completely; glaze as desired (see pages 72–73).

12 to 16 servings.

Chocolate Swirl Cake

This elegant cake creates its own chocolate swirl design. (It's not magic—it's the syrup!)

1 cup butter or margarine, softened
2 cups sugar
2 teaspoons vanilla
3 eggs
2¾ cups unsifted all-purpose flour
1 teaspoon baking soda
½ teaspoon salt
1 cup buttermilk or sour milk*
1 cup chocolate-flavored syrup
¼ teaspoon baking soda
1 cup flaked coconut (optional)

Cream butter or margarine, sugar and vanilla in large mixer bowl until light and fluffy. Add eggs; beat well. Combine flour, 1 teaspoon baking soda and the salt; add alternately with buttermilk or sour milk to creamed mixture. Combine syrup and ¼ teaspoon baking soda; blend into 2 cups batter.

Add coconut to remaining batter; pour into greased and floured 12-cup Bundt pan or 10-inch tube pan. Pour chocolate batter over vanilla batter in pan; *do not mix.* Bake at 350° about 70 minutes or until cake tester comes out clean. Cool 15 minutes; remove from pan. Cool completely; glaze or frost as desired (see pages 68–74).

12 to 16 servings.

*To sour milk: Use 1 tablespoon vinegar plus milk to equal 1 cup.

Feathery Fudge Cake

2½ blocks (2½ ounces) unsweetened baking chocolate
¾ cup butter or margarine, softened
2 cups sugar
1 teaspoon vanilla
2 eggs
2¼ cups unsifted all-purpose flour
1¼ teaspoons baking soda
½ teaspoon salt
1⅓ cups water

Melt baking chocolate in top of double boiler over hot, not boiling, water; cool slightly. Cream butter or margarine, sugar and vanilla in large mixer bowl until light and fluffy. Add eggs and cooled chocolate; blend well. Combine flour, baking soda and salt; add alternately with water to creamed mixture.

Pour into two greased and floured 9-inch layer pans. Bake at 350° for 35 to 40 minutes or until cake tester comes out clean. Cool 10 minutes; remove from pans. Cool completely; frost as desired (see pages 68–74).

8 to 10 servings.

Cocoa Streusel Cake

1 cup butter or margarine, softened
2 cups sugar
2 eggs
1 cup sour cream
1 teaspoon grated lemon peel
1 teaspoon lemon juice
2 cups unsifted all-purpose flour
1 teaspoon baking powder
¼ teaspoon salt
1 cup chopped nuts
½ cup flaked coconut
¼ cup unsweetened cocoa
¼ cup sugar
1 teaspoon cinnamon
3 tablespoons butter or margarine, melted
Confectioners' sugar

Cream 1 cup butter or margarine, 2 cups sugar and the eggs in large mixer bowl until light and fluffy. Blend in sour cream, lemon peel and lemon juice. Combine flour, baking powder and salt; blend into creamed mixture. Combine nuts, coconut, cocoa, ¼ cup sugar and the cinnamon in small mixing bowl; stir in 3 tablespoons melted butter or margarine. Set aside.

Pour half the batter into greased and floured 12-cup Bundt pan or 10-inch tube pan; sprinkle with half the nut mixture. Carefully spread remaining batter over nut mixture and top with remaining nut mixture. Bake at 350° for 1 hour or until cake tester comes out clean. Cool 10 minutes; remove from pan. Cool completely; sprinkle with confectioners' sugar.

12 to 16 servings.

Cocoa Bundt Cake

¾ cup butter or margarine, softened
1⅔ cups sugar
2 eggs
1 teaspoon vanilla
¾ cup sour cream

2 cups unsifted all-purpose flour
⅔ cup unsweetened cocoa
½ teaspoon salt
2 teaspoons baking soda
1 cup buttermilk or sour milk*

Cream butter or margarine, sugar, eggs and vanilla in large mixer bowl until light and fluffy; blend in sour cream. Combine flour, cocoa and salt. Stir baking soda into buttermilk or sour milk; add alternately with dry ingredients to creamed mixture. Beat 2 minutes on medium speed.

Pour into greased and floured 9- or 12-cup Bundt pan. Bake at 350° for 45 to 50 minutes or until cake tester comes out clean. Cool 10 minutes; remove from pan. Cool completely; glaze as desired (see pages 72–73).

12 to 16 servings.

*To sour milk: Use 1 tablespoon vinegar plus milk to equal 1 cup.

Chocolate Spice Cake

Applesauce gives this spice-fragrant cake extra moistness.

1¾ cups unsifted all-purpose flour
1¼ cups sugar
⅓ cup unsweetened cocoa
2 teaspoons baking soda
1 teaspoon cinnamon
½ teaspoon nutmeg
¼ teaspoon allspice

⅛ teaspoon salt
1½ cups applesauce
½ cup milk
½ cup butter or margarine, melted
1 teaspoon vanilla
1 cup chopped nuts (optional)
½ cup raisins

Combine flour, sugar, cocoa, baking soda, cinnamon, nutmeg, allspice and salt in large mixer bowl. Stir in applesauce, milk, butter or margarine and vanilla; blend well. Add nuts and raisins.

Pour into greased and floured 9-cup Bundt pan or 13 x 9-inch pan. Bake at 350° for 55 to 60 minutes for Bundt pan or 40 to 45 minutes for oblong pan, or until cake tester comes out clean. Cool 15 minutes; remove from pan. Cool completely. Glaze or frost as desired (see pages 68–74).

8 to 10 servings.

Fudgey Pecan Cake

¾ cup butter, melted
1½ cups sugar
1½ teaspoons vanilla
3 egg yolks
½ cup plus 1 tablespoon
 unsweetened cocoa
½ cup unsifted all-purpose
 flour
3 tablespoons vegetable oil

3 tablespoons water
¾ cup finely chopped pecans
3 egg whites, at room
 temperature
⅛ teaspoon cream of tartar
⅛ teaspoon salt
 Royal Glaze (page 53)
 Pecan halves (optional)

Line bottom of 9-inch springform pan with aluminum foil; butter foil and side of pan. Set pan aside. Combine ¾ cup melted butter, the sugar and vanilla in large mixer bowl; beat well. Add egg yolks, one at a time, beating well after each addition. Blend in cocoa, flour, oil and water; beat well. Stir in chopped pecans. Beat egg whites, cream of tartar and salt in small mixer bowl until stiff peaks form. Carefully fold into chocolate mixture. Pour into prepared pan. Bake at 350° for 45 minutes or until top begins to crack slightly. (Cake will not test done in center.) Cool 1 hour. Cover; chill until firm. Remove side of pan.

Prepare Royal Glaze. Pour over cake, allowing glaze to run down side. With narrow metal spatula, spread glaze evenly on top and side. Allow to harden. Garnish with pecan halves.

10 to 12 servings.

Royal Chocolate Cake

¼ cup butter, melted
½ cup sugar
6 tablespoons unsweetened cocoa
¾ cup butter, softened
¾ cup sugar
6 egg yolks, at room temperature
1¼ cups finely chopped blanched almonds
6 egg whites, at room temperature
⅛ teaspoon salt
Royal Glaze (below)
Sweetened whipped cream (optional)

Butter 9-inch springform pan; line bottom with wax paper. Butter paper; dust bottom and sides with fine, dry bread crumbs. Tap pan lightly to shake out excess crumbs. Set aside.

Combine ¼ cup melted butter, ½ cup sugar and the cocoa in large mixer bowl until smooth; set aside. Cream ¾ cup softened butter and ¾ cup sugar in small mixer bowl until light and fluffy. Add egg yolks, one at a time, beating well after each addition. Add reserved cocoa mixture on low speed just until blended. Blend in chopped almonds just until mixed. Beat egg whites and salt in small mixer bowl until soft peaks form. Gradually fold about a fourth of the egg whites at a time into chocolate mixture.

Pour into prepared pan. Bake at 375° for 20 minutes; without opening oven door, decrease temperature to 350° and continue to bake for 40 to 45 minutes or until cake has a soft, moist spot only in the center. Cool completely; remove side of pan.

Prepare Royal Glaze. Pour over cake, allowing glaze to run down side. With narrow metal spatula, spread glaze evenly over top and around side. Allow to harden. Serve with sweetened whipped cream.

10 to 12 servings.

Royal Glaze
Break 8 blocks (8 ounces) semi-sweet baking chocolate into small pieces. Combine baking chocolate pieces and ½ cup heavy or whipping cream in small saucepan. Cook over very low heat, stirring constantly, until chocolate is melted and mixture is smooth; *do not boil*. Remove from heat; cool, stirring occasionally, until mixture begins to thicken, 10 to 15 minutes.

Marble Chiffon Cake

⅓ cup unsweetened cocoa
2 tablespoons sugar
¼ cup water
2 tablespoons vegetable oil
2 cups unsifted all-purpose flour
1½ cups sugar
3 teaspoons baking powder
1 teaspoon salt
½ cup vegetable oil
7 egg yolks, at room temperature
¾ cup cold water
2 teaspoons vanilla
7 egg whites, at room temperature
½ teaspoon cream of tartar
Chocolate Glaze (below)

Combine cocoa, 2 tablespoons sugar, ¼ cup water and 2 tablespoons oil in small mixing bowl until smooth; set aside. Combine flour, 1½ cups sugar, the baking powder and salt in large mixer bowl; add ½ cup oil, the egg yolks, ¾ cup cold water and the vanilla. Beat on low speed until combined. Beat 5 minutes on high speed. With second set of beaters, beat egg whites and cream of tartar in large mixer bowl until stiff peaks form.

Pour batter in thin stream over entire surface of egg whites; fold in lightly by hand. Remove a third of the batter to another bowl; gently fold in chocolate mixture. Pour half the vanilla batter into ungreased 10-inch tube pan; spread half the chocolate batter over vanilla. Repeat layers; gently swirl with spatula or knife for marbled effect. Bake at 325° for 65 to 70 minutes or until top springs back when touched lightly. Invert cake over funnel or bottle until completely cool. Loosen cake from pan; invert onto serving plate. Glaze with Chocolate Glaze.

12 to 16 servings.

Chocolate Glaze

2 tablespoons butter or margarine
¼ cup unsweetened cocoa
3 tablespoons water
½ teaspoon vanilla
1¼ cups confectioners' sugar

Melt butter or margarine in small saucepan over low heat. Stir in cocoa and water. Cook, stirring constantly, until mixture thickens; *do not boil*. Remove from heat. Stir in vanilla. Gradually add confectioners' sugar; beat until smooth.

On facing page—Mousse-Filled Cocoa Chiffon Cake (page 56); Marble Chiffon Cake (this page)

Mousse-Filled Cocoa Chiffon Cake

1¾ cups sugar	¾ cup cold water
1½ cups unsifted cake flour	2 teaspoons vanilla
⅔ cup unsweetened cocoa	7 egg whites, at room
2 teaspoons baking powder	temperature
1 teaspoon salt	½ teaspoon cream of tartar
½ teaspoon baking soda	¼ cup sugar
½ cup vegetable oil	Mousse Filling (below)
7 egg yolks	Chocolate Cream (below)

Combine 1¾ cups sugar, the flour, cocoa, baking powder, salt and baking soda in large mixing bowl. Make a "well" in mixture and add in order: oil, egg yolks, water and vanilla. Beat until smooth. Beat egg whites and cream of tartar in large mixer bowl until foamy. Gradually add ¼ cup sugar and beat until stiff peaks form. Gradually pour chocolate batter over beaten egg whites, gently folding just until blended. Pour into ungreased 10-inch tube pan. Bake at 325° for 1 hour and 20 minutes or until top springs back when touched lightly. Meanwhile, prepare Mousse Filling and Chocolate Cream.

Invert cake over funnel or bottle until completely cool. Loosen cake from pan; invert onto serving plate. Slice a ¾-inch-thick layer from top of cake; set aside. Being careful to leave 1-inch-thick walls and base, cut a neat cavity in cake. With a fork, remove section of cake between the cuts. Spoon Mousse Filling into cavity. Replace top of cake; press gently. Frost cake with Chocolate Cream. Chill several hours.

12 to 16 servings.

Mousse Filling

1 envelope unflavored gelatine	⅔ cup sugar
2 tablespoons cold water	1½ cups heavy or whipping
⅓ cup water	cream
⅓ cup unsweetened cocoa	2 teaspoons vanilla

Sprinkle gelatine onto 2 tablespoons water in small bowl; set aside to soften. Bring ⅓ cup water to boil in small saucepan; stir in cocoa over low heat until smooth and thickened. Add softened gelatine, stirring until dissolved. Remove from heat; stir in sugar. Cool to room temperature. Whip cream with vanilla until stiff peaks form. Gradually add chocolate while beating on low speed just until well blended. Chill 30 minutes.

Chocolate Cream

Combine ¾ cup confectioners' sugar and 6 tablespoons unsweetened cocoa in small mixer bowl. Add 1½ cups heavy or whipping cream and ¾ teaspoon vanilla; beat until stiff. Cover; chill.

Chocolate Pound Cake

1½ cups butter or margarine, softened
3 cups sugar
2 teaspoons vanilla
5 eggs
1½ teaspoons instant coffee granules
¼ cup hot water

2 cups unsifted all-purpose flour
¾ cup unsweetened cocoa
1 teaspoon salt
½ teaspoon baking powder
1 cup buttermilk or sour milk*
Confectioners' sugar

Cream butter or margarine, sugar and vanilla in large mixer bowl 5 minutes on medium speed. Add eggs, one at a time, beating well after each addition. Dissolve coffee granules in hot water. Combine flour, cocoa, salt and baking powder; add alternately with coffee and buttermilk or sour milk to creamed mixture, beating just until mixture is blended.

Pour into well-greased and floured 12-cup Bundt pan or 10-inch tube pan. Bake at 325° for 1 hour and 20 to 25 minutes or until cake tester comes out clean. Cool 20 minutes; remove from pan. Cool completely; sprinkle with confectioners' sugar.

12 to 16 servings.

*To sour milk: Use 1 tablespoon vinegar plus milk to equal 1 cup.

Mini Chip Pound Cake

1 cup butter or margarine, softened
1 cup sugar
1 cup packed light brown sugar
1½ teaspoons vanilla
3 eggs
2½ cups unsifted all-purpose flour

2 teaspoons baking powder
½ teaspoon salt
1 cup milk
1½ cups semi-sweet chocolate Mini Chips
Chocolate Satin Glaze (page 73)

Cream butter or margarine, sugar, brown sugar and vanilla in large mixer bowl until light and fluffy. Add eggs, one at a time, beating well after each addition. Combine flour, baking powder and salt; add alternately with milk to creamed mixture, beating just until smooth. Stir in Mini Chips.

Pour into well-greased and floured 12-cup Bundt pan or 10-inch tube pan. Bake at 350° for 65 to 70 minutes or until cake tester comes out clean. Remove from pan; cool completely. Glaze with Chocolate Satin Glaze.

12 to 16 servings.

Chocolate-Strawberry Chiffon Squares

1½ cups unsifted cake flour
1 cup sugar
½ cup unsweetened cocoa
¾ teaspoon baking soda
½ teaspoon salt
1 cup buttermilk or sour milk
½ cup vegetable oil
2 egg yolks
2 egg whites
½ cup sugar
Berry Cream (below)
Fresh strawberries

Combine cake flour, 1 cup sugar, the cocoa, baking soda and salt in large mixer bowl. Add buttermilk or sour milk, oil and egg yolks; beat until smooth. Beat egg whites in small mixer bowl until foamy; gradually add ½ cup sugar, beating until very stiff peaks form. Gently fold egg whites into chocolate batter. Pour into greased and floured 13 x 9-inch pan. Bake at 350° for 30 to 35 minutes or until cake springs back when touched lightly in center. Cool in pan on wire rack. Just before serving, prepare Berry Cream; frost top of cake. Cut into squares and garnish with strawberry halves. Refrigerate leftovers.

10 to 12 servings.

Berry Cream
Mash or puree 1 cup sweetened sliced strawberries in blender or food processor to measure ½ cup. Whip 1 cup heavy or whipping cream until stiff; gently fold in puree, 1 teaspoon vanilla and, if desired, 2 or 3 drops red food color.

Aztec Sunburst Cake

The name of this upside-down cake honors its chocolate ancestry. Be creative in arranging the fruit in a handsome pattern.

¼ cup butter or margarine, melted
½ cup packed light brown sugar
2 tablespoons light corn syrup
1 can (16 ounces) pear halves, about 4 halves
7 maraschino cherries, cut into quarters
¼ cup chopped pecans
½ cup plus 2 tablespoons butter or margarine, softened

1¼ cups sugar
1 teaspoon vanilla
2 eggs
1½ cups unsifted all-purpose flour
¼ cup unsweetened cocoa
½ teaspoon baking soda
½ teaspoon salt
½ cup buttermilk or sour milk*
Sweetened whipped cream (optional)

Combine ¼ cup melted butter or margarine, the brown sugar and corn syrup in 9-inch square pan; spread evenly over bottom of pan. Drain pear halves; slice each half lengthwise into 4 sections and arrange in sunburst design over mixture in pan. Arrange cherries and pecans between pear sections, in center and at corners.

Cream ½ cup plus 2 tablespoons butter or margarine, the sugar and vanilla in large mixer bowl. Add eggs; beat well. Combine flour, cocoa, baking soda and salt; add alternately with buttermilk or sour milk to creamed mixture.

Carefully pour batter over fruit and nuts in pan. Bake at 350° for 45 to 50 minutes or until cake tester comes out clean. Immediately invert onto serving plate. Serve warm or cold with sweetened whipped cream.

8 to 10 servings.

*To sour milk: Use 1½ teaspoons vinegar plus milk to equal ½ cup.

Chocolate Zucchini Cake

3 eggs
1½ cups sugar
1 teaspoon vanilla
½ cup vegetable oil
2 cups unsifted all-purpose flour
⅓ cup unsweetened cocoa
1 teaspoon baking powder
1 teaspoon baking soda
1 teaspoon cinnamon
¼ teaspoon salt
¾ cup buttermilk or sour milk*
2 cups coarsely shredded raw zucchini
1 cup chopped nuts
½ cup raisins
Creamy Chocolate Glaze (optional, below)

Beat eggs in large mixer bowl on high speed until foamy. Gradually add sugar and vanilla; beat until thick and lemon colored. Gradually add oil; beat until combined. Combine flour, cocoa, baking powder, baking soda, cinnamon and salt; add alternately with buttermilk or sour milk to egg mixture in two additions, beginning and ending with flour mixture. Fold zucchini into batter. Stir in nuts and raisins.

Pour into greased and floured 12-cup Bundt pan. Bake at 350° for 50 to 55 minutes or until cake tester comes out clean. Cool 10 minutes; invert onto serving plate. Cool completely; glaze with Creamy Chocolate Glaze.

12 to 16 servings.

*To sour milk: Use 2 teaspoons vinegar plus milk to equal ¾ cup.

Creamy Chocolate Glaze

3 tablespoons sugar
2 tablespoons water
½ cup semi-sweet chocolate Mini Chips
1 tablespoon marshmallow creme
1 to 2 teaspoons hot water

Combine sugar and 2 tablespoons water in small saucepan; bring to boil. Remove from heat; immediately add Mini Chips and stir until melted. Blend in marshmallow creme; add hot water, ½ teaspoon at a time, until glaze is desired consistency.

Chocolate Chip Carrot Cake

Popular carrot cakes—like zucchini cakes—are especially moist. Chocolate chips and cinnamon enhance the subtle flavor of the carrots in our recipe.

1 ½ cups unsifted all-purpose flour
¾ cup sugar
½ cup packed light brown sugar
1 ¼ teaspoons baking soda
1 teaspoon cinnamon
½ teaspoon salt
3 eggs
¾ cup vegetable oil

1 ½ teaspoons vanilla
2 cups grated carrots
2 cups (12-ounce package) semi-sweet chocolate Mini Chips
½ cup chopped walnuts
Cream Cheese Frosting (below)

Combine flour, sugar, brown sugar, baking soda, cinnamon and salt in large mixer bowl. Beat eggs, oil and vanilla in small mixer bowl; add to dry ingredients. Blend well. Stir in carrots, Mini Chips and walnuts. Pour into greased and floured 13 x 9-inch pan. Bake at 350° for 35 to 40 minutes or until cake tester comes out clean. Cool completely; frost with Cream Cheese Frosting.

10 to 12 servings.

Cream Cheese Frosting

Beat 1 package (3 ounces) cream cheese, softened, and ¼ cup softened butter or margarine in small mixer bowl until smooth and well blended. Gradually add 2 cups confectioners' sugar; stir in 1 teaspoon vanilla. Beat until smooth.

Chip-Apple Snackin' Cake

2 eggs
½ cup vegetable oil
¼ cup apple juice
1 teaspoon vanilla
1¾ cups unsifted all-purpose flour
1 cup sugar
½ teaspoon baking soda
½ teaspoon salt
½ teaspoon cinnamon
1½ cups diced peeled tart apples
¾ cup semi-sweet chocolate Mini Chips
½ cup chopped nuts
Confectioners' sugar or whipped topping (optional)

Beat eggs slightly in large mixing bowl; add oil, apple juice and vanilla. Combine flour, sugar, baking soda, salt and cinnamon; add to egg mixture, blending well. Stir in apples, Mini Chips and nuts.

Pour into greased and floured 9-inch square pan. Bake at 350° for 40 to 45 minutes or until cake begins to pull away from edges of pan. Cool in pan. Just before serving, sprinkle top with confectioners' sugar or serve with dollop of whipped topping sprinkled with cinnamon.

8 to 10 servings.

Cocoa-Coconut Snackin' Cake

¼ cup butter or margarine, melted
⅓ cup unsweetened cocoa
1 cup sour cream
1¼ cups unsifted all-purpose flour
1 cup sugar
¾ teaspoon baking soda
¼ teaspoon salt
2 eggs, beaten
1 cup flaked coconut
½ cup chopped nuts

Combine melted butter or margarine and cocoa; blend in sour cream. Combine flour, sugar, baking soda and salt in large mixing bowl. Blend in cocoa mixture and eggs until dry ingredients are moistened. Stir in coconut and nuts.

Spread in greased 9-inch square pan. Bake at 350° for 30 to 35 minutes or until cake tester comes out clean. Cool in pan.

8 to 10 servings.

Cocoa-Spice Snackin' Cake

¼ cup butter or margarine, melted
¼ cup unsweetened cocoa
¾ cup applesauce
1¼ cups unsifted all-purpose flour
1 cup sugar
¾ teaspoon baking soda
½ teaspoon cinnamon
¼ teaspoon nutmeg
¼ teaspoon salt
1 egg, beaten
½ cup chopped nuts

Combine melted butter or margarine and cocoa; blend in applesauce. Combine flour, sugar, baking soda, cinnamon, nutmeg and salt in large mixing bowl. Blend in cocoa mixture and egg until dry ingredients are moistened. Stir in nuts.

Spread in greased 9-inch square pan. Bake at 350° for 30 to 35 minutes or until cake tester comes out clean. Cool in pan.

8 to 10 servings.

Easy Pumpkin Cake

1 package (18½ ounces) regular yellow cake mix
4 teaspoons pumpkin pie spice
2 teaspoons baking soda
1¾ cups (16-ounce can) pumpkin
¼ cup water
¼ cup vegetable oil
3 eggs
1 cup semi-sweet chocolate Mini Chips
Chocolate Glaze (below)
Chopped nuts (optional)

Combine dry cake mix, pumpkin pie spice, baking soda, pumpkin, water, oil and eggs in large mixer bowl; beat on low speed until moistened. Beat 2 minutes on medium speed until smooth. Stir in Mini Chips. Pour into greased and floured 12-cup Bundt pan. Bake at 350° for 45 to 50 minutes or until top springs back when touched lightly. Cool 10 minutes; remove from pan. Cool completely. Drizzle with Chocolate Glaze and sprinkle with chopped nuts.

12 to 16 servings.

Chocolate Glaze

Combine 2 tablespoons sugar and 2 tablespoons water in small saucepan; cook over medium heat, stirring constantly, until mixture boils and sugar is dissolved. Remove from heat; immediately add ½ cup semi-sweet chocolate chips, stirring until melted. Continue stirring until glaze is desired consistency.

Tiger-Stripe Cake

1 package (18½ ounces) regular yellow cake mix	2 cups milk
⅔ cup sugar	2 tablespoons butter or margarine
¼ cup unsweetened cocoa	½ teaspoon vanilla
2½ tablespoons cornstarch	

Prepare cake mix as directed on package; bake in greased and floured 13 x 9-inch pan as directed. Remove from oven; immediately poke holes at 1-inch intervals down through entire cake with handle of wooden spoon or with plastic drinking straw. Cool 20 minutes.

Meanwhile, combine sugar, cocoa and cornstarch in medium saucepan; gradually stir in milk. Cook over medium heat, stirring constantly, until mixture comes to a full rolling boil; stir in butter or margarine and vanilla. Immediately pour hot mixture over warm cake, making sure that entire top is covered and that mixture flows into holes. Press plastic wrap onto surface of topping; chill until firm, at least 2 hours. Cut into pieces; serve cold. Store, covered, in refrigerator.

12 to 14 servings.

Checkerboard Cake

1 package (18½ ounces) white cake mix (pudding-in-the-mix type)	3 tablespoons boiling water
1 envelope unflavored gelatine	1 cup chocolate-flavored syrup
¼ cup cold water	Chocolate Whipped Cream (page 244)

Prepare cake mix as directed on package; bake in greased and floured 13 x 9-inch pan as directed. Cool 15 minutes. With a fork, carefully pierce cake in pan to full depth of cake, making parallel rows about 1 inch apart, covering both length and width of cake. Sprinkle gelatine onto cold water in small mixing bowl; let stand 5 minutes to soften. Stir in boiling water until gelatine is dissolved; stir in syrup. Pour chocolate mixture over cooled cake, making sure that entire top is covered and that mixture flows into holes. Cover; chill until firm, about 5 hours. Cut into pieces; serve with Chocolate Whipped Cream.

12 to 14 servings.

Ice-Itself Chocolate Layer Cake

Our simple-to-make version of a German chocolate cake. For best results, follow the directions exactly: Covering the layers with foil at the right moment keeps the topping soft.

1 cup flaked coconut
½ cup chopped pecans
⅓ cup packed light brown sugar
3 tablespoons butter or margarine, melted
3 tablespoons evaporated milk
2 tablespoons light corn syrup
½ cup butter or margarine, softened

1 cup plus 2 tablespoons sugar
1 egg
½ teaspoon vanilla
1¼ cups plus 2 tablespoons unsifted all-purpose flour
⅓ cup unsweetened cocoa
1 teaspoon baking soda
½ teaspoon salt
1 cup buttermilk

Line two 8-inch layer pans with foil; butter foil. Combine coconut, pecans, brown sugar, 3 tablespoons melted butter or margarine, the evaporated milk and corn syrup in small bowl. Spread half the mixture evenly over bottom of each pan.

Cream ½ cup butter or margarine and the sugar in large mixer bowl until light and fluffy. Add egg and vanilla; blend well. Combine flour, cocoa, baking soda and salt; add alternately with buttermilk to creamed mixture. Carefully spread half the batter into each prepared pan; do not mix with coconut topping. Bake at 350° for 30 to 35 minutes or until top springs back when touched. Invert immediately onto wire rack; gently remove foil and discard. Cover layers loosely with foil to keep topping soft. Cool completely; place one layer on top of other. Keep well covered.

8 to 10 servings.

Chocolate-Peanut Butter Marble Cake

¼ cup unsweetened cocoa
2 tablespoons confectioners' sugar
2 tablespoons butter or margarine, softened
2 tablespoons hot water
1 cup peanut butter chips
1 tablespoon shortening
1 package (18½ ounces) white cake mix (pudding-in-the-mix type)
½ cup packed light brown sugar
1¼ cups water
3 eggs

Combine cocoa, confectioners' sugar, butter or margarine and 2 tablespoons hot water in small mixing bowl until smooth; set aside. Melt peanut butter chips and shortening in top of double boiler over hot, not boiling, water; set aside. Combine dry cake mix, brown sugar, 1¼ cups water, the eggs and melted peanut butter mixture in large mixer bowl; beat on low speed until moistened. Beat 2 minutes on medium speed until smooth. Add 1½ cups batter to reserved cocoa mixture; blend well. Pour remaining batter into greased and floured 13 x 9-inch pan; spoon dollops of chocolate batter on top. Swirl with knife or spatula for marbled effect. Bake at 350° for 40 to 45 minutes or until cake tester comes out clean. Cool; frost as desired (see pages 68–74).

10 to 12 servings.

Chocolatetown Cupcakes

½ cup butter or margarine, softened
1 cup sugar
1 teaspoon vanilla
4 eggs
1¼ cups unsifted all-purpose flour
¾ teaspoon baking soda
1½ cups (1-pound can) chocolate-flavored syrup

Cream butter or margarine, sugar and vanilla in large mixer bowl until light and fluffy. Add eggs; beat well. Combine flour and baking soda; add alternately with syrup to creamed mixture. Fill paper-lined muffin cups (2½ inches in diameter) half full with batter. Bake at 375° for 15 to 20 minutes or until cake tester comes out clean. Cool; frost as desired (see pages 68–74).

About 2½ dozen cupcakes.

Banana Chocolicious Cupcakes

1 package (18½ ounces) regular banana cake mix	1⅓ cups water
⅔ cup sugar	¼ cup vegetable oil
⅓ cup unsweetened cocoa	2 eggs
	1 cup mashed ripe bananas

Combine dry cake mix, sugar, cocoa, water, oil, eggs and mashed bananas in large mixer bowl; beat on low speed until moistened. Beat 2 minutes on medium speed until smooth. Fill paper-lined muffin cups (2½ inches in diameter) ⅔ full with batter. Bake at 350° for 15 to 20 minutes or until cake tester comes out clean. Cool completely; frost as desired (see pages 68–74).

About 2½ dozen cupcakes.

Creme-Filled Cupcakes

These luscious cupcakes are a snap to fill: You can use a pastry tube to squeeze in the Vanilla Creme.

¾ cup shortening	½ cup unsweetened cocoa
1¼ cups sugar	1 teaspoon baking soda
2 eggs	½ teaspoon salt
1 teaspoon vanilla	1 cup milk
1¾ cups unsifted all-purpose flour	Vanilla Creme (below)

Cream shortening and sugar in large mixer bowl. Add eggs and vanilla; blend well. Combine flour, cocoa, baking soda and salt; add alternately with milk to creamed mixture. Fill paper-lined muffin cups (2½ inches in diameter) ⅔ full with batter. Bake at 375° for 20 to 25 minutes or until cake tester comes out clean. Cool completely.

Prepare Vanilla Creme; spoon into pastry tube with open star tip. Insert tip into center of top of cupcake; gently squeeze until cupcake begins to peak. Cover top with swirl of filling. (Or cut a 1½-inch cone from top of cupcake. Fill; replace cone. Swirl filling over top.)

About 2 dozen cupcakes.

Vanilla Creme

Combine ¼ cup unsifted all-purpose flour and ½ cup milk in small saucepan; cook over low heat, stirring constantly with wire whisk, until mixture thickens and just begins to boil. Remove from heat; chill. Cream ¼ cup softened butter or margarine and ¼ cup shortening in large mixer bowl; blend in 2 teaspoons vanilla, ¼ teaspoon salt and the chilled flour mixture. Gradually add 4 cups confectioners' sugar; beat to spreading consistency.

Chocolate Buttercream Frosting

	1 cup frosting	2 cups frosting
Unsweetened cocoa:		
Light flavor	2 tablespoons	¼ cup
Medium flavor	¼ cup	½ cup
Dark flavor	⅓ cup	¾ cup
Confectioners' sugar	1 cup	2⅔ cups
Butter or margarine, softened	3 tablespoons	6 tablespoons
Milk or water	2 tablespoons	4 to 5 tablespoons
Vanilla	½ teaspoon	1 teaspoon

In small bowl, combine amount of cocoa for flavor you prefer with confectioners' sugar. Cream butter or margarine and ½ cup of cocoa mixture in small mixer bowl. Add remaining cocoa mixture, milk or water and vanilla; beat to spreading consistency. For a glossier texture, add 1 tablespoon light corn syrup to the mixture.

Chocolate Fudge Frosting

	1 cup frosting	2 cups frosting
Butter or margarine	3 tablespoons	⅓ cup
Unsweetened cocoa:		
Light flavor	2 tablespoons	3 tablespoons
Medium flavor	¼ cup	⅓ cup
Dark flavor	½ cup	⅔ cup
Confectioners' sugar	1⅓ cups	2⅔ cups
Milk	2 to 3 tablespoons	⅓ cup
Vanilla	½ teaspoon	1 teaspoon

Melt butter or margarine in small saucepan over medium heat. Add amount of cocoa for flavor you prefer. Cook over medium heat, stirring constantly, until mixture just begins to boil. Remove from heat. Pour into small mixer bowl; cool completely. Add confectioners' sugar alternately with milk, beating to spreading consistency. Blend in vanilla.

Creamy Chocolate Frosting

3 tablespoons butter or margarine
3 blocks (3 ounces) unsweetened baking chocolate

3 cups confectioners' sugar
¼ teaspoon salt
½ cup milk
1 teaspoon vanilla

Melt butter or margarine in small saucepan; add baking chocolate and cook over very low heat, stirring constantly, until chocolate is melted and mixture is smooth. Pour into small mixer bowl. Add confectioners' sugar, salt, milk and vanilla; beat until well blended. Chill 10 to 15 minutes or until spreading consistency.

About 2 cups frosting.

Seven-Minute Cocoa Frosting

2 egg whites
1½ cups sugar
⅓ cup water

¼ cup unsweetened cocoa
1½ teaspoons vanilla

Combine egg whites, sugar and water in top of a double boiler over boiling water; beat about 7 minutes on high speed or until frosting holds its shape. Remove from heat; carefully fold in cocoa and vanilla.

About 3 cups frosting.

Quick Chocolate Frosting

4 blocks (4 ounces) unsweetened baking chocolate
¼ cup butter or margarine

3 cups confectioners' sugar
1 teaspoon vanilla
⅛ teaspoon salt
⅓ cup milk

Melt baking chocolate with butter or margarine in small saucepan over very low heat. Pour into small mixer bowl; add confectioners' sugar, vanilla and salt. Blend in milk; beat to spreading consistency. (If frosting is too thick, add additional milk, 1 teaspoonful at a time, until frosting is desired consistency.)

About 2 cups frosting.

Chocolate Whipped Cream Frosting

	8-inch layer cake	9-inch layer cake	9-inch torte (3 layers)
Heavy or whipping cream	1 cup	1½ cups	2 cups
Chocolate-flavored syrup, chilled	½ cup (5.5-ounce can)	⅔ cup	1 cup
Vanilla	½ teaspoon	½ teaspoon	1 teaspoon

Combine cream, syrup and vanilla in mixer bowl. Beat to spreading consistency. Spread on cake layers; refrigerate until ready to serve.

Chocolate Cream Cheese Frosting

3 packages (3 ounces each) cream cheese, softened
⅓ cup butter or margarine, softened

5 cups confectioners' sugar
1 cup unsweetened cocoa
5 to 7 tablespoons light cream

Blend cream cheese and butter or margarine in large mixer bowl. Combine confectioners' sugar and cocoa; add alternately with light cream to cream cheese mixture. Beat to spreading consistency.

About 3 cups frosting.

Chocolate-Coconut Frosting

⅓ cup sugar
1 tablespoon cornstarch
¾ cup evaporated milk
1 milk chocolate bar (4 ounces), broken into pieces

1 tablespoon butter or margarine
1 cup flaked coconut
½ cup chopped nuts

Combine sugar and cornstarch in small saucepan; blend in evaporated milk. Cook over medium heat, stirring constantly, until mixture boils; remove from heat. Add chocolate bar pieces and butter or margarine; stir until chocolate is melted and mixture is smooth. Stir in coconut and nuts. Immediately spread on cake.

About 2 cups frosting.

On facing page—Chocolatetown Cupcakes (page 66) frosted with Chocolate-Coconut Frosting (this page) and Chocolate Buttercream Frosting (page 68); Creme-Filled Cupcakes (page 67)

Hershey Icing

½ cup butter or margarine, softened
3⅔ cups confectioners' sugar
½ cup (5.5-ounce can) chocolate-flavored syrup
1 milk chocolate bar (4 ounces), broken into pieces
2 to 3 tablespoons milk

Cream butter or margarine and confectioners' sugar in small mixer bowl; blend in syrup. Melt chocolate bar pieces in top of double boiler over hot, not boiling, water; add to syrup mixture. Add milk; beat to spreading consistency.

About 3 cups frosting.

Mocha Frosting

5 tablespoons butter or margarine, softened
1 egg yolk
3 tablespoons unsweetened cocoa
2½ cups confectioner's sugar
3 tablespoons hot strong black coffee*
1 teaspoon vanilla

Cream butter or margarine and egg yolk in small mixer bowl; blend in cocoa. Add confectioners' sugar alternately with hot coffee; beat well. Stir in vanilla.

About 1½ cups frosting.

*Or ½ teaspoon instant coffee granules plus 3 tablespoons boiling water.

Chocolate Glaze

¼ cup unsweetened cocoa
3 tablespoons water
2 tablespoons butter or margarine
1 tablespoon light corn syrup
½ teaspoon vanilla
1 to 1¼ cups confectioners' sugar

Combine cocoa, water, butter or margarine and corn syrup in small saucepan. Cook over low heat, stirring constantly, until mixture thickens; remove from heat. Stir in vanilla. Gradually add confectioners' sugar; beat until smooth and thickened.

About ¾ cup glaze.

Chocolate Satin Glaze

2 tablespoons sugar
2 tablespoons water

½ cup semi-sweet chocolate Mini Chips

Combine sugar and water in small saucepan; cook over medium heat, stirring constantly, until mixture boils and sugar is dissolved. Remove from heat; immediately add Mini Chips, stirring until melted. Continue stirring until glaze is desired consistency.

About ½ cup glaze.

Quick Chocolate Glaze

3 tablespoons chocolate-flavored syrup

⅔ cup confectioners' sugar

Combine syrup and confectioners' sugar in small mixing bowl until smooth. Add water, a few drops at a time, or additional confectioners' sugar until glaze is desired consistency.

About ⅓ cup glaze.

Cocoa Cream Filling

2 tablespoons butter or margarine
½ cup sugar
¼ cup unsweetened cocoa

⅓ cup light cream
1 cup confectioners' sugar
¼ teaspoon vanilla

Melt butter or margarine in top of double boiler over hot, not boiling, water. Stir in sugar, cocoa and light cream; cook and stir 1 minute. Cool; add confectioners' sugar and vanilla. Beat to spreading consistency.

About ¾ cup filling.

Classic Chocolate Buttercream

This classic recipe takes a little time and care to make, but it's worth it when you want an extravagantly rich filling or frosting.

1 cup sugar
½ teaspoon cream of tartar
½ cup water
5 egg yolks
1 cup butter, softened

1 tablespoon rum
2 blocks (2 ounces)
   unsweetened baking
   chocolate, melted

Combine sugar, cream of tartar and water in small heavy saucepan. Cook over medium heat, stirring constantly, until sugar dissolves and syrup is clear. Continue cooking over medium heat, without stirring, until syrup reaches 238°F (soft-ball stage) or until syrup, when dropped into very cold water, forms a soft ball that flattens when removed from water.

Meanwhile, beat egg yolks in small mixer bowl on high speed until thick and lemon colored, about 2 minutes. With mixer on high speed, slowly pour hot syrup in a thin stream over egg yolks, beating constantly until thick and cooled, about 5 minutes. Beat in butter, 1 tablespoon at a time. Add rum and melted chocolate; beat until well blended. Place in bowl of ice water; chill 15 to 20 minutes. Remove from water; beat on high speed until filling is thick enough to spread.

About 2½ cups filling or frosting.

Pies
& Pastries

Fudge Brownie Pie

2 eggs
1 cup sugar
½ cup butter or margarine,
    melted
½ cup unsifted all-purpose flour
⅓ cup unsweetened cocoa

¼ teaspoon salt
1 teaspoon vanilla
½ cup chopped nuts (optional)
   Ice cream
   Hot Fudge Sauce (below)

Beat eggs in small mixer bowl; blend in sugar and melted butter or margarine. Combine flour, cocoa and salt; add to butter mixture. Stir in vanilla and nuts.

Pour into lightly greased 8-inch pie pan. Bake at 350° for 25 to 30 minutes or until almost set (pie will not test done). Cool; cut into wedges. Serve wedges topped with scoop of ice cream and drizzled with Hot Fudge Sauce.

6 to 8 servings.

Hot Fudge Sauce

¾ cup sugar
½ cup unsweetened cocoa
⅔ cup (5.3-ounce can)
   evaporated milk

⅓ cup light corn syrup
⅓ cup butter or margarine
1 teaspoon vanilla

Combine sugar and cocoa in small saucepan; blend in evaporated milk and corn syrup. Cook over medium heat, stirring constantly, until mixture boils; boil and stir 1 minute. Remove from heat; stir in butter or margarine and vanilla. Serve warm.

Fudge Pecan Pie

½ cup sugar
⅓ cup unsweetened cocoa
⅓ cup unsifted all-purpose flour
¼ teaspoon salt
1¼ cups light corn syrup
3 eggs
3 tablespoons butter or
   margarine, melted

1½ teaspoons vanilla
½ cup chopped pecans
9-inch unbaked pastry shell
Pecan halves
Mocha Whipped Cream
   (optional, below)

Combine sugar, cocoa, flour, salt, corn syrup, eggs, melted butter or margarine and vanilla in large mixer bowl; beat 30 seconds on medium speed *(do not overbeat)*. Stir in chopped pecans.

Pour into unbaked pastry shell. Bake at 350° for 55 to 60 minutes; immediately arrange pecan halves on top. Cool. (For fullest flavor, cover and let stand one day before serving.) Serve with Mocha Whipped Cream.

8 servings.

Mocha Whipped Cream

Whip ½ cup heavy or whipping cream and 1 tablespoon confectioners' sugar until stiff. Dissolve ¼ teaspoon instant coffee granules in 1 teaspoon water; carefully stir into sweetened whipped cream.

Variation

Fudge Walnut Pie: Substitute dark corn syrup for light corn syrup, 1 tablespoon imitation maple flavor for vanilla and chopped walnuts and walnut halves for chopped pecans and pecan halves. Prepare and bake as directed above.

Chocolatetown Bourbon Pie

Our town's chocolate rendition of a Kentucky classic.

½ cup butter, softened
2 eggs, beaten
2 tablespoons bourbon
1 cup sugar
½ cup unsifted all-purpose flour
1 cup semi-sweet chocolate Mini Chips
1 cup chopped pecans or walnuts
9-inch unbaked pastry shell
Sweetened whipped cream (optional)

Cream butter in small mixer bowl; add eggs and bourbon. Combine sugar and flour; add to creamed mixture. Stir in Mini Chips and nuts. Pour into unbaked pastry shell. Bake at 350° for 45 to 50 minutes or until golden brown. Cool about 1 hour; serve warm. Garnish with sweetened whipped cream.

8 servings.

Chocolate Marble Cheesepie

Chocolate Crumb Crust (below)
¼ cup unsweetened cocoa
2 tablespoons milk
1⅓ cups (14-ounce can) sweetened condensed milk*
1 teaspoon vanilla
½ cup heavy or whipping cream
4 packages (3 ounces each) cream cheese, softened
2 tablespoons lemon juice
2 teaspoons vanilla

Prepare Chocolate Crumb Crust. Combine cocoa, milk and ⅔ cup of the sweetened condensed milk in small saucepan. Cook over low heat, stirring constantly, until mixture boils. Remove from heat; stir in 1 teaspoon vanilla. Cool completely.

Whip cream until stiff; fold into chocolate mixture. Beat cream cheese in small mixer bowl until light and fluffy. Gradually beat in remaining condensed milk, lemon juice and 2 teaspoons vanilla. Alternately spoon cheese mixture and chocolate mixture into prepared crust; swirl with knife or spatula for marbled effect. Chill until firm.

8 servings.

*Do not use evaporated milk.

Chocolate Crumb Crust
Combine 1¼ cups graham cracker crumbs, ¼ cup unsweetened cocoa and ¼ cup sugar in small mixing bowl. Blend in ¼ cup melted butter or margarine. Press mixture firmly onto bottom and up side of 9-inch pie pan; freeze.

Chocolate Cheesepie

1 cup graham cracker crumbs
¼ cup sugar
¼ cup butter or margarine, melted
4 packages (3 ounces each) cream cheese, softened
1¼ cups sugar
Dash salt

3 eggs, at room temperature
½ teaspoon vanilla
2 blocks (2 ounces) unsweetened baking chocolate, melted
1 cup sour cream
⅓ cup sugar
½ teaspoon vanilla

Combine crumbs, ¼ cup sugar and the melted butter or margarine in small mixing bowl. Press mixture firmly onto bottom and up side of 9-inch pie pan. Chill. Beat cream cheese in small mixer bowl until light and fluffy; gradually add 1¼ cups sugar and the salt. Add eggs, one at a time, beating well after each addition. Stir in ½ teaspoon vanilla and the melted chocolate until completely blended. Pour into prepared crust. Bake at 375° for 20 minutes or until center is almost set. Remove from oven; cool 1 hour.

Blend sour cream, ⅓ cup sugar and ½ teaspoon vanilla in small mixing bowl. Spread over top of cooled pie. Bake at 375° for 10 minutes. Cool to room temperature. Cover; chill until firm.

8 servings.

Chocolate Shoo-Fly Pie

A chewy chocolate version of a Pennsylvania Dutch favorite.

¼ teaspoon baking soda
1⅓ cups boiling water
1½ cups (1-pound can) chocolate-flavored syrup
1 teaspoon vanilla
1⅓ cups unsifted all-purpose flour

½ cup sugar
¼ teaspoon baking soda
¼ teaspoon salt
⅓ cup butter or margarine
9-inch unbaked pastry shell
Cinnamon

Dissolve ¼ teaspoon baking soda in boiling water; stir in syrup and vanilla. Set aside. Combine flour, sugar, ¼ teaspoon baking soda and the salt in medium mixing bowl; cut in butter or margarine until mixture resembles coarse crumbs. Set aside 1 cup each of chocolate mixture and crumbs; gently combine remaining chocolate and crumbs, stirring just until crumbs are moistened (mixture will be lumpy).

Pour reserved 1 cup chocolate mixture into unbaked pastry shell; evenly pour in chocolate-crumb mixture. Sprinkle with remaining 1 cup crumbs; dust with cinnamon. Bake at 375° for 1 hour. Cool completely.

8 servings.

Black Bottom Pie

9-inch baked pastry shell or
  crumb crust
½ cup sugar
⅓ cup unsweetened cocoa
¼ cup butter
1 envelope unflavored gelatine
¼ cup cold water
½ cup sugar
¼ cup cornstarch
2 cups milk
4 eggs, separated
1 teaspoon vanilla
2 tablespoons rum
½ cup sugar
  Grated chocolate

Bake pastry shell or crumb crust; set aside. Combine ½ cup sugar, the cocoa and butter in medium bowl; set aside. Combine gelatine and cold water in small bowl; place bowl in pan of simmering water to dissolve gelatine. Combine ½ cup sugar, the cornstarch, milk and egg yolks in medium saucepan. Cook over medium heat, stirring constantly, until mixture boils; boil and stir 1 minute. Remove from heat; measure 1½ cups of the custard and blend into cocoa-sugar mixture. Add vanilla and pour into cooled shell or crust; chill until set.

Combine dissolved gelatine with remaining custard; add rum and set aside. Beat egg whites until foamy; gradually add ½ cup sugar and beat until stiff peaks form. Fold gelatine-custard mixture into beaten egg whites. Chill 15 minutes or until partially set. Spoon over chocolate custard in prepared crust. Chill until set. Garnish with grated chocolate before serving.

8 servings.

Mocha Cream Pie

9-inch baked pastry shell or
  crumb crust
1⅓ cups sugar
⅓ cup unsweetened cocoa
⅓ cup cornstarch
2 teaspoons instant coffee
  granules
¼ teaspoon salt
3 cups milk
3 tablespoons butter or
  margarine
1½ teaspoons vanilla

Bake pastry shell or crumb crust; set aside. Combine sugar, cocoa, cornstarch, coffee granules and salt in medium saucepan; gradually add milk, stirring until smooth. Cook over medium heat, stirring constantly, until mixture boils; boil and stir 3 minutes. Remove from heat; blend in butter or margarine and vanilla. Pour into cooled shell or crust; press plastic wrap onto surface. Chill 3 to 4 hours or until firm.

8 servings.

Classic Chocolate Cream Pie

9-inch baked pastry shell or crumb crust
2½ blocks (2½ ounces) unsweetened baking chocolate
3 cups milk
1⅓ cups sugar
3 tablespoons flour
3 tablespoons cornstarch
½ teaspoon salt
3 egg yolks
2 tablespoons butter or margarine
1½ teaspoons vanilla
3 egg whites, at room temperature
¼ teaspoon cream of tartar
6 tablespoons sugar

Bake pastry shell or crumb crust; set aside. Melt baking chocolate with 2 cups of the milk in medium saucepan over medium heat, stirring constantly. Cook and stir *just* until mixture boils; remove from heat. Combine 1⅓ cups sugar, the flour, cornstarch and salt in small mixing bowl. Blend egg yolks with remaining 1 cup milk; add to dry ingredients. Blend into chocolate mixture in saucepan. Cook over medium heat, stirring constantly, until mixture boils; boil and stir 1 minute. Remove from heat; blend in butter or margarine and vanilla. Pour into cooled shell or crust.

Beat egg whites and cream of tartar in small mixer bowl until foamy. Gradually add 6 tablespoons sugar; beat until stiff peaks form. Spread meringue onto hot pie filling, carefully sealing meringue to edge of crust. Bake in preheated 350° oven for 8 to 10 minutes or until lightly browned. Cool to room temperature; chill several hours or overnight.

8 servings.

Variation
Rum Cream Pie: Substitute 3 to 4 tablespoons light rum for the vanilla.

Chocolate Banana Cream Pie

9-inch baked pastry shell or
  crumb crust
1 1/4 cups sugar
1/3 cup unsweetened cocoa
1/3 cup cornstarch
1/4 teaspoon salt
3 cups milk

3 tablespoons butter or
  margarine
1 1/2 teaspoons vanilla
2 medium bananas, sliced
  Sweetened whipped cream
  Additional banana slices

Bake pastry shell or crumb crust; set aside. Combine sugar, cocoa, cornstarch and salt in medium saucepan; gradually add milk, stirring until smooth. Cook over medium heat, stirring constantly, until mixture boils; boil and stir 3 minutes. Remove from heat; blend in butter or margarine and vanilla. Pour into bowl; press plastic wrap onto surface. Cool to room temperature.

Cover bottom of cooled shell or crust with small amount of filling. Arrange banana slices over filling; cover with remaining filling. Chill 3 to 4 hours or until firm. Garnish with sweetened whipped cream and banana slices.

8 servings.

Chocolate Coconut Cream Pie

Some flavors just seem to have been created to team up with chocolate: Coconut is one of the best.

9-inch baked pastry shell or crumb crust
⅔ cup sugar
⅓ cup cornstarch
¼ teaspoon salt
3 cups milk
3 egg yolks, beaten
1 tablespoon butter or margarine
2 teaspoons vanilla
½ cup flaked coconut
3 tablespoons unsweetened cocoa
3 tablespoons sugar
2 tablespoons milk
Sweetened whipped cream (optional)

Bake pastry shell or crumb crust; set aside. Combine ⅔ cup sugar, the cornstarch, salt and 3 cups milk in medium saucepan. Blend in egg yolks. Cook over medium heat, stirring constantly, until mixture boils; boil and stir 1 minute. Remove from heat; stir in butter or margarine and vanilla. Pour 1½ cups cooked mixture into small bowl; stir in coconut. Set aside.

Combine cocoa, 3 tablespoons sugar and 2 tablespoons milk in small bowl; blend into remaining cooked mixture in saucepan. Cook over medium heat, stirring constantly, until mixture begins to boil; remove from heat.

Pour 1 cup chocolate mixture into cooled shell or crust; spread coconut mixture over chocolate. Top with remaining chocolate mixture; spread evenly. Press plastic wrap onto surface. Cool; chill several hours or overnight. Top with sweetened whipped cream.

8 servings.

Chocolate Mousse Pie

9-inch baked pastry shell or crumb crust
1 package (8 ounces) cream cheese, softened
½ cup unsweetened cocoa
1 cup confectioners' sugar
1½ teaspoons vanilla
2 cups heavy or whipping cream
Chocolate curls and sweetened whipped cream (optional)

Bake pastry shell or crumb crust; set aside. Beat cream cheese and cocoa in large mixer bowl until fluffy and well blended. Gradually add confectioners' sugar; blend well. Stir in vanilla. Whip cream until stiff; fold into cheese mixture.

Pour into cooled shell or crust; chill until firm. Garnish with chocolate curls and sweetened whipped cream.

8 servings.

Chocolate Silk Pie

Crumb Crust (below)
½ cup butter or margarine, softened
½ cup sugar
2 blocks (2 ounces) unsweetened baking chocolate, melted and cooled
3 egg yolks, at room temperature
1 teaspoon vanilla
3 egg whites, at room temperature
¼ cup sugar
½ cup heavy or whipping cream
Coffee Topping (below)

Prepare Crumb Crust; set aside. Cream butter or margarine and ½ cup sugar in small mixer bowl until light and fluffy. Add cooled chocolate; beat well. Add egg yolks, one at a time, beating well after each addition; stir in vanilla. Beat egg whites until foamy; gradually add ¼ cup sugar, beating until stiff peaks form. Fold egg white mixture into chocolate mixture. Whip cream until stiff; fold into chocolate mixture.

Pour into prepared crust. Cover; chill until firm. Garnish with dollops of Coffee Topping.

8 servings.

Crumb Crust
Combine 1½ cups vanilla wafer crumbs (about 45 wafers) and ⅓ cup melted butter or margarine in small mixing bowl. Press mixture firmly onto bottom and up side of 9-inch pie pan. Bake at 350° for 10 minutes. Cool.

Coffee Topping
Combine ½ cup heavy or whipping cream, 1 teaspoon instant coffee granules and 2 tablespoons confectioners' sugar in small mixer bowl; beat until stiff peaks form.

Crumb Crusts

Whether you're using graham crackers or vanilla wafers, you'll need 1½ cups crumbs to make a 9-inch crust. That will call for:

about 20 graham cracker squares
about 45 vanilla wafers

Hershey Bar Pie

*One of our most popular pies—
it tastes like a Hershey Bar! The
dough for the unusual and
beautiful petal crust also doubles
as chocolate refrigerator
cookies—just follow the baking
instructions in the recipe on
page 194.*

Chocolate Petal Crust
  (below)
1 milk chocolate bar
  (8 ounces), broken into
  pieces
⅓ cup milk
1½ cups miniature or 15 large
  marshmallows

1 cup heavy or whipping cream
Sweetened whipped cream
  (optional)
Cherry pie filling, chilled
  (optional)

Prepare Chocolate Petal Crust; set aside. Melt chocolate bar pieces with milk in top of double boiler over hot, not boiling, water. Add marshmallows, stirring until melted; cool completely.

Whip cream until stiff; carefully fold into chocolate mixture. Spoon into prepared crust. Cover; chill several hours or until firm. Garnish with sweetened whipped cream or chilled cherry pie filling.

8 servings.

Chocolate Petal Crust

½ cup butter or margarine,
  softened
1 cup sugar
1 egg
1 teaspoon vanilla

1¼ cups unsifted all-purpose
  flour
½ cup unsweetened cocoa
¾ teaspoon baking soda
¼ teaspoon salt

Cream butter or margarine, sugar, egg and vanilla in large mixer bowl. Combine flour, cocoa, baking soda and salt; add to creamed mixture. Shape soft dough into two rolls, 1½ inches in diameter. Cut one roll into ⅛-inch slices; arrange slices, edges touching, on bottom and up side of greased 9-inch pie pan. (Small spaces in crust will not affect pie.) Bake at 375° for 8 to 10 minutes. Cool.

Enough dough for 2 crusts.

Note: Remaining roll of dough may be frozen for later use.

Brandy Alexander Pie

Chocolate Petal Crust
  (page 85)
30 large marshmallows
½ cup milk
 1 cup (6-ounce package) semi-
    sweet chocolate chips

 1 teaspoon vanilla
 1 to 2 tablespoons brandy
 1 to 2 tablespoons crème de
    cacao
 2 cups heavy or whipping cream
   Chocolate leaves (optional)

Prepare Chocolate Petal Crust; set aside. Combine marshmallows and milk in medium saucepan; cook over low heat, stirring constantly, until marshmallows are melted and mixture is smooth. Pour half the marshmallow mixture into small bowl; set aside. Add chocolate chips to the remaining marshmallow mixture; return to low heat and stir until chips are melted. Remove from heat and stir in vanilla; cool to room temperature. Stir brandy and crème de cacao into reserved marshmallow mixture; chill until mixture mounds slightly when dropped from a spoon.

Whip cream until stiff. Fold 2 cups of the whipped cream into cooled chocolate mixture; spoon into cooled crust. Blend remaining whipped cream into chilled brandy mixture; spread over chocolate mixture. Chill about 2 hours or until firm. Just before serving, garnish with chocolate leaves.

8 servings.

Chocolate Bavarian Pie

9-inch baked crumb crust
 1 envelope unflavored gelatine
 1 cup milk
⅔ cup sugar
 6 tablespoons unsweetened
    cocoa

 1 tablespoon light corn syrup
 2 tablespoons butter or
    margarine
¾ cup milk
¾ teaspoon vanilla
 1 cup heavy or whipping cream

Bake crumb crust; set aside. Sprinkle gelatine onto 1 cup milk in medium saucepan; let stand 5 minutes to soften. Combine sugar and cocoa; add to mixture in saucepan. Stir in corn syrup. Cook over medium heat, stirring constantly, until mixture boils; remove from heat. Add butter or margarine; stir until melted. Blend in ¾ cup milk and the vanilla. Pour into large mixer bowl. Cool to room temperature; chill until almost set.

Whip cream until stiff. Whip chocolate mixture on medium speed until smooth. Blend half the whipped cream into chocolate mixture on low speed just until smooth. Pour into cooled crust; chill until set. Top with remaining chilled whipped cream.

On facing page, from top—Brandy Alexander Pie (this page); Black Bottom Pie (page 80)

8 servings.

Coconutty Chocolate Chiffon Pie

An all-time favorite pie, but with a scrumptious difference: a crunchy coconut crust (excellent for a number of other chocolatey fillings, too).

Coconut Crust (below)
1 envelope unflavored gelatine
¼ cup cold water
¾ cup sugar
½ cup unsweetened cocoa
½ teaspoon salt
1¼ cups milk
3 egg yolks, beaten
1 cup heavy or whipping cream
3 egg whites

Prepare Coconut Crust; set aside. Sprinkle gelatine onto cold water in small mixing bowl; let stand several minutes to soften. Combine sugar, cocoa and salt in small saucepan; stir in milk and egg yolks. Cook over low heat, stirring constantly, until mixture thickens; *do not boil*. Remove from heat; stir in gelatine until dissolved. Chill until slightly thickened.

Whip cream until stiff; fold into chocolate mixture. Beat egg whites until stiff peaks form; fold into chocolate mixture. Pour into prepared crust. Cover; chill until firm.

8 servings.

Coconut Crust
Combine ¼ cup melted butter or margarine, ½ teaspoon vanilla and 3 cups flaked coconut in medium mixing bowl. Press mixture firmly onto bottom and up side of 9-inch pie pan. Bake at 375° for 6 to 8 minutes or until lightly browned. Cool.

Cacao Chiffon Pie

10-inch baked pastry shell
2 envelopes unflavored gelatine
1 cup chocolate-flavored syrup
3 egg yolks, beaten
¼ cup crème de cacao
3 egg whites, at room temperature
⅓ cup sugar
1 cup heavy or whipping cream

Bake pastry shell; set aside. Blend gelatine into syrup in medium saucepan; let soften about 10 minutes. Stir in egg yolks. Cook over low heat, stirring constantly, until gelatine is dissolved and mixture is hot; *do not boil*. Remove from heat; stir in crème de cacao. Cover; chill until mixture mounds slightly when dropped from a spoon.

Beat egg whites until foamy; gradually add sugar, beating until stiff peaks form. Whip cream until stiff. Fold beaten egg whites and whipped cream into chocolate mixture. Pour into cooled pastry shell; press plastic wrap onto surface. Chill until firm.

8 to 10 servings.

Ice Cream Pie

When you want "something ice cream"—but something different.

Chocolate Crumb Crust
(below)

2 quarts ice cream
Classic Chocolate Sauce (below)

Prepare Chocolate Crumb Crust. Spread about half the ice cream evenly in crust; top with scoops of remaining ice cream. Cover; freeze until firm. Serve topped with Classic Chocolate Sauce.

8 servings.

Note: Use your favorite flavor of ice cream — peach, coffee, peppermint or butter pecan, for example.

Chocolate Crumb Crust

1½ cups vanilla wafer crumbs
(about 45 wafers)
6 tablespoons unsweetened
cocoa

⅓ cup confectioners' sugar
6 tablespoons butter or
margarine, melted

Combine crumbs, cocoa and confectioners' sugar in medium mixing bowl. Gradually add butter or margarine, stirring to coat crumb mixture completely. Press mixture firmly onto bottom and up side of 9-inch pie pan; freeze.

Classic Chocolate Sauce

1 cup sugar
6 tablespoons unsweetened
cocoa
¾ cup evaporated milk

¼ cup butter or margarine
⅛ teaspoon salt
½ teaspoon vanilla

Combine sugar and cocoa in small saucepan; blend in evaporated milk. Add butter or margarine and salt. Cook over medium heat, stirring constantly, until mixture just begins to boil. Remove from heat; add vanilla. Serve warm.

Strawberry Chocolate Pie

1½ cups vanilla wafer crumbs (about 45 wafers)
⅓ cup unsweetened cocoa
⅓ cup confectioners' sugar
6 tablespoons butter or margarine, melted
¾ cup chocolate-flavored syrup
½ cup sweetened condensed milk*

1 egg yolk, beaten
1 teaspoon vanilla
1 cup heavy or whipping cream**
1 egg white
1 tablespoon sugar
 Topping (below)
 Chocolate Butterflies (optional, page 270)

Combine crumbs, cocoa and confectioners' sugar in medium mixing bowl; gradually add butter or margarine, stirring to completely coat crumb mixture. Press mixture firmly onto bottom and up side of 9-inch pie pan; freeze.

Combine syrup, sweetened condensed milk and egg yolk in small heavy saucepan. Cook over medium heat, stirring constantly, until mixture boils. Remove from heat; add vanilla. Cool; chill thoroughly. Whip cream until stiff; fold into chocolate mixture. Beat egg white until foamy; add sugar and beat until stiff peaks form. Fold into chocolate cream mixture. Pour into prepared crust. Cover; freeze until firm.

Prepare Topping; spoon onto frozen chocolate filling. Cover; freeze until serving time. Garnish with Chocolate Butterflies.

8 servings.

*Do not use evaporated milk.
**Do not use non-dairy whipped topping.

Topping
Whip 1 cup heavy or whipping cream until stiff; fold in ⅔ cup well-drained pureed sweetened strawberries, 2 tablespoons sugar and 2 tablespoons light corn syrup.

Chocolate-Cherry Tarts

2 blocks (2 ounces)
   unsweetened baking
   chocolate
2 tablespoons butter or
   margarine, softened
½ cup sugar
1 egg
½ teaspoon vanilla

1¼ cups unsifted all-purpose
   flour
⅛ teaspoon baking soda
¼ teaspoon salt
   Cherry-Cheese Filling
   (below)
12 maraschino cherries, well
   drained and cut in half

Cut 24 three-inch circles of heavy-duty aluminum foil; set aside. Melt baking chocolate in top of double boiler over hot, not boiling, water; cool slightly. Cream butter or margarine and sugar in large mixer bowl until light and fluffy; blend in cooled chocolate. Add egg and vanilla; beat well. Combine flour, baking soda and salt; blend into chocolate mixture.

Roll pastry to ⅛-inch thickness on lightly floured pastry cloth; cut circles with 3-inch cookie cutter. Place each on a foil circle. With thumb and forefinger, turn up edges of dough at five points, forming a star. Place on cookie sheet.

Prepare Cherry-Cheese Filling; spoon 1 tablespoon into each star. Bake at 350° for 10 to 12 minutes or until set. Remove from oven; top each tart with a cherry half. Cool completely; carefully remove foil. Cover; chill thoroughly.

2 dozen tarts.

Cherry-Cheese Filling

Combine 1 package (8 ounces) cream cheese, softened, ½ cup sugar and 1 egg in small mixer bowl; blend well. Fold in ½ cup well-drained chopped maraschino cherries.

Chocolate-Filled Cream Puffs

1 cup water
½ cup butter or margarine
¼ teaspoon salt
1 cup unsifted all-purpose flour

4 eggs
Chocolate Cream Filling
(below)
Confectioners' sugar

Heat water, butter or margarine and salt to rolling boil in medium saucepan. Add flour all at once; stir vigorously over low heat about 1 minute or until mixture leaves side of pan and forms a ball. Remove from heat; add eggs, one at a time, beating well after each addition until smooth and velvety.

Drop by scant ¼ cupfuls onto ungreased cookie sheet. Bake at 400° for 35 to 40 minutes or until puffed and golden brown. While puff is warm, horizontally slice off small portion of top; reserve tops. Remove any soft filaments of dough; cool. Prepare Chocolate Cream Filling; fill puffs. Replace tops; dust with confectioners' sugar. Chill.

About 12 cream puffs.

Chocolate Cream Filling

1¼ cups sugar
⅓ cup unsweetened cocoa
⅓ cup cornstarch
¼ teaspoon salt
3 cups milk

3 egg yolks, slightly beaten
2 tablespoons butter or
   margarine
1½ teaspoons vanilla

Combine sugar, cocoa, cornstarch and salt in medium saucepan; stir in milk. Cook over medium heat, stirring constantly, until mixture boils; boil and stir 1 minute. Remove from heat. Gradually stir small amount of chocolate mixture into egg yolks; blend well. Return egg mixture to chocolate mixture in pan; stir and heat just until boiling. Remove from heat; blend in butter or margarine and vanilla. Pour into bowl; press plastic wrap onto surface. Cool.

Variation

Miniature Cream Puffs: Drop dough by level teaspoonfuls onto ungreased cookie sheet. Bake at 400° for about 15 minutes. Fill as directed above. Glaze with Chocolate Glaze (page 72).

About 8 dozen miniature cream puffs.

Napoleons

Now you can conjure up fragile Napoleons, just like any skilled pastry chef; the secret here is easy-to-use frozen puff pastry. The chocolate filling, however, is your own homemade creation—and not a bit difficult.

2 sheets (17¼-ounce package) frozen puff pastry
Chocolate Cream Filling (below)

Vanilla Frosting (below)
Chocolate Glaze (below)

Thaw folded pastry sheets for 20 minutes; gently unfold. Roll each on floured surface to 15 x 12-inch rectangle. Place on ungreased cookie sheets; prick each sheet thoroughly with fork. Bake at 350° for 18 to 22 minutes or until puffy and lightly browned. Cool completely on cookie sheets. Prepare Chocolate Cream Filling.

Cut one rectangle lengthwise into 3 equal pieces. Place one piece on serving plate; spread with a fourth of the Chocolate Cream Filling. Top with second piece of pastry; spread with a fourth of the filling. Place remaining piece of pastry on top; set aside. Repeat procedure with remaining pastry and filling.

Prepare Vanilla Frosting; spread half the frosting on each rectangle. Prepare Chocolate Glaze; drizzle half the glaze in decorative design over frosting on each rectangle. Cover; chill at least 1 hour or until filling is firm. Cut each rectangle into 6 pieces.

12 servings.

Chocolate Cream Filling

½ cup sugar
3 tablespoons cornstarch
1½ cups milk
3 egg yolks, beaten

¾ cup semi-sweet chocolate Mini Chips
½ teaspoon vanilla

Combine sugar, cornstarch and milk in medium saucepan. Cook over medium heat, stirring constantly, until mixture just begins to boil. Remove from heat. Gradually stir small amount of mixture into egg yolks; blend well. Return egg mixture to mixture in pan. Cook over medium heat, stirring constantly, 1 minute. Remove from heat; add Mini Chips and vanilla, stirring until chips are melted and mixture is smooth. Press plastic wrap onto surface. Cool; chill thoroughly.

Vanilla Frosting

Combine 1½ cups confectioners' sugar, 1 tablespoon light corn syrup, ¼ teaspoon vanilla and 1 to 2 tablespoons hot water in small mixer bowl; beat to spreading consistency.

Chocolate Glaze

Melt ¼ cup butter or margarine in small saucepan. Remove from heat; stir in ⅓ cup unsweetened cocoa until smooth. Cool slightly.

On facing page, top to bottom—Chocolate-Filled Cream Puffs (page 93); Chocolate-Almond Tarts (page 96); Napoleons (this page)

Chocolate-Almond Tarts

Chocolate Tart Shells (below)
¾ cup sugar
¼ cup unsweetened cocoa
2 tablespoons cornstarch
2 tablespoons flour
¼ teaspoon salt
2 cups milk

2 egg yolks, slightly beaten
2 tablespoons butter or
    margarine
¼ teaspoon almond extract
    Sweetened whipped cream
    (optional)
    Sliced almonds

Prepare Chocolate Tart Shells; set aside. Combine sugar, cocoa, cornstarch, flour and salt in medium saucepan; blend in milk and egg yolks. Cook over medium heat, stirring constantly, until mixture boils; boil and stir 1 minute. Remove from heat; blend in butter or margarine and almond extract.

Pour into Chocolate Tart Shells; press plastic wrap onto surface. Chill. Garnish tops with sweetened whipped cream and sliced almonds.

6 tarts.

Chocolate Tart Shells

1½ cups vanilla wafer crumbs
    (about 45 wafers)
⅓ cup confectioners' sugar

¼ cup unsweetened cocoa
6 tablespoons butter or
    margarine, melted

Combine crumbs, confectioners' sugar, cocoa and melted butter or margarine in medium mixing bowl; stir until completely blended. Divide mixture among six 4-ounce tart pans; press mixture firmly onto bottoms and up sides of pans. Bake at 350° for 5 minutes. Cool.

Cheesecakes

Hershey Bar Cheesecake

Almond Crust (below)
1 milk chocolate bar
   (8 ounces), broken into
   pieces
4 packages (3 ounces each)
   cream cheese, softened
¾ cup sugar
2 tablespoons unsweetened
   cocoa

Dash salt
2 eggs
½ teaspoon vanilla
Sour Cream Topping
   (optional, below)
Chopped almonds (optional)

Prepare Almond Crust; set aside. Melt chocolate bar pieces in top of double boiler over warm water. Meanwhile, beat cream cheese until light and fluffy. Combine sugar, cocoa and salt; add to cream cheese mixture. Beat in eggs and vanilla. Add melted chocolate; beat just until blended (*do not overbeat*).

Pour into prepared crust. Bake at 325° for 40 minutes. Turn off oven; let cheesecake remain in oven 30 minutes without opening door. Remove from oven; cool completely. Chill thoroughly. Spread Sour Cream Topping over cheesecake; garnish with chopped almonds.

8 to 10 servings.

Almond Crust
Combine ¾ cup graham cracker crumbs, ⅔ cup chopped slivered almonds and 2 tablespoons sugar. Add ¼ cup melted butter or margarine; mix well. Press mixture onto bottom and up side of 8-inch layer pan with removable bottom.

Sour Cream Topping
Combine ½ cup sour cream, 2 tablespoons sugar and ½ teaspoon vanilla.

No-Bake Chocolate Cheesecake

Crumb-Nut Crust (below)
1½ cups semi-sweet chocolate chips
1 package (8 ounces) plus 1 package (3 ounces) cream cheese, softened
⅓ cup sugar
¼ cup butter, softened
1½ teaspoons vanilla
1 cup heavy or whipping cream
Peach Topping (below)
Grated chocolate (optional)

Prepare Crumb-Nut Crust; set aside. Melt chocolate chips in top of double boiler over hot, not boiling, water, stirring until smooth. Combine cream cheese and sugar in large mixer bowl; add butter, beating until smooth. Blend in vanilla. Beat in melted chocolate all at once. Whip cream until stiff; fold into chocolate mixture.

Spoon into prepared crust; chill while preparing Peach Topping. Spoon topping onto chocolate layer and chill thoroughly. Garnish with grated chocolate.

10 to 12 servings.

Crumb-Nut Crust

About 5 ounces almonds or pecans
¾ cup vanilla wafer crumbs
¼ cup confectioners' sugar
¼ cup butter or margarine, melted

If using almonds, toast in shallow baking pan at 350° for 8 to 10 minutes, stirring frequently; cool. Chop nuts very finely in food processor or blender. Measure 1 cup chopped nuts and combine with wafer crumbs and confectioners' sugar in mixing bowl; drizzle with butter or margarine. Mix well. Press onto bottom and up side of 9-inch springform pan.

Note: You may substitute 1¾ cups graham cracker crumbs for the nuts and vanilla wafer crumbs.

Peach Topping

1 teaspoon unflavored gelatine
1 tablespoon cold water
2 tablespoons boiling water
1 cup heavy or whipping cream
2 tablespoons sugar
1 teaspoon vanilla
½ cup sweetened diced peaches, drained

Sprinkle gelatine onto cold water in small glass dish; allow to stand a few minutes to soften. Add boiling water and stir until gelatine is dissolved. Whip cream and sugar until stiff; beat in gelatine mixture and vanilla. Fold in diced peaches.

On facing page—No-Bake Chocolate Cheesecake (this page); Strawberry Chocolate Chip Cheesecake (page 100)

Strawberry Chocolate Chip Cheesecake

An unusual strawberry-flavored cheesecake with tasty bits of chocolate throughout. An ideal ending for al fresco entertaining.

Pastry Crust (below)
3 packages (8 ounces each) cream cheese, softened
¾ cup sugar
1 package (10 ounces) frozen sliced strawberries with syrup, thawed
⅔ cup unsifted all-purpose flour

3 eggs
1 teaspoon strawberry extract
4 or 5 drops red food color
1 cup semi-sweet chocolate Mini Chips
Sweetened whipped cream (optional)
Fresh strawberries (optional)

Prepare Pastry Crust; set aside. Beat cream cheese and sugar in large mixer bowl until smooth. Puree strawberries with syrup in food processor or blender; add to cream cheese mixture. Blend in flour, eggs, strawberry extract and food color. Stir in Mini Chips.

Pour into prepared crust. Bake at 450° for 10 minutes; without opening oven door, decrease temperature to 250° and continue to bake for 50 to 60 minutes or until set. Cool; loosen cake from side of pan. Cover; chill several hours or overnight. Serve topped with sweetened whipped cream and strawberries.

10 to 12 servings.

Pastry Crust
Cream ⅓ cup softened butter or margarine and ⅓ cup sugar in small mixer bowl; blend in 1 egg. Add 1¼ cups unsifted all-purpose flour; mix well. Spread dough on bottom and 1½ inches up side of 9-inch springform pan. Bake at 450° for 5 minutes; cool.

Peanutty-Cocoa Marble Cheesecake

A change-of-pace cheesecake: The flavor's like that of a chocolate-peanut butter cup.

Peanutty-Cocoa Crust (below)
3 packages (8 ounces each) cream cheese, softened
¾ cup sugar
½ cup sour cream
1 tablespoon vanilla

3 eggs
3 tablespoons flour
¼ cup unsweetened cocoa
¼ cup sugar
1 tablespoon vegetable oil
1¼ cups peanut butter chips
¼ cup milk

Prepare Peanutty-Cocoa Crust; set aside. Beat cream cheese, ¾ cup sugar, the sour cream and vanilla in large mixer bowl until light and fluffy. Blend in eggs and flour. Mix cocoa, ¼ cup sugar and the oil with 1½ cups of the cream cheese mixture. Melt peanut butter chips with milk in top of double boiler over hot, not boiling, water; gradually add to remaining cream cheese mixture. Beat 5 minutes on high speed.

Spoon peanut butter and cocoa mixtures alternately onto prepared crust; swirl with knife or spatula for marbled effect. Bake at 450° for 10 minutes; without opening oven door, decrease temperature to 250° and continue to bake 30 minutes. Turn off oven; let cheesecake remain in oven 30 minutes without opening door. Remove from oven; cool completely. Chill thoroughly.

10 to 12 servings.

Peanutty-Cocoa Crust

1¼ cups vanilla wafer crumbs
¼ cup unsweetened cocoa
¼ cup confectioners' sugar
¼ cup butter or margarine, melted

¾ cup peanut butter chips, chopped

Combine wafer crumbs, cocoa, confectioners' sugar and melted butter or margarine. Stir in chopped peanut butter chips. Press onto bottom of 9-inch springform pan or 9-inch square pan.

Marble Cheesecake

Graham Crust (page 107)
3 packages (8 ounces each) cream cheese, softened
¾ cup sugar
½ cup sour cream
2 teaspoons vanilla
3 tablespoons flour
3 eggs
¼ cup unsweetened cocoa
¼ cup sugar
1 tablespoon vegetable oil
½ teaspoon vanilla

Prepare Graham Crust; set aside. Combine cream cheese, ¾ cup sugar, the sour cream and 2 teaspoons vanilla in large mixer bowl; beat on medium speed until smooth. Add flour, 1 tablespoon at a time, blending well. Add eggs; beat well. Combine cocoa and ¼ cup sugar in small bowl. Add oil, ½ teaspoon vanilla and 1½ cups of the cream cheese mixture; mix until well blended.

Spoon plain and chocolate mixtures alternately into prepared crust, ending with dollops of chocolate on top; gently swirl with knife or spatula for marbled effect. Bake at 450° for 10 minutes; without opening oven door, decrease temperature to 250° and continue to bake 30 minutes. Turn off oven; let cheesecake remain in oven 30 minutes without opening door. Remove from oven; loosen cake from side of pan. Cool completely; chill thoroughly.

10 to 12 servings.

Peanut Butter Cheesecake

Peanut Butter-Chocolate
   Crust (below)
1 package (8 ounces) cream
   cheese, softened
1 tablespoon lemon juice
1½ cups peanut butter chips
1⅓ cups (14-ounce can)
   sweetened condensed
   milk*
1 cup heavy or whipping
   cream
   Sliced fresh fruit

Prepare Peanut Butter-Chocolate Crust; set aside. Beat cream cheese with lemon juice in large mixer bowl until light and fluffy. Combine peanut butter chips and sweetened condensed milk in medium saucepan. Cook over low heat, stirring constantly, until chips are melted and mixture is smooth. Add warm mixture to cream cheese mixture.

Whip cream until stiff; fold into peanut butter mixture. Pour onto prepared crust; chill several hours or overnight. Garnish with sliced fruit before serving.

10 to 12 servings.

*Do not use evaporated milk.

Peanut Butter-Chocolate Crust

1¼ cups vanilla wafer crumbs
¼ cup unsweetened cocoa
¼ cup confectioners' sugar
¼ cup butter or margarine,
   melted
½ cup peanut butter chips,
   chopped

Combine wafer crumbs, cocoa, confectioners' sugar and melted butter or margarine. Stir in chopped peanut butter chips. Press onto bottom of 9-inch springform pan.

Cocoa Cheesecake

Graham Crust (below)
2 packages (8 ounces each) cream cheese, softened
¾ cup sugar
½ cup unsweetened cocoa
1 teaspoon vanilla
2 eggs
1 cup sour cream
2 tablespoons sugar
1 teaspoon vanilla

Prepare Graham Crust; set aside. Beat cream cheese, ¾ cup sugar, the cocoa and 1 teaspoon vanilla in large mixer bowl until light and fluffy. Add eggs; blend well. Pour into prepared crust. Bake at 375° for 20 minutes. Remove from oven; cool for 15 minutes.

Combine sour cream, 2 tablespoons sugar and 1 teaspoon vanilla; stir until smooth. Spread evenly over baked filling. Bake at 425° for 10 minutes. Cool; chill several hours or overnight.

10 to 12 servings.

Graham Crust
Combine 1½ cups graham cracker crumbs, ⅓ cup sugar and ⅓ cup melted butter or margarine. Press mixture onto bottom and half-way up side of 9-inch springform pan.

Frozen Chocolate Cheesecake

Chocolate Graham Crust (page 105)
1 envelope unflavored gelatine
½ cup water
½ cup unsweetened cocoa
½ teaspoon instant coffee granules
1⅓ cups (14-ounce can) sweetened condensed milk*
1½ teaspoons vanilla
2 packages (8 ounces each) cream cheese, softened
3½ cups (8-ounce container) frozen non-dairy whipped topping, thawed
Sliced strawberries (optional)

Prepare Chocolate Graham Crust; chill. Mix gelatine and water in small saucepan; heat and stir until dissolved. Combine cocoa and coffee granules in small bowl. Gradually add gelatine mixture to cocoa mixture; blend well until mixture is smooth. Stir in sweetened condensed milk and vanilla.

Beat cream cheese in large mixer bowl until fluffy; gradually blend in cocoa mixture. Fold in whipped topping. Pour onto prepared crust. Freeze 4 hours or until firm. Garnish with strawberries.

10 to 12 servings.

*Do not use evaporated milk.

Frozen Marble Cheesecake

Chocolate Graham Crust (below)

1⅓ cups (14-ounce can) sweetened condensed milk*

¾ cup chocolate-flavored syrup

1 teaspoon vanilla

4 packages (3 ounces each) cream cheese, softened

2 tablespoons lemon juice

2 teaspoons vanilla

1 cup heavy or whipping cream, whipped

Prepare Chocolate Graham Crust; cover and freeze while preparing filling. Combine ⅓ cup of the sweetened condensed milk and the syrup in small saucepan. Cook over medium heat, stirring constantly, until mixture boils. Remove from heat. Stir in 1 teaspoon vanilla; chill. Beat cream cheese in large mixer bowl until light and fluffy. Gradually beat in remaining 1 cup sweetened condensed milk, the lemon juice and 2 teaspoons vanilla. Whip cream until stiff; fold into chilled chocolate mixture.

Spoon half the chocolate mixture onto frozen crumb crust. Spoon cream cheese mixture and remaining chocolate mixture alternately onto crust; swirl with knife or spatula for marbled effect. Freeze at least 4 hours or until firm. Remove from freezer 10 to 15 minutes before serving.

10 to 12 servings.

*Do not use evaporated milk.

Chocolate Graham Crust
Combine 1¼ cups graham cracker crumbs, ¼ cup unsweetened cocoa and ¼ cup sugar in small bowl. Add ⅓ cup melted butter or margarine; mix well. Press mixture onto bottom of 9-inch springform pan.

Chocolate Ricotta Cheesecake

The sensuous, delicate tartness of ricotta gives this cheesecake richness and texture apart from the rest.

Graham Crust (below)
3 cups ricotta or low-fat cottage cheese
1 cup sugar
4 eggs
1 cup heavy or whipping cream
⅛ teaspoon salt
⅓ cup unsweetened cocoa
¼ cup unsifted all-purpose flour
½ teaspoon vanilla
Glazed Fruit (below)
Sweetened whipped cream (optional)

Prepare Graham Crust; set aside. Place ricotta or cottage cheese, sugar and eggs in food processor or blender container; process or blend until smooth. Add heavy or whipping cream, salt, cocoa, flour and vanilla; process until smooth.

Pour into prepared crust. Bake at 350° about 1 hour and 15 minutes or until set. Turn off oven; open door and let cheesecake remain in oven 1 hour. Cool completely; chill thoroughly. Just before serving, arrange Glazed Fruit on top of cheesecake. With pastry tube, make a border of sweetened whipped cream around edge.

10 to 12 servings.

Graham Crust
Combine 1 cup graham cracker crumbs, 2 tablespoons sugar and ¼ cup melted butter or margarine. Press mixture onto bottom and ½ inch up side of 9-inch springform pan. Bake at 350° for 8 to 10 minutes; cool.

Glazed Fruit
Stir about 1 cup sliced nectarines or peaches, pitted sweet cherries, fresh blueberries, strawberries and/or canned pineapple chunks with ¼ cup fruit preserves until fruit pieces are well coated.

Party Chocolate Cheesecake Cups

Individual little cheesecakes can be created well ahead of the party rush.

Graham Shells (below)
2 packages (8 ounces each) cream cheese, softened
1 cup sour cream
1¼ cups sugar
⅓ cup unsweetened cocoa
2 tablespoons flour
3 eggs
1 teaspoon vanilla
Topping (below)
Cherry pie filling

Prepare Graham Shells; set aside. Combine cream cheese and sour cream in large mixer bowl. Combine sugar, cocoa and flour; add to cream cheese mixture, blending well. Add eggs, one at a time, beating well after each addition. Blend in vanilla.

Fill each prepared cup almost full with cheese mixture (mixture rises only slightly during baking). Bake at 300° for 45 to 50 minutes. Turn off oven; let cheese cups remain in oven 45 minutes without opening door. Prepare Topping; spread 2 teaspoons on each cup. Cool completely; chill thoroughly. Garnish with dollop of cherry pie filling just before serving.

2 dozen desserts.

Graham Shells
Line 24 muffin cups (2½ inches in diameter) with paper baking cups. Combine 1½ cups graham cracker crumbs, ⅓ cup sugar and ¼ cup melted butter or margarine. Press about 1 tablespoon onto bottom of each cup.

Topping
Combine 1 cup sour cream, 2 tablespoons sugar and 1 teaspoon vanilla; stir until sugar is dissolved.

Soufflés & Fondues

Chocolate Rum Soufflé

2 envelopes unflavored
   gelatine
½ cup cold water
1¼ cups milk
6 egg yolks, at room
   temperature
3 tablespoons butter
2 teaspoons vanilla
6 egg whites, at room
   temperature

¼ teaspoon cream of tartar
⅓ cup sugar
1½ cups (1-pound can)
   chocolate-flavored syrup
3 tablespoons rum
1½ cups heavy or whipping
   cream
Chopped nuts or macaroon
   crumbs
Chocolate curls

Measure length of aluminum foil to fit around 1-quart soufflé dish; fold in half lengthwise. Lightly oil one side of collar; tape securely to outside of dish (oiled side in), allowing collar to extend 4 inches above rim. Set aside.

Sprinkle gelatine onto water in medium saucepan; let stand 3 to 4 minutes to soften. Combine milk and egg yolks; blend into softened gelatine. Add butter. Cook over medium heat, stirring constantly, until mixture just begins to boil. Remove from heat; blend in vanilla. Pour into large bowl; press plastic wrap directly onto surface. Cool; chill, stirring occasionally, until mixture mounds when dropped from a spoon.

Beat egg whites with cream of tartar in large mixer bowl until foamy; gradually add sugar, beating until stiff peaks form. Beat gelatine mixture in large mixer bowl on high speed just until smooth; blend in syrup and rum. Fold chocolate mixture into beaten egg whites. Whip cream until stiff; fold into chocolate mixture, blending well. Pour into prepared dish; cover and chill several hours or overnight. Just before serving, carefully remove foil. Gently pat nuts or macaroon crumbs onto side of soufflé. Garnish top with chocolate curls.

6 to 8 servings.

Cold Mocha Soufflé

Cold soufflés have a unique cloudlike texture. The delicate mocha flavor of this beautiful dessert is subtly echoed in the topping.

2 envelopes unflavored gelatine
½ cup sugar
⅓ cup unsweetened cocoa
1 tablespoon instant coffee granules
2¼ cups milk
3 egg yolks, beaten

½ teaspoon vanilla
1 cup heavy or whipping cream
3 egg whites, at room temperature
¼ cup sugar
Cozumel Whipped Cream (optional, below)
Chocolate curls (optional)

Measure length of aluminum foil to fit around 1-quart soufflé dish; fold in thirds lengthwise. Lightly oil one side of collar; tape securely to outside of dish (oiled side in), allowing collar to extend 3 inches above rim of dish. Set aside.

Combine gelatine, ½ cup sugar, the cocoa and coffee granules in medium saucepan; blend in milk and egg yolks. Let stand 2 minutes. Stir over low heat until gelatine is completely dissolved and mixture coats a metal spoon; *do not boil.* Remove from heat; add vanilla. Pour into large bowl and chill, stirring occasionally, until mixture mounds slightly when dropped from a spoon.

Whip cream until stiff; fold into chocolate mixture. Beat egg whites in small mixer bowl until soft peaks form; gradually add ¼ cup sugar and beat until stiff peaks form. Fold into chocolate mixture. Pour into prepared dish; chill until set, at least 4 hours. Just before serving, carefully remove foil. Garnish with Cozumel Whipped Cream and chocolate curls.

6 to 8 servings.

Cozumel Whipped Cream
Beat ½ cup heavy or whipping cream with 1 tablespoon confectioners' sugar in small bowl until stiff. Fold in 1 to 2 teaspoons coffee-flavored liqueur.

Chocolate-Peanut Soufflé

A chocolate soufflé with the surprise crunch of peanuts. The sauce is opulent yet simple to make.

1¼ cups milk
3 blocks (3 ounces) unsweetened baking chocolate
¾ cup sugar
2 tablespoons plus 1½ teaspoons cornstarch
¼ cup cold milk
1½ teaspoons vanilla
6 egg yolks, at room temperature

½ cup finely chopped unsalted peanuts
7 egg whites, at room temperature
½ teaspoon salt
Sauce Supreme (below)
Sweetened whipped cream (optional)

Butter 1½-quart soufflé dish. Measure length of aluminum foil to fit around soufflé dish; fold in thirds lengthwise. Lightly oil one side of collar; tape securely to outside of dish (oiled side in), allowing collar to extend 2 inches above rim. Sprinkle dish and collar with sugar; set aside.

Heat 1¼ cups milk and the baking chocolate in small saucepan over low heat, stirring constantly, until chocolate is melted. Combine sugar and cornstarch in medium saucepan. Gradually stir in ¼ cup cold milk; stir in chocolate mixture. Cook over medium heat, stirring constantly with wire whisk, until mixture thickens and boils; boil and stir 1 minute. Remove from heat; stir in vanilla.

Beat egg yolks in small mixer bowl until very thick and lemon colored, about 5 minutes; fold into chocolate mixture. Stir in peanuts. Beat egg whites and salt in large mixer bowl until stiff peaks form. Fold chocolate mixture into beaten egg whites.

Pour into prepared dish. Place dish in larger pan; place in oven on bottom rack. Pour hot water into pan to depth of 1 inch. Bake at 350° about 1½ hours or until cake tester inserted halfway between edge and center comes out clean. Carefully remove foil. Serve immediately with warm Sauce Supreme and sweetened whipped cream.

6 to 8 servings.

Sauce Supreme

2 tablespoons sugar
2 tablespoons cornstarch
⅛ teaspoon salt

1 cup water
¼ cup coffee-flavored liqueur

Combine sugar, cornstarch and salt in small saucepan; gradually stir in water. Cook over medium heat, stirring constantly, until mixture thickens and boils. Remove from heat; stir in liqueur.

Chocolate-Almond Soufflé

¼ cup butter or margarine
⅓ cup unsweetened cocoa
¼ cup unsifted all-purpose flour
1 cup milk
¾ teaspoon almond extract
4 egg yolks, at room
    temperature
½ cup sugar

¾ cup ground almonds (about
    3 ounces whole)
4 egg whites, at room
    temperature
2 tablespoons sugar
    Almond Whipped Cream
    (below)

Grease bottom only of 1-quart soufflé dish. Measure length of aluminum foil to fit around soufflé dish; fold in thirds lengthwise. Lightly oil one side of collar; tape securely to outside of dish (oiled side in), allowing collar to extend 3 inches above rim. Set aside.

Melt butter or margarine in small saucepan over low heat. Remove from heat; stir in cocoa and flour, blending well. Gradually blend in milk. Cook over low heat, stirring constantly, until mixture is smooth and thick and just begins to boil. Remove from heat; stir in almond extract. Press plastic wrap directly onto surface; cool 20 minutes.

Beat egg yolks and ½ cup sugar in small mixer bowl until thick and lemon colored. Fold ground almonds and reserved cocoa mixture into egg mixture; set aside. Beat egg whites in large mixer bowl until foamy; gradually add 2 tablespoons sugar, beating until stiff peaks form. Fold cocoa mixture into egg whites just until blended.

Pour into prepared dish. Place dish in larger pan; place in oven on bottom rack. Pour hot water into pan to depth of 1 inch. Bake at 350° for 60 to 65 minutes or until cake tester inserted halfway between edge and center comes out clean. Carefully remove foil. Serve immediately with Almond Whipped Cream.

4 to 6 servings.

Almond Whipped Cream
Beat ½ cup heavy or whipping cream, 1 tablespoon confectioners' sugar and ⅛ teaspoon almond extract or 1 teaspoon amaretto in small mixer bowl until stiff.

Hot Chocolate Soufflé

While they're a little more complicated to make than some desserts, dramatic hot soufflés are well worth the extra effort. Important to serve immediately.

¾ cup unsweetened cocoa
¾ cup sugar
½ cup unsifted all-purpose flour
¼ teaspoon salt
2 cups milk
6 egg yolks, well beaten
2 tablespoons butter

1 teaspoon vanilla
8 egg whites, at room temperature
¼ teaspoon cream of tartar
¼ cup sugar
Sweetened whipped cream

Lightly butter 2½-quart soufflé dish; sprinkle with sugar. Measure length of heavy-duty aluminum foil to fit around soufflé dish; fold in thirds lengthwise. Lightly oil one side of collar; tape securely to outside of dish (oiled side in), allowing collar to extend at least 2 inches above rim. Set aside.

Combine cocoa, ¾ cup sugar, the flour and salt in medium saucepan; gradually blend in milk. Cook over medium heat, stirring constantly with wire whisk, until mixture boils; remove from heat. Gradually stir small amount of chocolate mixture into beaten egg yolks; blend well. Return egg mixture to chocolate mixture in pan. Add butter and vanilla, stirring until combined. Set aside; cool to lukewarm.

Beat egg whites with cream of tartar in large mixer bowl until soft peaks form. Add ¼ cup sugar, 2 tablespoons at a time, beating until stiff peaks form. Gently fold a third of the chocolate mixture into beaten egg whites. Fold in remaining chocolate mixture, half at a time, just until combined.

Gently pour mixture, without stirring, into prepared dish; smooth top with spatula. Place dish in larger pan; place in oven on bottom rack. Pour hot water into pan to depth of 1 inch. Bake at 350° for 1 hour and 10 minutes or until cake tester inserted halfway between edge and center comes out clean. Carefully remove foil. Serve immediately with sweetened whipped cream.

8 to 10 servings.

Soufflé Success Tips

● To help the soufflé collar stand straight, fasten seam with a straight pin or paper clip. And be sure the bottom of the collar doesn't touch the water bath.

● Don't "overfold"! For a high, light soufflé, fold chocolate mixture into beaten egg whites *very* gently.

Individual Fudge Soufflés

½ cup butter or margarine,
   softened
1¼ cups sugar
1 teaspoon vanilla
4 eggs
⅔ cup milk
½ teaspoon instant coffee
   granules

⅔ cup unsifted all-purpose flour
⅔ cup unsweetened cocoa
1½ teaspoons baking powder
1 cup heavy or whipping cream
2 tablespoons confectioners'
   sugar

Grease and sugar eight 5- or 6-ounce ramekins or custard cups; set aside. Cream butter or margarine, sugar and vanilla in large mixer bowl until light and fluffy. Add eggs, one at a time, beating well after each addition. Scald milk; remove from heat and add coffee granules, stirring until dissolved. Combine flour, cocoa and baking powder; add alternately with milk-coffee mixture to creamed mixture. Beat 1 minute on medium speed.

Divide batter evenly among prepared ramekins. Place in two 8-inch square pans; place pans in oven. Pour hot water into pans to depth of ⅛ inch. Bake at 325° for 45 to 50 minutes or until cake tester inserted halfway between edge and center comes out clean. Remove pans from oven and allow ramekins to stand in water 5 minutes. Remove ramekins from water; cool slightly. Serve in ramekins or invert onto dessert dishes. Beat cream with confectioners' sugar until stiff; spoon onto warm soufflés.

8 servings.

Black Forest Fondue

2 jars (12 ounces each)
   maraschino cherries with
   stems
1 milk chocolate bar (8 ounces)

1 Special Dark chocolate bar
   (8 ounces)
½ cup light cream
3 tablespoons kirsch

Drain cherries; set aside. (Cherries may be placed on flat tray in freezer for at least one hour before serving, if desired.) Break chocolate bars into pieces; place in medium saucepan with light cream. Cook over very low heat, stirring constantly, until chocolate is melted and mixture is smooth. Remove from heat; add kirsch. If mixture thickens, stir in additional light cream, a tablespoon at a time. Pour into fondue pot or chafing dish; dip cherries into warm fondue.

About 2 cups fondue.

Mt. Gretna Chocolate Fondue

Dessert fondues are fun for guests and easy on the host. Mt. Gretna Fondue—enlivened with the flavor of peanut butter—is named for a resort town near Hershey.

4 blocks (4 ounces)
  unsweetened baking
  chocolate
1 cup light cream

1 cup sugar
¼ cup creamy peanut butter
1½ teaspoons vanilla
  Fondue Dippers (below)

Combine chocolate and cream in medium saucepan. Cook over low heat, stirring constantly, until chocolate melts and mixture is smooth. Add sugar and peanut butter; continue cooking until slightly thickened. Remove from heat; stir in vanilla. Pour into fondue pot or chafing dish; serve warm with Fondue Dippers.

About 2 cups fondue.

Fondue Dippers

In advance, prepare a selection of the following: marshmallows; angel food, sponge or pound cake pieces; strawberries; grapes; pineapple chunks; mandarin orange segments; cherries; fresh fruit slices. (Drain fruit well. Brush fresh fruit with lemon juice.)

Chocolate-Marshmallow Fondue

3½ blocks (3½ ounces) unsweetened baking chocolate
1⅓ cups (14-ounce can) sweetened condensed milk*

½ cup marshmallow creme
1 tablespoon milk
1½ teaspoons vanilla
1 tablespoon creamy peanut butter (optional)
Fondue Dippers (page 117)

Combine baking chocolate and sweetened condensed milk in medium saucepan. Cook over low heat, stirring constantly, until chocolate is melted and mixture is smooth. Blend in marshmallow creme and milk. Remove from heat; stir in vanilla and peanut butter. Pour into fondue pot or chafing dish; serve warm with selection of Fondue Dippers.

About 2 cups fondue.

*Do not use evaporated milk.

Puddings, Mousses & Bavarians

Chocolate Custard Pudding

¾ cup sugar
⅓ cup unsweetened cocoa
2 tablespoons cornstarch
2 tablespoons flour
¼ teaspoon salt

2 cups milk
2 egg yolks, beaten
2 tablespoons butter or margarine
1 teaspoon vanilla

Combine sugar, cocoa, cornstarch, flour and salt in medium saucepan; blend in milk and egg yolks. Cook over medium heat, stirring constantly, until mixture boils; boil and stir 1 minute. Remove from heat; blend in butter or margarine and vanilla. Pour into bowl or individual dessert dishes; press plastic wrap directly onto surface. Cool; chill until set.

4 to 6 servings.

Variations

Chocolate Custard Parfaits: Alternate layers of cold pudding and sweetened whipped cream or whipped topping in parfait glasses; top with fruit.

Chocolate Custard Pie: Pour hot pudding into 8-inch baked pie shell or crumb crust; press plastic wrap directly onto surface. Chill. Top with dollops of sweetened whipped cream before serving.

Classic Chocolate Pudding

2 blocks (2 ounces) unsweetened baking chocolate
2½ cups milk
1 cup sugar
¼ cup cornstarch
½ teaspoon salt
3 egg yolks, slightly beaten
1 tablespoon butter
1 teaspoon vanilla
Sweetened whipped cream (optional)

Combine baking chocolate with 1½ cups of the milk in medium saucepan; cook over low heat, stirring constantly with wire whisk, until chocolate is melted and mixture is smooth. Combine sugar, cornstarch and salt in medium mixing bowl; blend in remaining 1 cup milk and the egg yolks. Gradually add to chocolate mixture, stirring constantly.

Cook over medium heat, stirring constantly, until mixture boils; boil and stir 1 minute. Remove from heat; add butter and vanilla. Pour into bowl or individual dessert dishes; press plastic wrap directly onto surface. Cool; chill until set. Serve topped with sweetened whipped cream.

4 to 6 servings.

Blender Cocoa Pudding

This delicately flavored chocolate pudding can be made in a flash.

¼ cup cold milk
1 envelope unflavored gelatine
¾ cup very hot milk
⅔ cup sugar
¼ cup unsweetened cocoa
1 teaspoon vanilla
½ cup heavy or whipping cream
¾ cup crushed ice
Sweetened whipped cream and sliced bananas (optional)

Pour cold milk into blender container. Sprinkle gelatine onto cold milk; let stand several minutes to soften. Add hot milk; blend 2 minutes on low speed or until gelatine is completely dissolved. Add sugar, cocoa and vanilla; blend well. Add cream and crushed ice; continue processing until ice is liquefied. Allow to stand several minutes to begin setting. Pour into bowl or individual dessert dishes. Cover; chill at least 20 minutes or until set. Garnish with sweetened whipped cream and sliced bananas.

4 or 5 servings.

Chocolate-Berry Parfaits

Chocolate Cream Pudding
  (page 122)
1 package (10 ounces) frozen
    sliced strawberries, thawed,
    or 1 cup sweetened sliced
    fresh strawberries

1 cup heavy or whipping
    cream*
¼ cup confectioners' sugar*
    Fresh strawberries (optional)

Prepare Chocolate Cream Pudding; cool completely. Drain straw-berries; puree in blender or sieve to equal ½ to ¾ cup. Beat cream and confectioners' sugar until stiff; fold in strawberry puree. Alternately layer chocolate pudding and strawberry cream in parfait glasses. Chill until set. Garnish with strawberries.

8 to 10 servings.

*You may substitute 2 cups frozen non-dairy whipped topping, thawed, for the cream and confectioners' sugar.

Chocolate Cream Pudding

1 cup sugar
¼ cup unsweetened cocoa
⅓ cup cornstarch
¼ teaspoon salt
3 cups milk

3 egg yolks, slightly beaten
2 tablespoons butter
1½ teaspoons vanilla
Fresh fruit (optional)

Combine sugar, cocoa, cornstarch and salt in heavy saucepan; add milk and egg yolks. Cook over medium heat, stirring constantly, until mixture boils; boil and stir 1 minute. Remove from heat; blend in butter and vanilla. Pour into bowl or individual dessert dishes; press plastic wrap directly onto surface. Cool; chill until set. Garnish with fresh fruit.

6 to 8 servings.

Chocolate Cheese Pudding

1 package (3 ounces) cream
    cheese, softened
⅔ cup sugar
⅓ cup unsweetened cocoa
¼ cup milk

1 teaspoon vanilla
1½ cups heavy or whipping
    cream
Fresh fruit (optional)

Beat cream cheese and sugar in small mixer bowl. Stir in cocoa, milk and vanilla; beat until smooth. Whip cream in large mixer bowl until stiff; fold in chocolate mixture. Spoon into bowl or individual dessert dishes. Cover; chill or freeze until firm. Garnish with fresh fruit.

6 to 8 servings.

Quick Chocolate Pudding for Two

⅓ cup sugar
2 tablespoons unsweetened
    cocoa
4½ teaspoons cornstarch

⅛ teaspoon salt
1 cup plus 2 tablespoons milk
1 tablespoon butter
½ teaspoon vanilla

Combine sugar, cocoa, cornstarch and salt in small saucepan; gradually stir in milk. Cook over medium heat, stirring constantly, until mixture boils; boil and stir 1 minute. Remove from heat; blend in butter and vanilla. Pour into two individual dessert dishes; carefully press plastic wrap directly onto surface. Cool; chill.

2 servings.

Chocolate Tapioca

These two recipes combine the reassuring old-fashioned pleasures of tapioca pudding with the unexpected flavor of chocolate.

¾ cup sugar
⅓ cup unsweetened cocoa
3 tablespoons quick-cooking tapioca

⅛ teaspoon salt
2¾ cups milk
1 egg, slightly beaten
1 teaspoon vanilla

Combine sugar, cocoa, tapioca and salt in medium saucepan; blend in milk and egg. Let stand 5 minutes. Cook over medium heat, stirring constantly, until mixture boils. Remove from heat; stir in vanilla. Pour into bowl or individual dessert dishes; press plastic wrap directly onto surface. Cool; chill until set.

4 to 6 servings.

Old-Fashioned Chocolate Tapioca

½ cup sugar
¼ cup unsweetened cocoa
3 tablespoons quick-cooking tapioca
2 cups milk
2 egg yolks, slightly beaten

1 tablespoon butter or margarine
1 teaspoon vanilla
2 egg whites
¼ cup sugar

Combine ½ cup sugar, the cocoa, tapioca, milk and egg yolks in medium saucepan. Let stand 5 minutes to soften. Cook over medium heat, stirring constantly, until mixture comes to full boil; boil and stir 1 minute. Remove from heat; stir in butter or margarine and vanilla. Cool slightly.

Beat egg whites in small mixer bowl until foamy; gradually beat in ¼ cup sugar until stiff peaks form. Fold into tapioca mixture. Pour into bowl or individual dessert dishes; press plastic wrap directly onto surface. Chill until set.

5 or 6 servings.

Chocolate Steamed Pudding

Generations of cooks have been proud of their steamed puddings; the texture's like that of a dense moist cake. Idea: Some Christmas, offer this instead of traditional plum pudding.

½ cup butter or margarine, softened
1½ cups sugar
2 teaspoons vanilla
2 eggs
2⅓ cups unsifted all-purpose flour
¾ cup unsweetened cocoa

1¼ teaspoons cinnamon
1 teaspoon baking soda
1½ cups milk
½ cup chopped nuts (optional)
Orange-Pineapple Sauce (below)
Peppermint Sauce (below)

Cream butter or margarine, sugar and vanilla in large mixer bowl. Add eggs; blend well. Combine flour, cocoa, cinnamon and baking soda; add alternately with milk to creamed mixture. Stir in nuts. Pour mixture into well-greased and sugared 2-quart heatproof mold. Grease sheet of aluminum foil and place, greased side down, over mold; fold down edges of foil around rim and tie securely with string.

Place rack in large kettle or saucepan; pour water into kettle to top of rack. Bring water to boil; place mold on rack. Cover kettle and steam pudding over simmering water about 1 hour and 45 minutes or until cake tester comes out clean. (Additional water may be needed.) Remove mold from kettle; cool 10 minutes. Unmold onto serving plate. Serve hot accompanied by Orange-Pineapple Sauce and/or Peppermint Sauce.

8 servings.

Orange-Pineapple Sauce

Combine 2 cups (15½-ounce can) undrained crushed pineapple, ¾ cup orange juice, ½ cup sugar and 4½ teaspoons cornstarch in medium saucepan. Cook over low heat, stirring constantly, until sauce thickens and bubbles.

Peppermint Sauce

⅓ cup light corn syrup
3 tablespoons crushed peppermint candy
1 tablespoon butter or margarine

1 cup marshmallow creme
2 tablespoons milk
½ teaspoon vanilla
1 or 2 drops red food color (optional)

Combine corn syrup, candy and butter or margarine in small saucepan. Cook over medium heat, stirring occasionally, until mixture boils; boil and stir 5 minutes. Remove from heat; blend in marshmallow creme, milk and vanilla. Stir in food color.

On facing page—Chocolate Steamed Pudding (this page) and Favorite Hot Cocoa (page 232)

Hot Fudge Coconut Pudding

1 cup unsifted all-purpose flour
⅔ cup sugar
⅓ cup unsweetened cocoa
2 teaspoons baking powder
½ teaspoon salt
½ cup milk
¼ cup vegetable oil
1 teaspoon vanilla
½ cup chopped nuts
¼ cup packed light brown sugar
¼ cup sugar
1 package (3⅛ ounces) vanilla pudding and pie filling mix*
¾ cup flaked coconut
1½ cups boiling water
Vanilla ice cream

Combine flour, ⅔ cup sugar, the cocoa, baking powder and salt in large mixing bowl. Blend in milk, oil and vanilla; stir in nuts. Spread in greased 8-inch square pan or 1½-quart shallow baking dish.

Combine brown sugar, ¼ cup sugar, the dry pudding and pie filling mix and coconut; sprinkle over batter. Carefully pour boiling water over mixture; *do not stir*. Bake at 350° for 45 minutes. Cool 10 minutes; serve warm with vanilla ice cream.

8 to 10 servings.

*Do not use instant mix.

Cinnamon Chocolate Dessert

1⅓ cups buttermilk baking mix
¾ cup sugar
⅓ cup unsweetened cocoa
½ teaspoon cinnamon
3 tablespoons butter or margarine, softened
¾ cup milk
1 egg
Vanilla ice cream
Cinnamon Chocolate Sauce (below)

Combine buttermilk baking mix, sugar, cocoa, cinnamon, butter or margarine, ¼ cup of the milk and the egg in large mixer bowl; beat 1 minute on medium speed. Add remaining ½ cup milk; blend well. Pour batter into greased and floured 8-inch square pan. Bake at 350° for 30 to 35 minutes or until cake tester inserted comes out clean. Cool; cut into pieces. Serve warm or cold topped with ice cream and Cinnamon Chocolate Sauce.

6 to 8 servings.

Cinnamon Chocolate Sauce
Combine 1 cup chocolate-flavored syrup and ¼ teaspoon cinnamon in small mixing bowl until well blended.

Mocha Fudge Pudding Cake

For fans of sumptuous down-home desserts, this has a double dividend: A layer of cake tops a moist pudding base. Add a scoop of ice cream and, if you dare, a hot fudge sauce.

¾ cup sugar
1 cup unsifted all-purpose flour
2 teaspoons baking powder
¼ teaspoon salt
½ cup butter or margarine
1 block (1 ounce) unsweetened baking chocolate
½ cup milk
1 teaspoon vanilla
½ cup sugar
½ cup packed light brown sugar
¼ cup unsweetened cocoa
1 cup hot strong coffee
Ice cream

Combine ¾ cup sugar, the flour, baking powder and salt in medium mixing bowl. Melt butter or margarine with baking chocolate in small saucepan over low heat; add to dry ingredients with milk and vanilla. Beat until smooth. Pour into 8- or 9-inch square pan.

Combine ½ cup sugar, the brown sugar and cocoa in small bowl; sprinkle evenly over batter. Pour coffee over top; *do not stir.* Bake at 350° for 40 minutes or until center is almost set. Serve warm with ice cream.

8 to 10 servings.

Brownie Fudge Dessert

½ cup unsweetened cocoa
1 cup butter
3 tablespoons vegetable oil
1 cup sugar
4 eggs, slightly beaten
2 teaspoons vanilla
½ cup unsifted all-purpose flour
30 pecan halves
Ice cream or sweetened whipped cream

Combine cocoa, butter and oil in top of double boiler over hot, not boiling, water; stir over low heat until butter is melted. Remove from heat; stir in sugar. Add eggs and vanilla just until well combined. Stir flour into mixture just until blended.

Pour batter into ungreased 9-inch square pan and arrange pecan halves evenly on top. Place pan with batter in 13 x 9-inch pan; place both in oven. Pour hot water to depth of 1 inch into 13 x 9-inch pan. Bake at 350° for 40 to 45 minutes or until knife inserted ½ inch from edge comes out clean and brownie-like crust has formed; *do not overbake.* Remove from water bath; let cool on wire rack until warm. Scoop onto serving plates and top with your favorite ice cream. Or chill, cut into squares and serve with sweetened whipped cream.

9 servings.

Pots de Crème au Chocolat

2 blocks (2 ounces) unsweetened baking chocolate, broken into pieces
1 cup light cream
⅔ cup sugar
2 egg yolks, slightly beaten
2 tablespoons butter
1 teaspoon vanilla
Sweetened whipped cream
Candied violets (optional)

Combine baking chocolate pieces and light cream in medium saucepan. Cook over low heat, stirring constantly with wire whisk, until chocolate flecks disappear and mixture boils. Add sugar and continue cooking and stirring until mixture begins to boil. Remove from heat; gradually add to beaten egg yolks. Stir in butter and vanilla. Pour into six crème pots or demitasse cups; press plastic wrap directly onto surface. Chill several hours or until set. Garnish with sweetened whipped cream and candied violets.

6 servings.

Blender Pots de Crème

1 egg
¼ cup unsweetened cocoa
¼ cup sugar
2 tablespoons butter, softened

2 tablespoons shortening
¼ teaspoon vanilla
⅓ cup hot milk
Sweetened whipped cream

Combine egg, cocoa, sugar, butter, shortening and vanilla in blender container; blend until smooth, scraping sides of container frequently. Add hot milk; blend on high speed until smooth, scraping sides of container occasionally. Pour into four crème pots or demitasse cups; press plastic wrap directly onto surface. Chill several hours or until set. Garnish with sweetened whipped cream.

4 servings.

Almond Chocolate Mousse

½ cup butter or margarine
1 cup semi-sweet chocolate
    Mini Chips
2 tablespoons amaretto
4 egg yolks, at room
    temperature
¼ cup sugar
3 tablespoons water

4 egg whites, at room
    temperature
¼ teaspoon cream of tartar
2 tablespoons sugar
    Sweetened whipped cream
    and slivered almonds
    (optional)

Melt butter or margarine in small saucepan; remove from heat. Add Mini Chips; stir until melted. Blend in amaretto; set aside. Beat egg yolks in small mixer bowl until thick and lemon colored. Heat ¼ cup sugar and the water in small saucepan until mixture boils rapidly; *immediately* pour hot mixture in thin stream into egg yolks, beating constantly. Continue beating 3 minutes on high speed or until doubled in volume. Carefully fold reserved chocolate mixture into egg yolk mixture; chill 20 minutes.

Beat egg whites with cream of tartar in large mixer bowl until foamy; gradually beat in 2 tablespoons sugar. Beat until stiff peaks form. Carefully fold beaten egg whites into chocolate mixture; spoon into 4-ounce dessert dishes. Chill several hours or until set. Garnish with sweetened whipped cream and almonds just before serving.

8 to 10 servings.

Chocolate Mousse à l'Orange

2 cups (12-ounce package) semi-sweet chocolate chips
1 block (1 ounce) unsweetened baking chocolate
6 tablespoons water
6 egg yolks, at room temperature
2 to 3 tablespoons orange-flavored liqueur
1½ cups heavy or whipping cream
6 egg whites, at room temperature
½ cup sugar
Sweetened whipped cream
Orange slices, cut into wedges

Melt chocolate chips, baking chocolate and water in top of double boiler over hot, not boiling, water; stir until smooth. Remove from heat. With wire whisk, beat egg yolks, one at a time, into chocolate mixture; cool to lukewarm. Stir in orange-flavored liqueur. Whip cream until stiff; fold into chocolate mixture.

Beat egg whites in large mixer bowl until foamy. Gradually add sugar; beat until stiff peaks form. Fold in chocolate-cream mixture. Spoon into dessert dishes. Cover; chill several hours or until firm. Garnish with whipped cream and orange wedges.

16 servings.

Double Chocolate Mousse

2 milk chocolate bars (8 ounces each)	2 egg yolks
	¼ cup butter
2 blocks (2 ounces) unsweetened baking chocolate	1 cup heavy or whipping cream
	18 ladyfingers, split
	4 egg whites
5 tablespoons water	Chopped almonds (optional)
2 tablespoons rum or brandy	Chocolate leaves (optional)

Break chocolate bars and baking chocolate into pieces. Melt with water and rum or brandy in top of double boiler over hot, not boiling, water, stirring until mixture is smooth. Remove from heat; blend in egg yolks. Add butter, 1 tablespoon at a time, stirring until blended; cool slightly. Whip cream until stiff; carefully fold into chocolate mixture. Chill 1 hour or until mixture begins to set.

Meanwhile, line bottom and side of 8- or 9-inch springform pan with ladyfingers, rounded sides touching pan. Beat egg whites until stiff but not dry. Carefully fold into chocolate mixture. Pour into ladyfinger-lined pan and chill 8 hours or overnight. Just before serving, remove side of pan. Garnish with chopped almonds and chocolate leaves.

10 to 12 servings.

Cocoa Bavarian Cream

2 envelopes unflavored gelatine	3 tablespoons butter
1½ cups cold milk	1¾ cups milk
1¼ cups sugar	1½ teaspoons vanilla
¾ cup unsweetened cocoa	10 to 12 ladyfingers, split
1 tablespoon light corn syrup	1 cup heavy or whipping cream

Sprinkle gelatine onto 1½ cups milk in medium saucepan; let stand 3 to 4 minutes to soften. Combine sugar and cocoa; add to gelatine mixture in saucepan. Add corn syrup. Cook over medium heat, stirring constantly, until mixture boils. Remove from heat; stir in butter until melted. Blend in 1¾ cups milk and the vanilla; pour into large mixer bowl. Cool; chill until almost set.

Meanwhile, line bottom and side of 1½-quart mold with ladyfingers, rounded sides touching mold. Whip cream until stiff. Beat chilled chocolate mixture until smooth. Add whipped cream to chocolate on low speed just until blended. Pour into ladyfinger-lined mold; chill until set. Unmold before serving.

12 servings.

Strawberry-Chocolate Bavarian Cream

Bavarians are a delightful contradiction: They're luxurious, yet ethereal. Nice after a weighty meal, and cooling when the temperature's tropical.

1 package (10 ounces) frozen sliced strawberries, thawed*
2 envelopes unflavored gelatine
½ cup sugar
1 cup semi-sweet chocolate chips

2¼ cups milk
1 teaspoon vanilla
1 cup heavy or whipping cream
Strawberry Cream (below)

Drain strawberries; reserve syrup. Add water to syrup to equal ¾ cup. Stir gelatine into liquid; set aside. Chill drained berries for use in Strawberry Cream.

Combine sugar, chocolate chips and ½ cup of the milk in medium saucepan. Cook over low heat, stirring constantly, until mixture is smooth and very hot. Add gelatine mixture, stirring until gelatine is completely dissolved. Remove from heat; add remaining 1¾ cups milk and the vanilla. Pour into bowl; chill, stirring occasionally, until mixture mounds when dropped from a spoon.

Whip cream until stiff; fold into chocolate mixture. Pour into oiled 5- or 6-cup mold; chill until firm. Unmold and garnish with Strawberry Cream.

8 to 10 servings.

*You may substitute 1 cup sweetened sliced fresh strawberries for the frozen.

Strawberry Cream
Mash or puree reserved strawberries from Bavarian Cream recipe to equal ½ cup. Whip 1 cup heavy or whipping cream and 1 teaspoon vanilla in small mixer bowl until stiff. Fold in strawberry puree and 2 or 3 drops red food color.

On facing page, from top—Strawberry-Chocolate Bavarian Cream (this page); Double Chocolate Mousse (page 131)

Nutty Crust Chocolate Cream

1 envelope unflavored gelatine	4 egg yolks, slightly beaten
¾ cup sugar	2 tablespoons butter or
6 tablespoons unsweetened	margarine
cocoa	1 teaspoon vanilla
¼ teaspoon salt	Nutty Crust (below)
1½ cups milk	1 cup heavy or whipping cream

Combine gelatine, sugar, cocoa and salt in medium saucepan; stir in milk. Cook over medium heat, stirring constantly with wire whisk, until mixture just begins to boil; remove from heat. Gradually stir hot mixture into beaten egg yolks; stir in butter or margarine and vanilla until blended. Chill mixture, stirring occasionally, until mixture mounds when dropped from a spoon.

Meanwhile, prepare Nutty Crust. Whip cream until stiff; fold into chilled chocolate mixture. Pour into prepared crust. Cover; chill until firm.

8 to 10 servings.

Nutty Crust
Combine 1 cup vanilla wafer crumbs, ¾ cup finely chopped pecans and ⅓ cup melted butter or margarine in small mixing bowl. Press mixture onto bottom and up side of 9-inch layer pan; chill.

Frozen Desserts

Party Chocolate-Strawberry Cups

1 cup graham cracker crumbs
¼ cup sugar
¼ cup butter or margarine, melted
1 envelope unflavored gelatine
½ cup cold water
2 milk chocolate bars (8 ounces each), broken into pieces
2 tablespoons water
1½ cups vanilla ice cream, softened
⅔ cup drained sweetened sliced strawberries*
1⅔ cups frozen non-dairy whipped topping, thawed

Combine crumbs, sugar and butter or margarine in small mixing bowl; press about 1 tablespoon onto bottom of each of 24 paper-lined muffin cups (2½ inches in diameter). Set aside.

Sprinkle gelatine onto ½ cup cold water in top of double boiler; place over hot, not boiling, water, stirring until gelatine is dissolved. Melt chocolate bars with gelatine mixture and 2 tablespoons water over warm water; stir until smooth. Cool slightly. Beat chocolate on high speed, gradually adding softened ice cream. Chill 15 minutes.

Meanwhile, puree strawberries in blender or mash with fork. Stir strawberry mixture into whipped topping. Fill each cup ¾ full with chocolate mixture; top with scant tablespoon strawberry topping. Cover and freeze. Serve with additional strawberry puree, if desired.

2 dozen desserts.

*You may substitute 1 package (10 ounces) frozen sliced strawberries, thawed and drained.

Sweet Cherry-Chocolate Bombe

1 package (16 ounces) golden pound cake mix
  Sweet Cherry Sauce (page 137)
3 tablespoons amaretto (optional)
¾ cup semi-sweet chocolate chips
1¼ cups heavy or whipping cream
1 teaspoon almond extract
1 package (5⅝ ounces) vanilla-flavored instant pudding and pie filling mix
2 cups milk
  Cocoa Whipped Cream (below)
  Fresh cherries (optional)
  Chocolate curls

Bake pound cake in 9¼ x 5¼ x 2¾-inch loaf pan as directed on package; cool completely. Meanwhile, prepare Sweet Cherry Sauce. When cool, remove cherries from sauce. Chop about half the cherries and set aside. Return remaining cherry halves to sauce and refrigerate.

Line 2½-quart bowl with aluminum foil. Cut pound cake into ½-inch-thick slices. Line prepared bowl with cake slices up to ½ inch from top, cutting some into triangles to fit; sprinkle with amaretto. Set aside remaining slices.

Melt chocolate chips in top of double boiler over hot, not boiling, water, stirring until melted. Cool slightly.

Whip cream and almond extract until soft peaks form. Prepare pudding and pie filling mix as directed on package, using only 2 cups milk. Gently fold almond whipped cream into prepared pudding. Divide mixture in half.

Stir reserved chopped cherries into one half of the pudding mixture (add few drops red food color, if desired); spread evenly over cake slices in bowl, completely covering cake. Gradually add remaining pudding mixture to warm melted chocolate, folding until well combined; use to fill center of mold. Top dessert with remaining cake slices, cutting some slices to fit and covering top completely. Cover with foil and freeze overnight.

To serve, unmold onto chilled plate; remove foil. Prepare Cocoa Whipped Cream; frost bombe. Decorate with fresh cherries and chocolate curls. Slice and serve with Sweet Cherry Sauce.

10 to 12 servings.

Cocoa Whipped Cream
Combine ⅓ cup sugar and 3 tablespoons unsweetened cocoa in small mixer bowl; add ¾ cup heavy or whipping cream and 1 teaspoon vanilla. Beat until stiff.

Sweet Cherry Sauce

2 cups fresh sweet cherries*
½ cup sugar
1 tablespoon cornstarch
　Dash salt
⅔ cup water
½ teaspoon vanilla or 1 table-
　spoon kirsch or orange-
　flavored liqueur

Wash cherries and cut in half. Remove pits; set cherries aside. Combine remaining ingredients in saucepan. Cook over medium heat, stirring constantly, until thickened. Add cherries and simmer 2 to 3 minutes; cool.

*You may substitute 1 can (16 ounces) sweet cherries for the fresh. Drain cherries, reserving ⅔ cup syrup; substitute syrup for water. Decrease sugar to ¼ cup; follow directions above.

Spread the cherry-pudding mixture evenly over cake slices in bowl, completely covering cake.

When ready to serve, unmold frozen dessert onto chilled plate and prepare Cocoa Whipped Cream.

Chocolate-Strawberry Beehive

A sensational-looking dessert, easier to prepare than it appears. Assemble the day before; freeze until you're ready to glaze and serve.

1½ teaspoons unflavored gelatine
½ cup milk
1 cup chocolate-flavored syrup
3 egg yolks, well beaten
2 tablespoons butter or margarine
1 teaspoon vanilla
¼ teaspoon instant coffee granules
Toasted Almond Crust (below)

1 cup frozen non-dairy whipped topping, thawed
⅔ cup pureed sweetened strawberries
2 tablespoons honey or light corn syrup
3 egg whites
¼ teaspoon cream of tartar
⅓ cup sugar
Chocolate Glaze (page 139)

Sprinkle gelatine onto milk in medium saucepan; let stand 3 to 4 minutes to soften. Gradually add syrup and egg yolks. Cook over medium heat, stirring constantly with wire whisk, until mixture just begins to boil. Remove from heat; stir in butter or margarine, vanilla and coffee granules. Pour into large mixer bowl; press plastic wrap onto surface. Chill until set, at least 1¼ hours. Meanwhile, prepare Toasted Almond Crust.

After chocolate mixture has set and just before removing from refrigerator, combine whipped topping, pureed strawberries and honey or corn syrup; set aside. Beat egg whites and cream of tartar in small mixer bowl until foamy; gradually add sugar and beat until stiff peaks form. Beat chocolate mixture on medium speed about 30 seconds or until smooth. Reduce speed to low; blend in egg white mixture.

Pour 1¼ cups of the chocolate mixture into crust-lined bowl. Carefully spoon strawberry mixture over chocolate, covering completely; top with remaining chocolate mixture. Cover with aluminum foil; freeze overnight. One hour before serving, unmold onto chilled plate; remove foil. Glaze with Chocolate Glaze; return to freezer until serving time.

10 to 12 servings.

Toasted Almond Crust
Line small mixer bowl or deep 1½-quart mixing bowl with aluminum foil. Spread 1 cup (4½-ounce can) slivered almonds on baking sheet; toast at 350° about 8 minutes or until golden brown, stirring occasionally. Cool; finely chop almonds. Thoroughly combine 1 cup vanilla wafer crumbs (about 30 wafers), the chopped almonds and ¼ cup melted butter or margarine. Press mixture firmly onto bottom and up side of prepared bowl; cover and freeze.

Chocolate Glaze

Combine ⅔ cup frozen non-dairy whipped topping, thawed, and ¼ cup chocolate-flavored syrup in small saucepan. Cook over medium-low heat, stirring constantly, until mixture begins to boil; boil and stir 1 minute. Remove from heat; stir in ½ teaspoon vanilla. Cool 5 minutes before using.

Regal Chocolate Mousse

3 blocks (3 ounces) unsweetened baking chocolate, broken into pieces
⅓ cup water
¾ cup sugar
⅛ teaspoon salt
3 egg yolks, well beaten
1 teaspoon vanilla
2 cups heavy or whipping cream

Combine baking chocolate and water in saucepan. Cook over low heat, stirring constantly with wire whisk, until smooth and well blended. Add sugar and salt; simmer 3 minutes, stirring constantly. Pour mixture slowly over egg yolks, stirring well. Cool; add vanilla. Whip cream until stiff; fold into chocolate mixture. Pour into 9-inch square pan; freeze 3 to 4 hours or until firm. Scoop into chilled individual dessert dishes.

6 to 8 servings.

Hershey Bar Mousse

1 milk chocolate bar (8 ounces), broken into pieces
¼ cup water
2 eggs, beaten
1 cup heavy or whipping cream
Sweetened whipped cream and chocolate curls (optional)

Combine chocolate bar pieces and ¼ cup water in top of double boiler over hot, not boiling, water; stir constantly until chocolate is melted and mixture is smooth. Add eggs; cook and stir over hot water about 2 minutes. Remove from heat; cool to room temperature.

Whip cream until stiff; carefully fold in cooled chocolate mixture. Spoon into 8-inch square pan. Freeze several hours or until completely frozen. When ready to serve, chill sherbet dishes. Cut mousse into squares; place one or two squares in each dish. Top with dollop of sweetened whipped cream and garnish with chocolate curls.

4 servings.

Frosty Chocolate-Peanut Butter Loaf

A handsome three-layer dessert in tones of beige and chocolate brown.

Crumb Crust (below)
1 cup chocolate-flavored syrup
½ cup sweetened condensed milk*
¼ teaspoon instant coffee granules (optional)
1 teaspoon vanilla
1½ cups heavy or whipping cream**

1 package (3 ounces) cream cheese, softened
¾ cup confectioners' sugar
⅓ cup peanut butter
⅓ cup milk
½ cup heavy or whipping cream
Additional chocolate-flavored syrup (optional)

Prepare Crumb Crust. Combine 1 cup syrup, the sweetened condensed milk and coffee granules in medium saucepan. Cook over medium heat, stirring constantly, until mixture boils; boil and stir 1 minute. Remove from heat; add vanilla. Cool; chill thoroughly. Whip 1½ cups cream until stiff; fold into chocolate mixture. Pour about half the chocolate mixture into prepared crust; freeze 1 hour. Refrigerate remaining chocolate filling.

Combine cream cheese and confectioners' sugar in large mixer bowl. Add peanut butter; beat until smooth. Gradually add milk; blend well. Whip ½ cup cream until stiff; fold into peanut butter mixture. Pour onto chocolate layer in loaf pan. Return to freezer 1 hour.

Carefully spoon remaining chocolate filling onto peanut butter layer. Sprinkle with crumbs reserved from crust; pat down lightly. Freeze several hours or overnight. To serve, unmold onto chilled plate; remove foil and slice. Drizzle with additional syrup.

10 to 12 servings.

*Do not use evaporated milk.
**Do not use whipped topping.

Crumb Crust
Combine 1 cup vanilla wafer crumbs (about 30 wafers), ½ cup chopped salted peanuts, 2 tablespoons confectioners' sugar and 3 tablespoons melted butter or margarine in small bowl. Pat ¾ cup of mixture onto bottom of aluminum-foil-lined 9½ x 5¼ x 2¾-inch loaf pan; place in freezer. Reserve remaining crumbs.

Marbled Mocha Squares

1 cup graham cracker crumbs
¼ cup unsweetened cocoa
¼ cup sugar
¼ cup butter or margarine, melted
4 teaspoons instant coffee granules
1 tablespoon hot water

1⅓ cups (14-ounce can) sweetened condensed milk*
⅔ cup chocolate-flavored syrup
1 cup chopped walnuts
2 cups heavy or whipping cream, whipped**
¼ cup chocolate-flavored syrup

Thoroughly combine graham cracker crumbs, cocoa and sugar in 9-inch square pan. Add melted butter or margarine; blend well. Pat crumbs firmly onto bottom of pan; set aside.

Dissolve coffee in hot water in large mixing bowl. Add sweetened condensed milk and ⅔ cup syrup; blend well. Fold in walnuts and whipped cream. Pour into prepared pan. Drizzle ¼ cup syrup over mixture; gently swirl with knife or spatula for marbled effect. Cover; freeze 6 hours or until firm. Cut into squares.

9 servings.

*Do not use evaporated milk.
**Do not use whipped topping.

Chocolate Tortoni

1 package (11 ounces) chocolate cream-filled sandwich cookies
1⅔ cups (13-ounce can) evaporated milk
¾ cup chocolate-flavored syrup
½ cup heavy or whipping cream

2 tablespoons rum or 1 teaspoon rum extract
1 tablespoon sugar
1 teaspoon vanilla
1 cup finely chopped walnuts
Additional chopped walnuts
9 maraschino cherries, well drained and cut into halves

Place cookies, a few at a time, in processor or blender; process or blend to form fine crumbs. Set aside. Pour evaporated milk into large mixer bowl. Place bowl and beaters in freezer until ice crystals form around edge of evaporated milk. Whip until stiff peaks form. Fold in syrup, cream, rum or rum extract, sugar, vanilla and cookie crumbs.

Pour into paper-lined muffin cups (2½ inches in diameter). Sprinkle with 1 cup chopped walnuts. Cover and freeze several hours or overnight. Top with additional chopped walnuts and maraschino cherry halves just before serving.

About 18 servings.

Chocolate Sundae Pizza

The "pizza" crust is actually a brownie. This is especially attractive with a variety of fruits—strawberries, blueberries, sliced bananas, kiwifruit, peaches.

¾ cup shortening
1 cup packed light brown sugar
1 egg
2¼ cups unsifted all-purpose flour
¼ teaspoon baking soda
¼ teaspoon cinnamon
¼ teaspoon salt
½ cup (5.5-ounce can) chocolate-flavored syrup
1 quart ice cream (any flavor)
Chocolate Caramel Sauce (below)
Fresh fruits

Cream shortening and brown sugar in large mixer bowl; add egg and blend well. Combine flour, baking soda, cinnamon and salt; add alternately with syrup to creamed mixture, blending well. Pat dough evenly onto greased 12-inch pizza pan, forming a thicker 1-inch-wide edge against rim of pan. Bake at 375° for 10 to 12 minutes or until top springs back when touched lightly. Cool completely.

Cut crust into 10 to 12 wedges, but do not remove from pan. Place small scoops of ice cream around edge. Wrap tightly; freeze until firm.

When ready to serve, prepare Chocolate Caramel Sauce. Arrange assorted fruits on "pizza." Pour warm sauce over ice cream. Serve immediately.

10 to 12 servings.

Chocolate Caramel Sauce
Combine ½ cup (5.5-ounce can) chocolate-flavored syrup, 3 tablespoons milk and 20 unwrapped light caramels in top of double boiler over hot, not boiling, water; stir until caramels are melted and mixture is smooth. Blend in 2 tablespoons butter or margarine. Keep sauce warm until serving time.

Hershey Bar Ice Cream

The wonderful flavor of the Great American Chocolate Bar, transformed into luscious homemade ice cream.

¼ cup sugar
2 tablespoons flour
½ teaspoon salt
1 cup light cream
2 eggs, slightly beaten

2 milk chocolate bars (8 ounces each), broken into pieces
2 teaspoons vanilla
3 cups light cream
1 cup heavy or whipping cream

Combine sugar, flour and salt in medium saucepan; add 1 cup light cream. Cook over medium heat, stirring constantly, until mixture boils; boil and stir 1 minute. Remove from heat. Gradually stir small amount of cooked mixture into eggs; blend well. Return egg mixture to cooked mixture in saucepan; stir until well blended. Add chocolate bar pieces; stir until melted. (If necessary, place over low heat until melted.)

Pour into large mixing bowl. Add vanilla, 3 cups light cream and the heavy or whipping cream; blend well. Chill. Freeze in ice cream freezer according to manufacturer's directions.

About 3 quarts ice cream.

Rich Chocolate Ice Cream

1¾ cups sugar
¼ cup unsifted all-purpose flour
¼ teaspoon salt
2 cups milk
2 eggs, slightly beaten

3½ blocks (3½ ounces) unsweetened baking chocolate, broken into pieces
1 tablespoon vanilla
4 cups light cream

Combine sugar, flour and salt in medium saucepan; gradually stir in milk. Blend in eggs; add baking chocolate. Cook over medium heat, stirring constantly, until mixture boils; boil and stir 1 minute. Remove from heat; add vanilla. Beat with wire whisk until mixture is smooth. Chill thoroughly. Add light cream to chilled mixture. Freeze in ice cream freezer according to manufacturer's directions. (For firmer ice cream, cover and freeze for several hours.)

About 2 quarts ice cream.

Variation
Chocolate Rum-Nut Ice Cream: Substitute 1 teaspoon rum extract for the vanilla. Sauté ¾ cup coarsely chopped nuts in 2 tablespoons butter over medium heat for 4 minutes, stirring occasionally. Add nuts after light cream is thoroughly blended into mixture.

Old-Fashioned Chocolate Ice Cream

2 cups sugar
⅔ cup unsweetened cocoa
¼ cup unsifted all-purpose flour
¼ teaspoon salt
2 cups milk

2 eggs, slightly beaten
1 tablespoon vanilla
4 cups light cream
1 cup heavy or whipping cream

Combine sugar, cocoa, flour and salt in medium saucepan; gradually stir in milk and eggs. Cook over medium heat, stirring constantly, until mixture just begins to boil. Remove from heat; blend in vanilla, light cream and heavy or whipping cream. Chill at least 1 hour. Freeze in ice cream freezer according to manufacturer's directions.

About 3 quarts ice cream.

Easy Homemade Chocolate Ice Cream

1⅓ cups (14-ounce can)
    sweetened condensed
    milk*

1 cup chocolate-flavored syrup
2 cups heavy or whipping cream,
    whipped

Combine sweetened condensed milk and syrup in large mixing bowl. Fold in whipped cream until blended. Pour into aluminum-foil-lined 9¼ x 5¼ x 2¾-inch loaf pan. Cover; freeze 6 hours or until firm.

About 8 servings.

*Do not use evaporated milk.

Refreshing Cocoa-Fruit Sherbet

This cool, festive fruit sherbet is a soothing response to a hot summer night.

1 medium-size ripe banana
1½ cups orange juice
1 cup half-and-half

½ cup sugar
¼ cup unsweetened cocoa

Slice banana into blender container. Add orange juice; blend until smooth. Add remaining ingredients; blend well. Pour into 9-inch square pan or two ice cube trays; freeze until hard around edges. Spoon mixture into blender container or large mixer bowl; blend until smooth. Pour into 1-quart mold; freeze until firm. To serve, unmold onto chilled plate and slice.

About 8 servings.

Ice Cream Sandwiches

½ cup shortening
1 cup sugar
1 egg
1 teaspoon vanilla
1½ cups plus 2 tablespoons
   unsifted all-purpose flour

⅓ cup unsweetened cocoa
½ teaspoon baking soda
½ teaspoon salt
¼ cup milk
   Ice cream (any flavor)

Combine shortening, sugar, egg and vanilla in large mixer bowl until well blended. Combine flour, cocoa, baking soda and salt; add alternately with milk to sugar mixture until ingredients are well blended. Cover and chill about 1 hour.

Drop by heaping tablespoonfuls onto ungreased cookie sheet. With palm of hand or bottom of glass, flatten each cookie into a 2¾-inch circle about ¼ inch thick. Bake at 375° for 8 to 10 minutes or until almost set. Cool 1 minute. Remove from cookie sheet; cool completely on wire rack.

Place scoop of slightly softened ice cream on flat side of one cookie; spread evenly with spatula. Top with another cookie, pressing lightly. Wrap and immediately place in freezer. Freeze until firm.

About 12 ice cream sandwiches.

For the Holidays

Holiday Chocolate Cookies

Use cookie-cutter shapes and food colors for the holiday you're celebrating (see our Valentine's Day hearts on page 149). Other ideas: shamrocks with green icing for St. Patrick's Day; orange icing on Halloween shapes; Christmas trees trimed with red and green icing garlands.

½ cup butter or margarine, softened
¾ cup sugar
1 egg
1 teaspoon vanilla
1½ cups unsifted all-purpose flour
⅓ cup unsweetened cocoa
½ teaspoon baking powder
½ teaspoon baking soda
¼ teaspoon salt
Decorator's Frosting (below)

Cream butter or margarine, sugar, egg and vanilla in large mixer bowl until light and fluffy. Combine remaining ingredients except Decorator's Frosting; add to creamed mixture, blending well.

Roll a small portion of dough at a time on lightly floured surface to ¼-inch thickness. (If too soft, chill dough until firm enough to roll.) Cut with 2½-inch cutter; place on ungreased cookie sheet. Bake at 325° for 5 to 7 minutes or until only a slight indentation remains when touched lightly. Cool 1 minute. Remove from cookie sheet; cool completely on wire rack. Prepare Decorator's Frosting and decorate with holiday designs or messages.

About 3 dozen cookies.

Decorator's Frosting

1½ cups confectioners' sugar
2 tablespoons shortening
2 tablespoons milk
½ teaspoon vanilla
Food color(s)

Combine all ingredients except food color(s) in small mixer bowl; beat until smooth and of spreading consistency. Tint with drops of food color(s), blending well.

Heavenly Heart Cake

¾ cup unsweetened cocoa
⅔ cup boiling water
¾ cup butter or margarine,
    softened
2 cups sugar
1 teaspoon vanilla
2 eggs
2 cups unsifted cake flour or
    1¾ cups unsifted
    all-purpose flour
1¼ teaspoons baking soda
¼ teaspoon salt
¾ cup buttermilk or sour milk*
    Glossy Chocolate Sour Cream
        Frosting (below)
    Creamy Buttercream Frosting
        (below)

Stir together cocoa and boiling water in small bowl until smooth; set aside. Cream butter or margarine, sugar and vanilla in large mixer bowl until light and fluffy; beat in eggs and cocoa mixture. Combine flour, baking soda and salt; add alternately with buttermilk or sour milk to creamed mixture.

Pour batter into two greased and floured heart-shaped pans. Bake at 350° for 30 to 35 minutes or until cake tester comes out clean. Cool 10 minutes; remove from pans. Cool completely. Frost with Glossy Chocolate Sour Cream Frosting and decorate as desired with Creamy Buttercream Frosting.

8 to 10 servings.

*To sour milk: Use 2 teaspoons vinegar plus milk to equal ¾ cup.

Note: If you don't have heart-shaped pans, bake cake as directed in two greased and floured pans: a 9-inch square and a 9-inch round. Slice round layer in half; arrange halves beside square layer as shown in diagram at left.

Glossy Chocolate Sour Cream Frosting
Melt 1½ cups semi-sweet chocolate chips in top of double boiler over hot, not boiling, water, stirring constantly until completely melted. Remove from heat; beat in ¾ cup sour cream, 2 cups confectioners' sugar and 1 teaspoon vanilla.

Creamy Buttercream Frosting
Combine 2 cups confectioners' sugar, ¼ cup softened butter or margarine, 2½ tablespoons milk, ½ teaspoon vanilla and a few drops red food color in small bowl until smooth and creamy.

On facing page—Heavenly Heart Cake (this page); Holiday Chocolate Cookies (page 147)

Valentine Mousse for Two

2 tablespoons sugar
½ teaspoon unflavored gelatine
¼ cup milk
½ cup semi-sweet chocolate
  Mini Chips

1 tablespoon orange-flavored
  liqueur or rum*
½ cup heavy or whipping cream
  Sweetened whipped cream

Combine sugar and gelatine in small saucepan; stir in milk. Let stand a few minutes to soften. Cook over medium heat, stirring constantly, until mixture just begins to boil. Remove from heat; immediately add Mini Chips, stirring until melted. Blend in liqueur or rum; cool to room temperature.

Whip cream until stiff; gradually add chocolate mixture, folding gently just until combined. Chill completely; garnish with sweetened whipped cream before serving.

2 servings.

*You may substitute 1 teaspoon vanilla for the liqueur or rum.

Cherry Chocolate Dessert Squares

For George's birthday: cheerful little cake squares instead of a cherry pie.

1 cup butter or margarine,
  softened
1½ cups sugar
¾ teaspoon almond extract
4 eggs
2 cups unsifted all-purpose flour

6 tablespoons unsweetened
  cocoa
2 cups (21-ounce can) cherry
  pie filling
  Sweetened whipped cream

Cream butter or margarine, sugar and almond extract in large mixer bowl until light and fluffy. Add eggs; beat 2 minutes on medium speed. Combine flour and cocoa; gradually add to egg mixture, blending well. Spread in greased 15½ x 10½ x 1-inch jelly roll pan.

Spoon heaping tablespoonfuls of cherry pie filling (three rows of five) over batter. Reserve remaining pie filling for garnish. Bake at 350° for 25 to 30 minutes or until top springs back when touched lightly in center. Cool. To serve, cut into squares; garnish with sweetened whipped cream and reserved cherry pie filling.

15 servings.

Chocolate-Cherry Mini-Tarts

2 cups confectioners' sugar
1 cup vanilla wafer crumbs
    (about 30 wafers)
1 cup ground almonds (about
    4 ounces whole)
½ cup unsweetened cocoa
6 to 7 tablespoons milk
    Cherry-Almond Filling (below)
    Candied cherry halves

Combine confectioners' sugar, wafer crumbs, ground almonds and cocoa in medium mixing bowl. Sprinkle in milk, mixing until ingredients are moistened and cling together. Shape into walnut-size pieces; place in small paper-lined muffin cups (1¾ inches in diameter). Press dough against bottom and up side of each cup to form shell; chill until firm. Prepare Cherry-Almond Filling; spoon into tart shells. Garnish with candied cherry halves. Chill until firm.

About 30 mini-tarts.

Cherry-Almond Filling

1 package (3 ounces) cream
    cheese, softened
2 cups confectioners' sugar
1 teaspoon vanilla
¼ teaspoon almond extract
½ cup coarsely chopped
    blanched almonds
¼ cup candied cherries,
    quartered

Beat cream cheese in small mixer bowl. Gradually add confectioners' sugar, vanilla and almond extract; beat until well blended. Stir in almonds and cherries.

Irish Hot Chocolate

3 tablespoons unsweetened
    cocoa
¼ cup plus 2 tablespoons sugar
    Dash salt
¼ cup hot water
3 cups milk
6 tablespoons Irish whiskey
    Sweetened whipped cream

Combine cocoa, sugar and salt in medium saucepan; blend in water. Cook over medium heat, stirring constantly, until mixture boils; boil and stir 2 minutes. Add milk. Stir and heat to serving temperature; *do not boil*. Remove from heat. Pour 1 tablespoon whiskey into each of six 6-ounce cups or goblets. Add hot cocoa; stir. Top with sweetened whipped cream. Serve immediately.

6 servings.

St. Patrick's Day Parfaits

For a less spiritous dessert, you may substitute a few drops of green food color for the crème de menthe.

3 cups miniature or 30 large marshmallows
½ cup milk
2 tablespoons green crème de menthe
1 cup semi-sweet chocolate chips

¼ cup confectioners' sugar
1½ cups heavy or whipping cream
Chocolate Cutouts (page 270)

Combine marshmallows and milk in medium saucepan; cook over low heat, stirring constantly, until marshmallows are melted and mixture is smooth. Measure 1 cup marshmallow mixture into small bowl. Blend in crème de menthe; set aside. Add chocolate chips and confectioners' sugar to marshmallow mixture remaining in saucepan; return to low heat and stir until chips are melted. Remove from heat; cool to room temperature.

Whip cream just until soft peaks form; fold 1½ cups into marshmallow-mint mixture. Fold remaining whipped cream into chocolate mixture. Alternately spoon chocolate and mint mixtures into parfait glasses. Chill thoroughly or freeze. Garnish with Chocolate Cutouts.

6 servings.

Easter Fondant Cups

2 milk chocolate bars (8 ounces each), broken into pieces
1 package (8 ounces) cream cheese, softened
½ cup butter or margarine, softened

3½ cups confectioners' sugar
½ teaspoon vanilla
Red and yellow food colors

Melt chocolate bar pieces in top of double boiler over hot, not boiling, water. Remove from heat. Place 10 small paper baking cups in miniature muffin cups (1½ inches in diameter). Using a narrow, soft-bristled pastry brush, thickly and evenly coat inside pleated surface and bottom of each cup with melted chocolate. (Reserve any remaining chocolate for touch-ups.) Chill 20 minutes or until set; coat any thin spots again. (If necessary, chocolate mixture may be reheated over hot water.) Cover tightly; chill until very firm, about 1 hour. Repeat procedure, coating 10 more cups.

Meanwhile, combine cream cheese and butter or margarine in large mixer bowl; beat until smooth and well blended. Gradually add confectioners' sugar and vanilla. Divide mixture in half. Mix 1 or 2 drops red food color into one part and 1 or 2 drops yellow food color into the other.

Remove chocolate cups from refrigerator. Carefully peel paper from each cup. Fill each with pastel fondant and decorate as desired. Cover and chill at least 1 hour. Store, covered, in refrigerator.

40 candies.

Fourth of July Flag Cake

One of the most colorful cakes ever, as bold and bright as a fireworks display.

1¾ cups unsifted all-purpose flour
1¾ cups sugar
¾ cup unsweetened cocoa
1½ teaspoons baking soda
1 teaspoon salt
⅔ cup butter or margarine, softened
1½ cups sour cream

2 eggs
1 teaspoon vanilla
Vanilla Buttercream Frosting (below)
½ pint blueberries
2 pints strawberries (of uniform size)

Combine flour, sugar, cocoa, baking soda and salt in large mixer bowl; blend in butter or margarine, sour cream, eggs and vanilla on low speed. Beat 3 minutes on medium speed.

Pour into greased and floured 13 x 9-inch pan. Bake at 350° for 35 to 40 minutes or until cake tester comes out clean. Cool 10 minutes; remove from pan. Cool completely.

Place cake on oblong serving tray or aluminum-foil-covered cardboard. Prepare Vanilla Buttercream Frosting; frost cake. Arrange blueberries in upper left corner of cake, creating a 4 x 5-inch rectangle. Arrange strawberries in rows for red stripes.

10 to 12 servings.

Vanilla Buttercream Frosting
Combine 3 cups confectioners' sugar and ⅓ cup softened butter or margarine in small mixer bowl. Add 1½ teaspoons vanilla and 2 to 3 tablespoons milk; beat to spreading consistency.

Variation
Coconut Flag Cake: Bake and frost cake as directed, but omit strawberries and blueberries. Instead, tint coconut as follows. For red coconut: Place 1 cup flaked coconut in small bowl or plastic bag. Dilute a few drops of red food color with ½ teaspoon milk; sprinkle onto coconut. Toss with fork or shake until evenly tinted. For blue coconut: Use ⅓ cup flaked coconut and blue food color. Proceed as directed for red. Use the blue coconut in the upper left corner. Alternate red and white coconut for the stripes.

Rich Chocolate Cupcakes

Halloween sorcery: While the cupcakes bake, a rich orange-flavored cream cheese topping becomes the filling! A delight for trick-or-treaters (or anybody, anytime).

Filling (below)
1¼ cups unsifted all-purpose flour
1 cup sugar
⅓ cup unsweetened cocoa
¾ teaspoon baking soda
½ teaspoon salt
1 cup buttermilk or sour milk*
⅓ cup vegetable oil
1 egg
1 teaspoon vanilla

Prepare Filling; set aside. Combine flour, sugar, cocoa, baking soda and salt in large mixer bowl. Add buttermilk or sour milk, oil, egg and vanilla; blend well. Fill paper-lined muffin cups (2½ inches in diameter) half full with batter. Spoon about 1 tablespoon Filling onto each cupcake. Bake at 350° for 20 to 25 minutes or until cake tester inserted in cake portion comes out clean. Cool completely.

About 2 dozen cupcakes.

*To sour milk: Use 1 tablespoon vinegar plus milk to equal 1 cup.

Filling

1 package (8 ounces) cream cheese, softened
⅓ cup sugar
2 teaspoons grated orange peel
⅛ teaspoon salt
2 drops red food color
2 drops yellow food color
1 egg
¾ cup semi-sweet chocolate Mini Chips

Blend cream cheese, sugar, orange peel, salt and food colors in small mixer bowl. Add egg; beat until smooth. Stir in Mini Chips.

Harvest Pumpkin Torte

4 eggs, separated
½ cup sugar
½ cup unsifted all-purpose flour
⅓ cup unsweetened cocoa
¼ cup sugar
½ teaspoon baking soda
¼ teaspoon salt

⅓ cup water
1 teaspoon vanilla
1 tablespoon sugar
Pumpkin Filling (below)
Chocolate Glaze (page 72)
Slivered almonds (optional)

Line 15½ x 10½ x 1-inch jelly roll pan with aluminum foil; generously grease foil. Set aside. Beat egg yolks in large mixer bowl 2 minutes on medium speed. Gradually add ½ cup sugar; continue beating 2 minutes. Combine flour, cocoa, ¼ cup sugar, the baking soda and salt; add alternately with water to egg yolk mixture on low speed just until batter is smooth. Add vanilla; set aside. Beat egg whites until foamy; add 1 tablespoon sugar and beat until stiff peaks form. Carefully fold into chocolate mixture.

Spread batter evenly in prepared pan. Bake at 375° for 14 to 16 minutes or until top springs back when touched lightly. Invert onto slightly dampened towel; carefully remove foil. Cool. Cut cake crosswise into 4 equal pieces. Place one piece on serving plate; spread with about ¾ cup of the Pumpkin Filling. Repeat layering with remaining cake and filling, ending with cake layer. Glaze top of cake with Chocolate Glaze; garnish with slivered almonds. Chill until serving time.

8 to 10 servings.

Pumpkin Filling

1 cup canned pumpkin
¼ cup unsifted all-purpose flour
⅓ cup butter, softened
3 tablespoons shortening

1 teaspoon cinnamon
¼ teaspoon nutmeg
1¾ cups confectioners' sugar

Combine pumpkin and flour in small saucepan. Cook over medium heat, stirring constantly, until mixture boils (mixture will be very thick). Remove from heat; cool thoroughly. Combine butter and shortening in small mixer bowl; add cinnamon and nutmeg. Gradually add confectioners' sugar; beat until light and fluffy. Slowly blend in pumpkin mixture. Chill until mixture begins to set.

Bûche de Noël

1 cup cake flour, sifted
⅓ cup unsweetened cocoa
⅛ teaspoon baking powder
    Dash salt
4 eggs, separated
1 cup sugar
¼ cup water

1 tablespoon butter or
    margarine, melted
1 teaspoon rum extract
    Mocha Filling (below)
    Chocolate Frosting (page 159)
    Meringue Mushrooms
      (page 274)

Line 15½ x 10½ x 1-inch jelly roll pan with aluminum foil; lightly grease foil. Set aside. Combine cake flour, cocoa, baking powder and salt in small mixing bowl; set aside.

Beat egg yolks and ⅔ cup sugar in large mixer bowl until light and fluffy. Beat egg whites in small mixer bowl until foamy; gradually add remaining ⅓ cup sugar, beating until stiff peaks form. Add flour mixture alternately with water to egg yolk mixture; stir in butter or margarine and rum extract. Carefully fold in beaten egg whites.

Spread batter evenly in prepared pan. Bake at 375° for 12 to 15 minutes or until top springs back when touched lightly. Cool in pan 5 minutes; invert onto towel sprinkled with confectioners' sugar. Carefully peel off foil. Trim crusty edges from cake and reserve. Immediately roll cake and towel together starting from narrow end; place on wire rack to cool completely.

Prepare Mocha Filling and Chocolate Frosting. Carefully unroll cake; remove towel. Spread cake with all but 2 tablespoons of Mocha Filling to within ½ inch of edges. Carefully reroll cake; place seam side down on serving plate. Using reserved crusty edges and remaining Mocha Filling, roll to form a "stump" of log and attach to one side of roll. Frost log and stump with Chocolate Frosting. Run fork tines over frosting to resemble bark. Chill about 2 hours before serving. Decorate with Meringue Mushrooms.

8 to 10 servings.

Mocha Filling

¼ cup butter or margarine,
    softened
2 cups confectioners' sugar
2 tablespoons unsweetened
    cocoa
1 tablespoon instant coffee
    granules

2 tablespoons hot water
1 tablespoon slivered orange
    peel (optional)
¼ cup sliced almonds

Cream butter or margarine in small mixer bowl; add confectioners' sugar and cocoa, beating until smooth. Dissolve coffee granules in hot water; beat into mixture until of spreading consistency. Stir in orange peel and almonds.

Chocolate Frosting

½ cup butter or margarine, softened
2½ cups confectioners' sugar
½ cup unsweetened cocoa
¼ cup evaporated milk

Cream butter or margarine in small mixer bowl. Combine confectioners' sugar and cocoa; add alternately with evaporated milk, beating until desired consistency.

Starting from the narrow end, roll the trimmed cake and towel together.

Form a "stump" with reserved crusty cake edges and filling; spread with filling and attach to side of rolled cake.

Holiday Chocolate Fruit-Nut Log

This original cake bakes right on top of its own filling, so all you have to do is roll it up and add a chocolate glaze. A tasty alternative for traditional holiday fruitcakes.

¼ cup butter or margarine, melted
Fruit-Nut Filling (below)
3 egg yolks, at room temperature
½ cup sugar
½ cup unsifted all-purpose flour
⅓ cup unsweetened cocoa
¼ cup sugar

½ teaspoon baking soda
¼ teaspoon salt
⅓ cup water
1 teaspoon vanilla
3 egg whites, at room temperature
1 tablespoon sugar
Chocolate Glaze (below)

Line 15½ x 10½ x 1-inch jelly roll pan with aluminum foil; spread with melted butter or margarine. Layer Fruit-Nut Filling in pan; set aside. Beat egg yolks in small mixer bowl 3 minutes on high speed. Gradually add ½ cup sugar; continue beating 2 minutes. Combine flour, cocoa, ¼ cup sugar, the baking soda and salt; add alternately with water to egg mixture just until blended. Add vanilla; set aside. Beat egg whites until foamy; add 1 tablespoon sugar and beat until stiff peaks form. Carefully fold beaten egg whites into chocolate mixture.

Spread batter evenly over filling in pan. Bake at 375° for 18 to 20 minutes or until top springs back when touched lightly. Invert onto slightly dampened towel; carefully remove foil. Starting at the 10-inch side, roll up cake, jelly-roll fashion; use towel to help roll, but do not roll towel inside cake. Cool completely on rack. Prepare Chocolate Glaze; pour over cake roll, spreading with spatula. Garnish as desired.

10 to 12 servings.

Fruit-Nut Filling
1 cup drained crushed pineapple
½ cup flaked coconut
½ cup chopped nuts

3 or 4 candied cherries, quartered
1 cup minus 1 tablespoon sweetened condensed milk*

Layer pineapple, coconut, nuts and candied cherries in prepared pan; drizzle with sweetened condensed milk.

Chocolate Glaze
Combine ⅓ cup sweetened condensed milk,* 2 tablespoons unsweetened cocoa and 2 tablespoons butter in small saucepan. Cook over medium heat, stirring constantly, until mixture thickens. Remove from heat; add ½ teaspoon vanilla.

*Do not use evaporated milk.

Christmas Poinsettia Pie

8- or 9-inch baked pastry shell
or crumb crust
1 teaspoon unflavored gelatine
1 tablespoon cold water
2 tablespoons boiling water
½ cup sugar
¼ cup unsweetened cocoa

1 cup heavy or whipping cream,
well chilled
1 teaspoon vanilla
Rum Cream Topping (below)
¼ cup flaked coconut
Red and green candied
cherries

Bake pastry shell or crumb crust; set aside. Sprinkle gelatine onto cold water in small bowl; let stand 1 minute to soften. Add boiling water; stir until gelatine is completely dissolved (mixture must be clear). Combine sugar and cocoa in chilled small mixer bowl; add cream and vanilla. Beat 30 seconds on low speed or until smooth; beat 1 minute on medium speed or until stiff peaks form. Gradually add gelatine mixture; beat until blended. Pour into cooled shell or crust. Spread Rum Cream Topping over chocolate filling; sprinkle with coconut. Chill at least 2 hours. Cut cherries into eighths; arrange to resemble poinsettia petals and leaves on top of pie.

6 to 8 servings.

Rum Cream Topping

½ teaspoon unflavored gelatine
1 tablespoon cold water
1 tablespoon boiling water
1 cup heavy or whipping cream

2 tablespoons confectioners'
sugar
2 teaspoons light rum or
¼ teaspoon rum extract

Sprinkle gelatine onto cold water in cup; let stand 1 minute to soften. Add boiling water; stir until gelatine is completely dissolved. Combine cream, confectioners' sugar and rum or rum extract in small mixer bowl. Blend well; gradually add gelatine mixture. Beat until stiff peaks form.

Cocoa Fruitcake

2 cups red candied cherries, cut in half
1½ cups pecan pieces
1 cup golden raisins
½ cup coarsely chopped candied pineapple
¾ cup butter or margarine, softened
1½ cups sugar
1 teaspoon vanilla
3 eggs
1 cup unsifted all-purpose flour
6 tablespoons unsweetened cocoa
½ teaspoon salt
¼ teaspoon baking powder
½ cup buttermilk or sour milk*

Combine cherries, pecans, raisins and pineapple in large bowl; set aside. Cream butter or margarine, sugar and vanilla in large mixer bowl until light and fluffy. Add eggs; beat well. Combine flour, cocoa, salt and baking powder; add alternately with buttermilk or sour milk to creamed mixture, beating just until blended. Stir in reserved fruit-nut mixture.

Pour into greased and floured 12-cup Bundt pan. Bake at 325° for 1 hour and 25 minutes or until cake tester comes out clean. Cool 10 minutes; remove from pan. Immediately wrap in aluminum foil. Allow to stand overnight before serving.

12 to 16 servings.

*To sour milk: Use 1½ teaspoons vinegar plus milk to equal ½ cup.

Christmas Kiss Kandies

¾ cup (3½-ounce package) slivered almonds
½ cup confectioners' sugar
1 tablespoon plus 2 teaspoons light corn syrup
1 teaspoon almond extract
⅛ teaspoon red food color
⅛ teaspoon green food color
24 Hershey's Kisses (6-ounce package), unwrapped
Sugar

Place slivered almonds in food processor; cover and process until very finely chopped. Pour into mixing bowl; add confectioners' sugar and blend well. Drizzle corn syrup and almond extract into almond mixture, stirring until blended.

Divide mixture in half. Add red food color to one half; add green food color to the other. With hands, mix each portion until the color is well blended and mixture clings together. Press about 1 teaspoon almond mixture around a Kiss, maintaining the Kiss shape. Roll in sugar. Store in airtight container.

About 2 dozen candies.

Hot Chocolate Eggnog

2 blocks (2 ounces) unsweetened baking chocolate, broken into pieces
4 cups milk
¾ cup sugar
¼ teaspoon salt
4 egg yolks, slightly beaten
⅓ cup light rum
3 tablespoons sugar
1 tablespoon unsweetened cocoa
4 egg whites, at room temperature
Sweetened whipped cream
Nutmeg

Combine baking chocolate pieces, milk, ¾ cup sugar, the salt and egg yolks in 4-quart saucepan. Cook over low heat, stirring constantly with wire whisk, until mixture is hot but not boiling. Add rum; beat with rotary beater until mixture is smooth. Combine 3 tablespoons sugar and the cocoa. Beat egg whites until foamy; gradually beat in sugar-cocoa mixture. Beat until stiff peaks form; fold into chocolate mixture. Pour into heatproof punch bowl or cups; top with sweetened whipped cream and sprinkle with nutmeg. Serve immediately.

10 to 12 servings (about 4 ounces each).

Mousse for a Crowd

End-of-the-year entertaining made easy.

5 cups (2½ twelve-ounce packages) semi-sweet chocolate chips
¾ cup water
¼ cup amaretto
12 egg yolks, at room temperature

3 cups heavy or whipping cream
1½ tablespoons amaretto
12 egg whites, at room temperature
4 tablespoons sugar

Combine chocolate chips, water and ¼ cup amaretto in top of double boiler over hot, not boiling, water; stir until mixture is smooth. With wire whisk, beat egg yolks, one at a time, into chocolate mixture; cool to room temperature. Beat cream and 1½ tablespoons amaretto in large bowl until soft peaks form. Fold a fourth of the cream into chocolate mixture; gently fold in remaining cream.

Beat half the egg whites in large mixer bowl until foamy; gradually add 2 tablespoons of the sugar, beating until stiff peaks form. Fold into chocolate mixture. Beat remaining egg whites in large mixer bowl until foamy; gradually add remaining 2 tablespoons sugar, beating until stiff peaks form. Fold into chocolate mixture. Spoon into one or two large serving bowls or individual dessert dishes. Cover; chill until firm.

36 servings (½ cup each).

Breads & Coffee Cakes

Chocolate-Raisin Batter Bread

⅔ cup milk
⅔ cup sugar
1½ teaspoons salt
¼ cup butter or margarine
2 packages active dry yeast
½ cup warm water

2 eggs, beaten
3 cups unsifted all-purpose flour
⅓ cup unsweetened cocoa
1 cup raisins
Confectioners' Glaze
  (optional, below)

Scald milk in small saucepan; stir in sugar, salt and butter or margarine. Set aside; cool to lukewarm. Dissolve yeast in warm water (105° to 115°F) in large mixer bowl; add milk mixture, eggs and 2⅓ cups of the flour. Beat 2 minutes on medium speed until smooth. Cover; let rise in warm place until doubled, about 1 hour. Stir down dough. Combine remaining ⅔ cup flour and cocoa; stir into dough. Add raisins.

Spoon into well-greased 10-inch tube pan. Cover; let rise in warm place until doubled, about 1 hour. Bake at 375° about 40 minutes or until bread is lightly browned and sounds hollow when tapped. Remove from pan; cool on wire rack. Glaze while warm with Confectioners' Glaze.

12 to 16 servings.

Confectioners' Glaze
Blend 1½ cups confectioners' sugar, 1 tablespoon shortening and 2 to 3 tablespoons milk in small mixer bowl until smooth.

Baked Boston Brown Bread

Simple-to-make chocolatey version of a Yankee favorite.

1 package (12 ounces) corn muffin mix
¼ cup unsweetened cocoa
3 tablespoons flour
2 tablespoons packed light brown sugar
1¼ cups milk
¾ cup chopped nuts
¾ cup raisins
¼ cup dark corn syrup
1 egg, beaten

Combine corn muffin mix, cocoa, flour and brown sugar in large mixing bowl. Add milk, stirring until dry ingredients are moistened; let stand 5 minutes. Stir in nuts, raisins, corn syrup and egg.

Divide batter equally among four well-greased miniature loaf pans (3¼ x 5¾ x 2¼ inches). Bake at 350° for 35 to 40 minutes or until cake tester comes out clean. Cool 5 minutes; remove from pans. Cool slightly. Slice; serve warm with butter, margarine or cream cheese.

4 loaves.

Variation

Baked Boston Brown Muffins: Fill greased muffin cups (2½ inches in diameter) ⅔ full with batter. Bake at 350° for 12 to 15 minutes or until cake tester comes out clean. Cool in pans 5 minutes; serve warm.

About 22 muffins.

Chocolate Tea Bread

¼ cup butter or margarine, softened
⅔ cup sugar
1 egg
1½ cups unsifted all-purpose flour
⅓ cup unsweetened cocoa
1 teaspoon baking soda
¼ teaspoon salt
1 cup buttermilk
¾ cup chopped walnuts
¾ cup raisins (optional)

Cream butter or margarine, sugar and egg in large mixer bowl until light and fluffy. Combine flour, cocoa, baking soda and salt in small mixing bowl; add alternately with buttermilk to creamed mixture. Beat on low speed just until blended; stir in nuts and raisins.

Pour into greased 8½ x 4½ x 2½-inch loaf pan. Bake at 350° for 55 to 60 minutes or until cake tester comes out clean. Remove from pan; cool completely on wire rack.

1 loaf.

Chocolate Chip Banana Bread

Always perfect for gift-giving, these banana breads offer something unexpected: the surprise of chocolate.

2 cups unsifted all-purpose flour
1 cup sugar
1 teaspoon baking powder
1 teaspoon salt
½ teaspoon baking soda
1 cup mashed ripe bananas
   (about 3 small)
½ cup shortening
2 eggs
1 cup semi-sweet chocolate
   Mini Chips
½ cup chopped walnuts

Grease the bottom only of a 9¼ x 5¼ x 2¾-inch loaf pan; set aside. Combine all ingredients except Mini Chips and walnuts in large mixer bowl; blend well on medium speed. Stir in Mini Chips and walnuts.

Pour into prepared pan. Bake at 350° for 60 to 70 minutes or until cake tester comes out clean. Cool 10 minutes; remove from pan. Cool completely on wire rack.

1 loaf.

Chocolate Banana Bread

1½ cups unsifted all-purpose
   flour
½ cup unsweetened cocoa
⅔ cup sugar
1 teaspoon baking powder
½ teaspoon baking soda
½ teaspoon salt
½ cup shortening
1 cup mashed ripe bananas
   (about 3 small)
2 eggs, beaten
   Confectioners' sugar
   (optional)

Combine flour, cocoa, sugar, baking powder, baking soda and salt in large mixing bowl; cut in shortening until mixture resembles coarse crumbs. Add mashed bananas and eggs; stir just until blended.

Pour into greased and floured 9¼ x 5¼ x 2¾-inch loaf pan. Bake at 350° for 50 to 55 minutes or until cake tester comes out clean. Cool 10 minutes; remove from pan. Cool completely on wire rack; sprinkle with confectioners' sugar.

1 loaf.

Variation
Fruited Chocolate Banana Bread: Add 1 cup raisins or finely chopped dried apricots to batter.

Chocolate Chip Date-Nut Loaves

1½ cups boiling water
1 cup chopped pitted dates
1¼ cups sugar
1 egg
1 tablespoon vegetable oil
2 teaspoons vanilla
2 cups unsifted all-purpose flour

2 teaspoons baking soda
½ teaspoon salt
¼ teaspoon baking powder
1 cup chopped nuts
1 cup semi-sweet chocolate Mini Chips

Pour the boiling water over dates in small mixing bowl; let stand 15 minutes. Beat sugar and egg in large mixer bowl 3 minutes on high speed. Blend in oil and vanilla. Combine flour, baking soda, salt and baking powder; add alternately with dates to egg mixture, blending well. Stir in nuts and Mini Chips.

Divide batter equally among four well-greased miniature loaf pans (3¼ x 5¾ x 2¼ inches). Bake at 350° for 35 to 40 minutes or until cake tester comes out clean. Cool 10 minutes; remove from pans. Cool completely on wire rack.

4 loaves.

Chocolate Chip Muffins

1½ cups unsifted all-purpose flour
½ cup sugar
2 teaspoons baking powder
½ teaspoon salt
½ cup milk
¼ cup vegetable oil

1 egg, beaten
½ cup semi-sweet chocolate Mini Chips
½ cup chopped nuts
¼ cup chopped maraschino cherries, well drained
2 teaspoons grated orange peel

Combine flour, sugar, baking powder and salt in medium mixing bowl. Add milk, oil and egg; stir just until blended. Stir in Mini Chips, nuts, cherries and orange peel.

Fill greased or paper-lined muffin cups (2½ inches in diameter) ⅔ full with batter. Bake at 400° for 25 to 30 minutes or until golden brown. Remove from pan; cool completely. Serve with butter, margarine or cream cheese.

About 12 muffins.

On facing page, clockwise from top—Chocolate Chip Muffins (this page); Chocolate Tea Bread (page 166); Chocolate Chip Banana Bread (page 167)

Cocoa Nut Bread

2¼ cups unsifted all-purpose flour
1¼ cups sugar
⅓ cup unsweetened cocoa
3½ teaspoons baking powder
1 teaspoon salt
1¼ cups milk
⅓ cup vegetable oil
1 egg
1 cup chopped nuts

Combine all ingredients in large mixer bowl; beat 30 seconds on medium speed, scraping side and bottom of bowl constantly. Pour into greased and floured 9¼ x 5¼ x 2¾-inch loaf pan. Bake at 350° for 60 to 65 minutes or until cake tester comes out clean. Cool 10 minutes; remove from pan. Cool completely on wire rack.

1 loaf.

Chocolate Streusel Coffee Cake

Extra good because chocolate chips are mixed into the crunchy topping.

Chocolate Streusel (below)
½ cup butter or margarine, softened
1 cup sugar
3 eggs
1 cup sour cream
1 teaspoon vanilla
2 cups unsifted all-purpose flour
1 teaspoon baking powder
1 teaspoon baking soda
¼ teaspoon salt

Prepare Chocolate Streusel; set aside. Cream butter or margarine and sugar in large mixer bowl until light and fluffy. Add eggs; blend well on low speed. Stir in sour cream and vanilla. Combine flour, baking powder, baking soda and salt; add to batter. Blend well.

Sprinkle 1 cup of the Chocolate Streusel into greased and floured 12-cup Bundt pan. Spread a third of the batter (about 1⅓ cups) in pan; sprinkle with half the remaining streusel (about 1 cup). Repeat layers, ending with batter on top. Bake at 350° for 50 to 55 minutes or until cake tester comes out clean. Cool 10 minutes; invert onto serving plate. Cool completely.

12 to 16 servings.

Chocolate Streusel

¾ cup packed light brown sugar
¼ cup unsifted all-purpose flour
¼ cup butter or margarine, softened
¾ cup chopped nuts
¾ cup semi-sweet chocolate Mini Chips

Combine brown sugar, flour and butter or margarine in medium mixing bowl until crumbly. Stir in nuts and Mini Chips.

Mocha-Chip Coffee Cake

Streusel Topping (below)
2 cups buttermilk baking mix
2 tablespoons sugar
1 tablespoon instant coffee granules

⅔ cup milk
1 egg
1 cup semi-sweet chocolate Mini Chips

Prepare Streusel Topping; set aside. Combine baking mix, sugar, coffee granules, milk and egg in large mixing bowl; beat vigorously for 30 seconds. Spread half the batter in greased 8-inch round pan; sprinkle with half the Mini Chips and half the Streusel Topping. Cover with remaining batter; repeat layers of Mini Chips and topping. Bake at 400° for 25 to 30 minutes or until cake tester comes out clean. Serve warm.

About 6 servings.

Streusel Topping

Using fork or pastry blender, combine ⅓ cup buttermilk baking mix, ⅓ cup packed light brown sugar, ½ teaspoon cinnamon and 2 tablespoons softened butter or margarine in small mixing bowl until crumbly.

Chocolate-Filled Braid

A beautiful braided bread with a cinnamon-fragrant, chocolate-rich filling.

Chocolate Filling (below)
2½ to 2¾ cups unsifted
    all-purpose flour
 2 tablespoons sugar
 ½ teaspoon salt
 1 package active dry yeast
 ½ cup milk

¼ cup water
½ cup butter or margarine
1 egg, at room temperature
   Melted butter (optional)
   Confectioners' Sugar Glaze
   (optional, below)

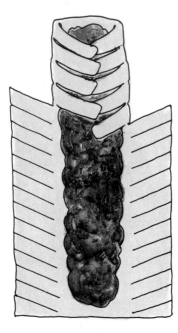

Prepare Chocolate Filling; set aside. Combine 1 cup of the flour, the sugar, salt and yeast in large mixer bowl; set aside. Combine milk, water and butter or margarine in small saucepan; cook over low heat until liquids are very warm (120° to 130°F) — butter or margarine does not need to melt. Gradually add to dry ingredients; beat 2 minutes on medium speed. Add egg and ½ cup of the flour; beat 2 minutes on high speed. Stir in enough additional flour to make a stiff dough. Cover; allow to rest 20 minutes.

Turn dough out onto well-floured board; roll into a 10 x 18-inch rectangle. Spread Chocolate Filling lengthwise down center third of dough. Cut 1-inch-wide strips diagonally along both sides of filling to within ¾ inch of filling. Alternately fold opposite strips of dough at an angle across filling. Carefully transfer to greased cookie sheet. Shape into ring, stretching slightly; pinch ends together. Cover loosely with wax paper brushed with vegetable oil; top with plastic wrap. Chill at least 2 hours or overnight.

Remove braid from refrigerator just before baking. Uncover dough; let stand at room temperature 10 minutes. Bake at 375° for 30 to 35 minutes or until lightly browned. Remove from cookie sheet; cool completely on wire rack. Brush with melted butter or drizzle with Confectioners' Sugar Glaze.

10 to 12 servings.

Chocolate Filling

¾ cup semi-sweet chocolate
   chips
 2 tablespoons sugar
⅓ cup evaporated milk

½ cup finely chopped nuts
1 teaspoon vanilla
¼ teaspoon cinnamon

Combine chocolate chips, sugar and evaporated milk in small pan. Cook over low heat, stirring constantly, until chips melt and mixture is smooth. Stir in nuts, vanilla and cinnamon. Cool.

Confectioners' Sugar Glaze

Beat 1 cup confectioners' sugar, 1 tablespoon softened butter or margarine, ½ teaspoon vanilla and 1 to 2 tablespoons milk in small mixer bowl until glaze is smooth and of desired consistency.

On facing page, from top—Cocoa Brunch Ring (page 175); Chocolate-Filled Braid (this page)

Chocolate Nut Loaves

5 to 5½ cups unsifted all-purpose flour
½ cup sugar
1 teaspoon salt
2 packages active dry yeast
1 cup sour cream
½ cup water
¼ cup milk
½ cup butter or margarine

4 egg yolks, at room temperature (reserve whites for filling)
Walnut-Chocolate Chip Filling (below)
Butter or margarine
Confectioners' sugar or Confectioners' Sugar Glaze (optional, page 172)

Combine 2 cups of the flour, the sugar, salt and yeast in large mixer bowl; set aside. Combine sour cream, water, milk and ½ cup butter or margarine in small saucepan; cook over low heat until liquids are very warm (120° to 130°F). Gradually add to dry ingredients; beat 2 minutes on medium speed. Add egg yolks and 1 cup of the flour; beat 2 minutes on high speed. Gradually stir in enough flour to make a soft dough. When dough becomes difficult to stir, turn out onto well-floured board. Knead in enough remaining flour until dough is elastic and forms a smooth ball (about 3 to 5 minutes). Cover; allow to rest 15 minutes.

Prepare Walnut-Chocolate Chip Filling; set aside. Divide dough into 4 equal pieces. On lightly floured board, roll out each piece of dough to a 10 x 12-inch rectangle. Spread 1 cup of the Walnut-Chocolate Chip Filling on each rectangle to within ½ inch of edges. Roll up dough from long side as for jelly roll; pinch edge to seal. Place on greased cookie sheet, sealed edges down, curving rolls to form crescent or spiral shapes. Cover; let rise in warm place until doubled, about 1 to 1½ hours.

Bake at 350° for 20 minutes. Loosely cover with aluminum foil; bake 10 to 15 minutes longer or until golden brown. Remove from oven; brush lightly with butter or margarine. Cool completely on wire rack. Just before serving, sprinkle with confectioners' sugar or glaze with Confectioners' Sugar Glaze. Garnish as desired.

4 loaves.

Walnut-Chocolate Chip Filling
Beat reserved 4 egg whites in large mixer bowl until foamy; gradually add ⅔ cup sugar and dash salt, beating until stiff peaks form. Fold in 4 cups ground walnuts (16-ounce bag shelled walnuts) and 2 cups (12-ounce package) semi-sweet chocolate Mini Chips; blend well.

Cocoa Brunch Rings

½ cup milk
½ cup sugar
1 teaspoon salt
½ cup butter or margarine
2 packages active dry yeast
½ cup warm water

2 eggs, slightly beaten
3½ to 3¾ cups unsifted
  all-purpose flour
¾ cup unsweetened cocoa
  Orange Filling (below)

Scald milk in small saucepan; stir in sugar, salt and butter or margarine. Set aside; cool to lukewarm. Dissolve yeast in warm water (105° to 115°F) in large mixer bowl; add milk mixture, eggs and 2 cups of the flour. Beat 2 minutes on medium speed until smooth. Combine 1½ cups of the flour and the cocoa; stir into yeast mixture.

Turn dough out onto well-floured board; knead in more flour until dough is smooth enough to handle. Knead about 5 minutes or until smooth and elastic. Place in greased bowl; turn to grease top. Cover; let rise in warm place until doubled, about 1 to 1½ hours. Punch down dough; turn over. Cover; let rise 30 minutes longer.

Prepare Orange Filling; set aside. Divide dough in half. On lightly floured board, roll out each half to a 9 x 13-inch rectangle. Spread a fourth of the Orange Filling on each rectangle to within ½ inch of edges; reserve remaining filling for frosting. Roll up dough from long side as for jelly roll; pinch edge to seal. Cut rolls into 1-inch slices. Place slices, sealed edges down, in two greased 4- to 6-cup ring molds. Tilt slices slightly, overlapping so filling shows. Cover; let rise in warm place until doubled, about 45 minutes. Bake at 350° for 20 to 25 minutes or until golden brown. Immediately remove from molds and place on serving plates. Frost with remaining Orange Filling or, if a glaze is preferred, stir in a few drops orange juice until of desired consistency; spoon over rings. Serve warm.

2 rings.

Orange Filling
Combine 3 cups confectioners' sugar, 6 tablespoons softened butter or margarine, ¼ cup orange juice and 4 teaspoons grated orange peel in small mixer bowl; beat on low speed until smooth.

Chocolate Waffles

For a truly different occasion, why not present a "chocolate brunch" and feature these waffles and Chocolate Chip Pancakes along with some of our coffee cakes and breakfast breads?

1 cup unsifted all-purpose flour
¾ cup sugar
½ cup unsweetened cocoa
½ teaspoon baking powder
½ teaspoon baking soda

¼ teaspoon salt
1 cup buttermilk or sour milk*
2 eggs
¼ cup butter or margarine, melted

Combine flour, sugar, cocoa, baking powder, baking soda and salt in medium mixing bowl. Add buttermilk or sour milk and eggs; beat just until blended. Gradually add melted butter or margarine, beating until smooth. Bake in waffle iron according to manufacturer's directions. Serve warm with pancake syrup or, for dessert, with ice cream, fruit-flavored syrups and, if desired, sweetened whipped cream or Chocolate Whipped Cream (page 244).

10 to 12 four-inch waffles.

*To sour milk: Use 1 tablespoon vinegar plus milk to equal 1 cup.

Chocolate Chip Pancakes

2 cups buttermilk baking mix
1 cup milk
2 eggs

½ cup semi-sweet chocolate Mini Chips

Combine buttermilk baking mix, milk and eggs in medium mixing bowl; beat until smooth. Stir in Mini Chips. For each pancake, pour 2 tablespoons batter onto hot, lightly greased griddle; bake until bubbles appear. Turn; bake other side until lightly browned. (For thinner pancakes, add 1 tablespoon milk to batter; pancakes should be at least ¼ inch thick.) Serve warm with butter or margarine; sprinkle with confectioners' sugar or top with syrup.

About 18 pancakes.

Cookies

Best Brownies

The timeless classic of chocolate cookery. Irresistible.

½ cup vegetable oil or melted
    butter
1 cup sugar
1 teaspoon vanilla
2 eggs
½ cup unsifted all-purpose flour

⅓ cup unsweetened cocoa
¼ teaspoon baking powder
¼ teaspoon salt
½ cup chopped nuts (optional)
    Creamy Brownie Frosting
    (page 180)

Blend oil or melted butter, sugar and vanilla in large mixing bowl. Add eggs; using a spoon, beat well. Combine flour, cocoa, baking powder and salt; gradually blend into egg mixture. Stir in nuts.

Spread in greased 9-inch square pan. Bake at 350° for 20 to 25 minutes or until brownie begins to pull away from edges of pan. Cool; frost with Creamy Brownie Frosting. Cut into squares.

About 16 brownies.

Rich Chocolate Brownies

½ cup sugar
¼ cup evaporated milk
¼ cup butter or margarine
8 blocks (8 ounces) semi-sweet
    baking chocolate, broken
    into pieces
2 eggs

1 teaspoon vanilla
¾ cup unsifted all-purpose flour
¼ teaspoon baking soda
¼ teaspoon salt
¾ cup chopped nuts (optional)
    Brownie Frosting (page 180)

Combine sugar, evaporated milk and butter or margarine in medium saucepan. Cook over medium heat, stirring occasionally, until mixture comes to a full rolling boil. Remove from heat; add chocolate pieces, stirring until melted. Beat in eggs and vanilla. Add flour, baking soda and salt; mix until smooth. Stir in nuts.

Spread in greased 9-inch square pan. Bake at 325° for 30 to 35 minutes or until brownie begins to pull away from edges of pan. Cool; frost with Brownie Frosting. Cut into squares.

About 16 brownies.

Peanut Butter Paisley Brownies

½ cup butter or margarine,
  softened
¼ cup peanut butter
1 cup sugar
1 cup packed light brown sugar
3 eggs

1 teaspoon vanilla
2 cups unsifted all-purpose flour
2 teaspoons baking powder
¼ teaspoon salt
½ cup (5.5-ounce can)
  chocolate-flavored syrup

Blend butter or margarine and peanut butter in large mixer bowl. Add sugar and brown sugar; beat well. Add eggs, one at a time, beating well after each addition. Blend in vanilla. Combine flour, baking powder and salt; add to peanut butter mixture.

Spread half the batter in greased 13 x 9-inch pan. Spoon syrup over top. Carefully spread with remaining batter. Swirl with spatula or knife for marbled effect. Bake at 350° for 35 to 40 minutes or until lightly browned. Cool; cut into squares.

About 3 dozen brownies.

Peanut Butter Chip Brownies

½ cup butter or margarine,
  softened
1 cup sugar
2 eggs
1 teaspoon vanilla
1¼ cups unsifted all-purpose
  flour

¼ cup unsweetened cocoa
¼ teaspoon baking soda
¾ cup chocolate-flavored syrup
1 cup peanut butter chips

Cream butter or margarine, sugar, eggs and vanilla in large mixer bowl until light and fluffy. Combine flour, cocoa and baking soda; add alternately with syrup to creamed mixture. Stir in peanut butter chips.

Spread in greased 13 x 9-inch pan. Bake at 350° for 30 to 35 minutes or until brownie begins to pull away from edges of pan. Cool; frost, if desired (see page 180). Cut into squares.

About 2 dozen brownies.

On facing page, clockwise from bottom—Best Brownies (page 177); Peanut Butter Paisley Brownies (this page); Scrumptious Chocolate Layer Bars (page 181)

Chewy Honey Brownies

⅓ cup butter or margarine, softened
½ cup sugar
2 teaspoons vanilla
⅓ cup honey
2 eggs
½ cup unsifted all-purpose flour
⅓ cup unsweetened cocoa
½ teaspoon salt
⅔ cup chopped nuts

Cream butter or margarine, sugar and vanilla in large mixer bowl; blend in honey. Add eggs; beat well. Combine flour, cocoa and salt; gradually add to creamed mixture. Stir in nuts.

Spread in greased 9-inch square pan. Bake at 350° for 25 to 30 minutes or until brownie begins to pull away from edges of pan. Cool; frost, if desired (below). Cut into squares.

About 16 brownies.

Creamy Brownie Frosting

3 tablespoons butter or margarine, softened
3 tablespoons unsweetened cocoa
1 tablespoon light corn syrup or honey
½ teaspoon vanilla
1 cup confectioners' sugar
1 to 2 tablespoons milk

Cream butter or margarine, cocoa, corn syrup or honey and vanilla in small mixer bowl. Add confectioners' sugar and milk; beat to spreading consistency.

About 1 cup frosting.

Brownie Frosting

2 blocks (2 ounces) unsweetened baking chocolate
2 tablespoons butter or margarine
1¾ cups confectioners' sugar
⅛ teaspoon salt
½ teaspoon vanilla
2 to 3 tablespoons water

Melt baking chocolate and butter or margarine in top of double boiler over hot, not boiling, water. Combine confectioners' sugar and salt in small mixing bowl; gradually add chocolate mixture and vanilla. Add water; beat to spreading consistency.

1 cup frosting.

Chewy Chocolate Bars

Lots 'n lots of oats and walnuts for great texture.

½ cup plus 3 tablespoons butter or margarine
½ cup unsweetened cocoa
1½ cups sugar
2 eggs
1 cup quick-cooking oats
¼ cup unsifted all-purpose flour
½ teaspoon baking powder
½ teaspoon salt
1 teaspoon vanilla
1 cup coarsely chopped walnuts

Melt butter or margarine in small saucepan over low heat; stir in cocoa. Pour mixture into small mixer bowl; gradually beat in sugar. Add eggs; beat well. Combine oats, flour, baking powder and salt; add to chocolate mixture, blending well. Stir in vanilla and walnuts.

Spread in greased 9-inch square pan. Bake at 350° for 30 to 35 minutes or until cookie begins to pull away from edges of pan. Cool slightly; cut into bars. Cool completely.

About 3 dozen bars.

Scrumptious Chocolate Layer Bars

2 cups (12-ounce package) semi-sweet chocolate chips
1 package (8 ounces) cream cheese
⅔ cup (5.3-ounce can) evaporated milk
1 cup chopped walnuts
¼ cup sesame seeds (optional)
½ teaspoon almond extract
3 cups unsifted all-purpose flour
1½ cups sugar
1 teaspoon baking powder
½ teaspoon salt
1 cup butter or margarine*
2 eggs
½ teaspoon almond extract

Combine chocolate chips, cream cheese and evaporated milk in medium saucepan. Cook over low heat, stirring constantly, until chips are melted and mixture is smooth. Remove from heat; stir in walnuts, sesame seeds and ½ teaspoon almond extract. Blend well; set aside.

Combine remaining ingredients in large mixer bowl; blend well with mixer until mixture resembles coarse crumbs.** Press half the mixture in greased 13 x 9-inch pan; spread with chocolate mixture. For topping, sprinkle rest of crumbs over filling. Bake at 375° for 35 to 40 minutes or until golden brown. Cool; cut into bars.

About 3 dozen bars.

*Do not use whipped or reduced-calorie products.
**If mixture softens and forms a stiff dough, pinch off small pieces to use as topping.

Chocolate-Cherry Squares

1 cup unsifted all-purpose flour	½ cup chopped nuts
⅓ cup butter or margarine	Filling (below)
½ cup packed light brown sugar	Red candied cherry halves

Combine flour, butter or margarine and brown sugar in large mixer bowl. Blend on low speed to form fine crumbs, about 2 to 3 minutes. Stir in nuts. Reserve ¾ cup crumb mixture for topping; pat remaining crumbs into ungreased 9-inch square pan. Bake at 350° for 10 minutes or until lightly browned. Prepare Filling; spread over warm crust. Sprinkle with reserved crumb mixture and garnish with cherry halves. Bake at 350° for 25 minutes or until lightly browned. Cool; cut into squares. Store in refrigerator.

About 3 dozen squares.

Filling

1 package (8 ounces) cream cheese, softened	1 egg
½ cup sugar	½ teaspoon vanilla
⅓ cup unsweetened cocoa	½ cup chopped red candied cherries
¼ cup milk	

Combine cream cheese, sugar, cocoa, milk, egg and vanilla in small mixer bowl; beat until smooth. Fold in cherries.

Chocolate-Filled Oatmeal Bars

1 cup butter or margarine, softened
2 cups packed light brown sugar
3 eggs
1 teaspoon vanilla
3 cups quick-cooking oats

2¼ cups unsifted all-purpose flour
1 teaspoon baking soda
½ teaspoon salt
Chocolate Filling (below)

Cream butter or margarine and brown sugar in large mixer bowl until light and fluffy. Add eggs and vanilla; beat well. Combine oats, flour, baking soda and salt; stir into creamed mixture.

Spread ⅔ of the mixture in greased 15½ x 10½ x 1-inch jelly roll pan. Prepare Chocolate Filling; spread evenly over oatmeal mixture in pan. Spoon small dollops of remaining oatmeal mixture evenly over top. Bake at 350° for 25 to 30 minutes or until golden brown. Cool; cut into bars.

About 5 dozen bars.

Chocolate Filling

2 cups (12-ounce package) semi-sweet chocolate chips
1⅓ cups (14-ounce can) sweetened condensed milk*

2 tablespoons butter or margarine
½ teaspoon salt
½ cup chopped nuts
1 teaspoon vanilla

Combine chocolate chips, sweetened condensed milk, butter or margarine and salt in medium saucepan; cook over low heat, stirring constantly, until chips and butter or margarine are melted and mixture is smooth. Stir in nuts and vanilla.

*Do not use evaporated milk.

Chocolate-Chip Chocolate Cookies

½ cup butter or margarine, softened
1 cup sugar
1 egg
1 teaspoon vanilla
1½ cups unsifted all-purpose flour
⅓ cup unsweetened cocoa
½ teaspoon baking soda
½ teaspoon salt
¼ cup milk
1 cup (6-ounce package) semi-sweet chocolate chips

Cream butter or margarine, sugar, egg and vanilla in large mixer bowl until light and fluffy. Combine flour, cocoa, baking soda and salt in small mixing bowl; add alternately with milk to creamed mixture, blending well. Stir in chocolate chips.

Drop by teaspoonfuls onto ungreased cookie sheet. Bake at 375° for 10 to 12 minutes or until almost set *(do not overbake)*. Cool 1 minute. Remove from cookie sheet; cool completely on wire rack.

About 3½ dozen cookies.

Chocolate Chip Whole Wheat Cookies

Nutritious whole wheat combines with chocolate chips for a delectable variation on everybody's favorite cookie.

1 cup unsifted whole wheat flour
½ teaspoon baking soda
½ teaspoon salt
¾ cup shortening
1½ cups packed light brown sugar
1 egg
¼ cup water
1 teaspoon vanilla
2 cups quick-cooking oats
1 cup raisins or chopped dried apricots
1 cup semi-sweet chocolate Mini Chips

Combine whole wheat flour, baking soda and salt in small mixing bowl; set aside. Cream shortening and brown sugar in large mixer bowl until light and fluffy. Add egg, water and vanilla; beat well. Stir reserved flour mixture into creamed mixture. Stir in oats, raisins or dried apricots and Mini Chips.

Drop by teaspoonfuls onto lightly greased cookie sheet; flatten slightly. Bake at 350° for 10 to 12 minutes or until golden brown. Remove from cookie sheet; cool completely on wire rack.

About 5 dozen cookies.

Oatmeal Chocolate Chip Cookies

¾ cup butter or margarine, softened
1 cup packed light brown sugar
½ cup sugar
1 egg
1 teaspoon vanilla
1 cup unsifted all-purpose flour
½ teaspoon baking soda
½ teaspoon salt
¼ cup milk
2½ cups quick-cooking oats
2 cups (12-ounce package) semi-sweet chocolate chips

Cream butter or margarine, brown sugar, sugar, egg and vanilla in large mixer bowl until light and fluffy. Combine flour, baking soda and salt in small mixing bowl; add alternately with milk to creamed mixture, blending well. Stir in oats and chocolate chips.

Drop by teaspoonfuls onto lightly greased cookie sheet. Bake at 375° for 10 to 12 minutes or until lightly browned. Remove from cookie sheet; cool completely on wire rack.

About 5 dozen cookies.

Note: Do not use vegetable shortening spray for greasing cookie sheet—it will cause cookies to flatten.

Traditional Chocolate Chip Cookies

1 cup butter, softened
¾ cup sugar
¾ cup packed light brown sugar
1 teaspoon vanilla
2 eggs
2¼ cups unsifted all-purpose flour
1 teaspoon baking soda
½ teaspoon salt
2 cups (12-ounce package) semi-sweet chocolate chips
1 cup chopped nuts (optional)

Cream butter, sugar, brown sugar and vanilla until light and fluffy. Add eggs; beat well. Combine flour, baking soda and salt; gradually add to creamed mixture. Beat well. Stir in chocolate chips and nuts.

Drop by teaspoonfuls onto ungreased cookie sheet. Bake at 375° for 8 to 10 minutes or until lightly browned. Cool slightly. Remove from cookie sheet; cool completely on wire rack.

About 6 dozen cookies.

Variation
Milk Chocolate Chip Cookies: Substitute 2 cups (11.5-ounce package) milk chocolate chips for the semi-sweet chocolate chips.

Mini Chip Sugar Cookies

⅓ cup butter or margarine, softened
¾ cup sugar
½ cup packed light brown sugar
1 egg
1 teaspoon vanilla
2 cups unsifted all-purpose flour

1 teaspoon baking soda
½ teaspoon baking powder
½ teaspoon salt
½ cup buttermilk or sour milk*
1½ cups semi-sweet chocolate Mini Chips

Cream butter or margarine, sugar and brown sugar in large mixer bowl until light and fluffy. Add egg and vanilla; beat well. Combine flour, baking soda, baking powder and salt; add alternately with buttermilk or sour milk to creamed mixture. Stir in Mini Chips.

Drop by teaspoonfuls onto ungreased cookie sheet. Bake at 350° for 10 to 12 minutes or until lightly browned. Remove from cookie sheet; cool on wire rack.

About 3 dozen cookies.

*To sour milk: Use 1½ teaspoons vinegar plus milk to equal ½ cup.

Reese's Chewy Chocolate Cookies

1¼ cups butter or margarine, softened
2 cups sugar
2 eggs
2 teaspoons vanilla
2 cups unsifted all-purpose flour

¾ cup unsweetened cocoa
1 teaspoon baking soda
½ teaspoon salt
2 cups (12-ounce package) peanut butter chips

Cream butter or margarine and sugar in large mixer bowl until light and fluffy. Add eggs and vanilla; beat well. Combine flour, cocoa, baking soda and salt; blend into creamed mixture. Stir in peanut butter chips.

Drop by teaspoonfuls onto ungreased cookie sheet. Bake at 350° for 8 to 9 minutes. *Do not overbake.* (Cookies will be soft; they will puff during baking and flatten upon cooling.) Cool until set, about 1 minute. Remove from cookie sheet; cool completely on wire rack.

About 4½ dozen cookies.

On facing page, clockwise from top—Traditional Chocolate Chip Cookies (page 185); Reese's Chewy Chocolate Cookies (this page); Chocolate Chip Whole Wheat Cookies (page 184); Chocolate Cookie Sandwiches (page 188)

Reese's Cookies

1 cup shortening, or ¾ cup
  butter or margarine,
  softened
1 cup sugar
½ cup packed light brown sugar
1 teaspoon vanilla

2 eggs
2 cups unsifted all-purpose flour
1 teaspoon baking soda
1 cup peanut butter chips
1 cup (6-ounce package) semi-
  sweet chocolate chips

Cream shortening or butter or margarine, sugar, brown sugar and vanilla in large mixer bowl until light and fluffy. Add eggs; beat well. Combine flour and baking soda; add to creamed mixture. Stir in peanut butter chips and chocolate chips.

Drop by teaspoonfuls onto ungreased cookie sheet. Bake at 350° for 10 to 12 minutes or until lightly browned. Cool slightly. Remove from cookie sheet; cool completely on wire rack.

About 5 dozen cookies.

Chocolate Cookie Sandwiches

Kids love this kind of filled cookie. Let junior chefs help make them for their lunch boxes (and impress their friends at school).

½ cup shortening
1 cup sugar
1 egg
1 teaspoon vanilla
1½ cups unsifted all-purpose
  flour

⅓ cup unsweetened cocoa
½ teaspoon baking soda
½ teaspoon salt
¼ cup milk
  Creme Filling (below)

Cream shortening, sugar, egg and vanilla in large mixer bowl until light and fluffy. Combine flour, cocoa, baking soda and salt; add alternately with milk to creamed mixture until ingredients are combined.

Drop by teaspoonfuls onto ungreased cookie sheet. Bake at 375° for 11 to 12 minutes or just until soft-set (*do not overbake*). Cool 1 minute. Remove from cookie sheet; cool completely on wire rack. Prepare Creme Filling. Spread bottom of one cookie with about 1 tablespoon filling; cover with another cookie. Repeat with remaining cookies.

About 15 filled cookies.

Creme Filling
Cream 2 tablespoons softened butter or margarine and 2 tablespoons shortening in small mixer bowl; gradually beat in ½ cup marshmallow creme. Blend in ¾ teaspoon vanilla and ⅔ cup confectioners' sugar; beat to spreading consistency.

Peanut Blossoms

¾ cup peanut butter
½ cup shortening
⅓ cup sugar
⅓ cup packed light brown
    sugar
1 egg
2 tablespoons milk
1 teaspoon vanilla

1½ cups unsifted all-purpose
    flour
1 teaspoon baking soda
½ teaspoon salt
  Sugar
54 Hershey's Kisses (9-ounce
    package), unwrapped

Blend peanut butter and shortening in large mixer bowl. Add ⅓ cup sugar and the brown sugar; cream until light and fluffy. Add egg, milk and vanilla; beat well. Combine flour, baking soda and salt; gradually add to creamed mixture. Blend well.

Shape dough into 1-inch balls; roll in sugar. Place on ungreased cookie sheet. Bake at 375° for 10 to 12 minutes or until lightly browned. Remove from oven; immediately place unwrapped Kiss on top of each cookie, pressing down so that cookie cracks around edge. Remove from cookie sheet; cool on wire rack.

About 4 dozen cookies.

Cocoa-Pecan Kiss Cookies

1 cup butter or margarine,
    softened
⅔ cup sugar
1 teaspoon vanilla
1⅔ cups unsifted all-purpose
    flour

¼ cup unsweetened cocoa
1 cup finely chopped pecans
54 Hershey's Kisses (9-ounce
    package), unwrapped
  Confectioners' sugar

Cream butter or margarine, sugar and vanilla in large mixer bowl until light and fluffy. Combine flour and cocoa; blend into creamed mixture. Add pecans; beat on low speed until well blended. Chill dough 1 hour or until firm enough to handle.

Shape scant tablespoon of dough around each unwrapped Kiss, covering Kiss completely; shape into balls. Place on ungreased cookie sheet. Bake at 375° for 10 to 12 minutes or until almost set. Cool slightly. Remove from cookie sheet; cool completely on wire rack. Roll in confectioners' sugar.

About 4½ dozen cookies.

Oatmeal Kiss Cookies

½ cup butter or margarine, softened
½ cup shortening
1 cup sugar
1 cup packed light brown sugar
2 eggs
2 cups unsifted all-purpose flour
1 teaspoon baking soda
1 teaspoon salt
2¼ cups quick-cooking oats
1 cup chopped nuts
72 Hershey's Kisses (14-ounce package), unwrapped

Blend butter or margarine and shortening in large mixer bowl. Gradually add sugar and brown sugar; cream until light and fluffy. Add eggs; beat well. Combine flour, baking soda and salt; blend into creamed mixture. Stir in oats and nuts.

Shape dough into 1-inch balls. Place on ungreased cookie sheet. Bake at 375° for 10 to 12 minutes or until lightly browned. Remove from oven; immediately press unwrapped Kiss on top of each cookie. Remove from cookie sheet; cool on wire rack.

About 6 dozen cookies.

Chocolate Almond Cookies

1 cup butter or margarine, softened
1 cup sugar
1 egg
½ teaspoon vanilla
½ teaspoon almond extract
2 cups unsifted all-purpose flour
½ cup unsweetened cocoa
¼ teaspoon baking powder
¼ teaspoon baking soda
⅛ teaspoon salt
Sugar
48 blanched almonds, whole or slivered

Cream butter or margarine and 1 cup sugar in large mixer bowl until light and fluffy. Add egg, vanilla and almond extract; beat well. Combine flour, cocoa, baking powder, baking soda and salt; blend into creamed mixture. Cover tightly; chill about 1 hour or until firm enough to handle.

Shape dough into 1-inch balls; roll in sugar. Place on ungreased cookie sheet; lightly press an almond or almond sliver into top of each ball of dough. Bake at 350° for 12 to 15 minutes or until set. Remove from cookie sheet; cool on wire rack.

About 4 dozen cookies.

Macaroon Kiss Cookies

⅓ cup butter or margarine, softened

1 package (3 ounces) cream cheese, softened

¾ cup sugar

1 egg yolk

2 teaspoons almond extract

2 teaspoons orange juice

1¼ cups unsifted all-purpose flour

2 teaspoons baking powder

¼ teaspoon salt

5 cups (14-ounce package) flaked coconut

54 Hershey's Kisses (9-ounce package), unwrapped

Cream butter or margarine, cream cheese and sugar in large mixer bowl until light and fluffy. Add egg yolk, almond extract and orange juice; beat well. Combine flour, baking powder and salt; gradually add to creamed mixture. Stir in 3 cups of the coconut. Cover tightly; chill 1 hour or until firm enough to handle.

Shape dough into 1-inch balls; roll in remaining coconut. Place on ungreased cookie sheet. Bake at 350° for 10 to 12 minutes or until lightly browned. Remove from oven; immediately press unwrapped Kiss on top of each cookie. Cool 1 minute. Carefully remove from cookie sheet; cool completely on wire rack.

About 4½ dozen cookies.

Forgotten Kiss Cookies

Delicate meringue cookies with a milk chocolate center. "Forget" them in the oven overnight.

2 egg whites, at room temperature
⅛ teaspoon cream of tartar
⅛ teaspoon salt

⅔ cup sugar
1 teaspoon vanilla
36 Hershey's Kisses (6-ounce package), unwrapped

Beat egg whites with cream of tartar and salt in small mixer bowl until soft peaks form. Gradually beat in sugar; continue beating until stiff peaks form. Add vanilla.

Drop meringue by half teaspoonfuls onto greased cookie sheet; top each with a Kiss. Cover Kiss *completely* with small teaspoonful of meringue. Place in a preheated 375° oven. Immediately turn off oven and let cookies remain in oven overnight or until completely dry.

About 2½ dozen cookies.

Chocolate Shortbread

1 cup butter, softened
1¼ cups confectioners' sugar
1½ teaspoons vanilla
½ cup unsweetened cocoa

1¾ cups unsifted all-purpose flour
Cocoa Glaze (below)

Cream butter, confectioners' sugar and vanilla in large mixer bowl; add cocoa. Gradually blend in flour. Roll or pat out on lightly floured surface to ½-inch thickness. Cut into rectangles (about 2¼ x 1½ inches) with decorative pastry cutter, if available.

Place on ungreased cookie sheet. With a fork, prick each cookie several times in a decorative pattern, piercing cookie through to bottom. Bake at 300° for 20 to 25 minutes or until firm. Cool slightly. Remove from cookie sheet; cool completely on wire rack. Drizzle Cocoa Glaze on top of cookies.

About 3½ dozen cookies.

Cocoa Glaze
Melt 1 tablespoon butter in small saucepan over low heat; add 1½ tablespoons unsweetened cocoa and 2 tablespoons water. Cook over low heat, stirring constantly, until mixture thickens; *do not boil.* Remove from heat. Blend in ¾ cup confectioners' sugar and ¼ teaspoon vanilla; beat until smooth.

Almond Choco-Chip Shortbread

1 cup butter, softened
½ cup sugar
2½ cups unsifted all-purpose flour

2 teaspoons almond extract
1 cup semi-sweet chocolate Mini Chips

Cream butter and sugar in large mixer bowl until light and fluffy. Add flour and almond extract; blend well. Stir in Mini Chips. Pat into greased 13 x 9-inch pan. Bake at 350° for 40 minutes or until golden brown. Cool 10 minutes; cut into squares.

About 3 dozen squares.

Coconut-Filled Chocolate Cookies

Coconut Filling (below)
½ cup butter or margarine, softened
1 cup confectioners' sugar
1 egg
1 teaspoon vanilla

1¼ cups unsifted all-purpose flour
⅓ cup unsweetened cocoa
½ teaspoon baking soda
½ teaspoon salt

Prepare Coconut Filling; chill. Cream butter or margarine, confectioners' sugar, egg and vanilla in small mixer bowl. Combine flour, cocoa, baking soda and salt; blend into creamed mixture. Cover and chill 20 minutes.

Divide dough in half; roll each half between wax paper into a 7 x 4½-inch rectangle. Shape half the chilled filling into 7-inch-long roll; place lengthwise on one rectangle of dough. Wrap dough around filling, sealing the long edge. Repeat procedure with remaining filling and dough. Wrap rolls tightly in wax paper; chill several hours or overnight.

Cut each roll into ¼-inch slices. Place slices on lightly greased cookie sheet. Bake at 375° for 8 to 10 minutes or until almost set. Cool slightly. Remove from cookie sheet; cool completely on wire rack.

About 4 dozen cookies.

Coconut Filling

1 package (3 ounces) cream cheese, softened
⅓ cup sugar
2 tablespoons flour

1 teaspoon vanilla
1 cup flaked or grated fresh coconut
½ cup chopped nuts (optional)

Beat cream cheese and sugar in small mixer bowl until creamy; add flour and vanilla. Stir in coconut and nuts. Cover and chill.

Chocolate Refrigerator Cookies

½ cup butter or margarine, softened
1 cup sugar
1 egg
1 teaspoon vanilla
1¼ cups unsifted all-purpose flour
½ cup unsweetened cocoa
¾ teaspoon baking soda
¼ teaspoon salt

Cream butter or margarine, sugar, egg and vanilla in large mixer bowl until light and fluffy. Combine flour, cocoa, baking soda and salt; blend into creamed mixture. Divide dough in half. Shape each half into a long roll, 1½ inches in diameter. Wrap in plastic wrap; chill several hours or overnight.

Cut each roll into ⅛-inch slices. Place on ungreased cookie sheet. Bake at 375° for 8 to 10 minutes or until almost set. Cool slightly. Remove from cookie sheet; cool completely on wire rack.

About 3 dozen cookies.

Chocolate Ladyfingers

3 egg yolks, at room temperature
¼ cup sugar
½ teaspoon vanilla
½ cup plus 1 tablespoon unsifted all-purpose flour
3 tablespoons unsweetened cocoa
3 egg whites, at room temperature
3 tablespoons sugar
Confectioners' sugar

Grease and flour ladyfinger mold pan; set aside. Beat egg yolks, ¼ cup sugar and the vanilla in small mixer bowl until very thick. Combine flour and cocoa in small mixing bowl; with mixer on low speed, add to yolk mixture, 1 tablespoon at a time. (The mixture will be extremely thick.)

Beat egg whites in large mixer bowl until foamy; gradually add 3 tablespoons sugar and beat until stiff peaks form. With mixer on lowest speed, beat a fourth of the beaten egg whites into yolks; fold in remaining whites by hand.

Fill prepared ladyfinger molds with batter. Sift confectioners' sugar generously over batter. Bake at 350° for 12 to 15 minutes or until cake tester comes out clean. Cool 5 minutes. Invert onto wire rack; cool completely.

About 12 ladyfingers.

Chocolate Florentines

You admire these lacy cookies in fine bakeries. A little like candy, they're definitely worth the extra effort.

½ cup butter
⅔ cup sugar
2 tablespoons milk
2 tablespoons light corn syrup
⅓ cup unsifted all-purpose flour

¼ cup Candied Orange Peel (below)
1 cup thinly sliced almonds
1 teaspoon vanilla
Chocolate Filling (below)

Line large cookie sheets with aluminum foil; smooth out wrinkles. Set aside. Combine butter, sugar, milk and corn syrup in medium saucepan. Cook over medium heat, stirring constantly, until mixture boils. Continue cooking, without stirring, until syrup reaches 230°F (thread stage) or until syrup spins a 2-inch thread when dropped from fork or spoon. Remove from heat; stir in flour, Candied Orange Peel, almonds and vanilla. Keep mixture warm over hot water or over very low heat to keep from hardening.

Drop mixture by *level* teaspoonfuls onto prepared cookie sheets, placing at least 4 inches apart (cookies will spread a great deal during baking). Bake at 350° for 10 to 12 minutes or until cookies are bubbly all over and a light brown caramel color. Remove from oven. Cool completely on cookie sheet. (Carefully slide foil off cookie sheet if you need to reuse sheet; prepare with foil for next use.) When the cookies are completely cool, gently peel off foil.

Prepare Chocolate Filling. With small spatula, spread thin layer of chocolate on flat side of one cookie, leaving ½-inch border around edge. Gently press on another cookie, flat sides together. Wrap individually in plastic wrap. Cover tightly; chill.

About 1 dozen filled cookies.

Candied Orange Peel
Making ½-inch-wide strips, cut off only the outer peel (no white membrane attached) of 1 large or 2 small navel oranges. Cut the strips into ⅛-inch pieces. Place orange strips, ¼ cup sugar and ½ cup water in small saucepan. Cook over very low heat until the bottom of the pan is covered only with glazed orange peel strips; do not allow to caramelize.

Chocolate Filling
Melt ⅔ cup semi-sweet chocolate chips in top of double boiler over hot, not boiling, water. Stir until smooth.

Chocolate Madeleines

Especially delicate—like little spongecake shells.

1¼ cups unsifted all-purpose flour
1 cup sugar
⅛ teaspoon salt
¾ cup butter, melted
5 tablespoons unsweetened cocoa

3 eggs
2 egg yolks
½ teaspoon vanilla
Chocolate Frosting (below)

Lightly grease the indentations of a madeleine mold pan (each shell is 3 x 2 inches); set aside. Combine flour, sugar and salt in medium saucepan. Combine melted butter and cocoa; stir into the dry ingredients. With a fork, lightly beat eggs, egg yolks and vanilla in small bowl until well blended; stir into chocolate mixture, blending well. Cook over very low heat, stirring constantly, until mixture is warm; *do not simmer or boil.* Remove from heat.

Fill each mold half full with batter (do not overfill). Bake at 350° for 8 to 10 minutes or until cake tester comes out clean. Invert onto wire rack; cool completely. Frost flat sides of cookies with Chocolate Frosting. Press frosted sides together, forming shells.

About 1½ dozen filled cookies.

Chocolate Frosting

2½ cups confectioners' sugar
¼ cup unsweetened cocoa
¼ cup butter, softened

4 to 5 tablespoons milk
1 teaspoon vanilla

Combine confectioners' sugar and cocoa in small mixing bowl. Cream butter and ½ cup of the confectioners' sugar-cocoa mixture in small mixer bowl until light and fluffy. Add remaining cocoa mixture alternately with milk; beat to spreading consistency. Stir in vanilla.

On facing page—at top, Chocolate Madeleines (this page); from left to right, Coconut-Filled Chocolate Cookies (page 193); Chocolate Florentines (page 195); Chocolate Spritz Cookies (page 198)

Chocolate Spritz Cookies

1 cup butter or margarine, softened
⅔ cup sugar
1 egg
1 teaspoon vanilla

2¼ cups unsifted all-purpose flour
⅓ cup unsweetened cocoa
½ teaspoon salt

Cream butter or margarine, sugar, egg and vanilla in large mixer bowl until light and fluffy. Combine flour, cocoa and salt; gradually add to creamed mixture.

Fill cookie press with dough. Press dough onto cool ungreased cookie sheet. Bake at 350° for 5 to 7 minutes or until set. Remove from cookie sheet; cool completely on wire rack.

About 4½ dozen cookies.

Choco-Coconut Gems

1 package (3 ounces) cream cheese, softened
½ cup butter or margarine, softened

1 cup unsifted all-purpose flour
Filling (below)
Sweetened whipped cream (optional)

Blend cream cheese and butter or margarine in small mixer bowl; stir in flour. Cover and chill 1 hour. Shape dough into 24 one-inch balls. Place in ungreased muffin cups (1¾ inches in diameter); press dough evenly against bottom and up side of each muffin cup.

Prepare Filling; spoon 2 level teaspoonfuls into each pastry-lined muffin cup. Bake at 350° for 20 to 25 minutes or until set. Cool; remove from pan. Garnish with dollops of sweetened whipped cream.

2 dozen cookies.

Filling

½ cup sugar
¼ cup unsweetened cocoa
1 egg, slightly beaten
3 tablespoons butter or margarine, melted

½ teaspoon vanilla
½ cup flaked coconut

Combine sugar, cocoa, egg, butter or margarine and vanilla in small bowl; stir just until smooth. Stir in coconut.

Petite Chocolate Tarts

2 packages (3 ounces each) cream cheese, softened
½ cup butter or margarine, softened
½ cup shortening
2 cups unsifted all-purpose flour
Filling (below)
Topping (optional, below)

Blend cream cheese, butter or margarine and shortening in large mixer bowl. Gradually add flour; beat well. Cover tightly; chill about 1 hour or until firm enough to handle. Shape dough into 48 one-inch balls. Place in ungreased muffin cups (1¾ inches in diameter); press dough evenly against bottom and up side of each muffin cup.

Prepare Filling; spoon 1 heaping teaspoonful into each pastry-lined muffin cup. Bake at 350° for 20 to 25 minutes. Cool; remove from pan. Garnish with dollops of Topping.

4 dozen cookies.

Filling

2 eggs
1 cup sugar
3 tablespoons cornstarch
½ cup butter or margarine, melted
¼ cup bourbon or apple juice
¾ cup semi-sweet chocolate Mini Chips
½ cup finely chopped pecans

Slightly beat eggs in small mixer bowl; gradually add sugar and cornstarch. Add melted butter or margarine and bourbon or apple juice; blend well. Stir in Mini Chips and pecans.

Topping

Combine ⅔ cup heavy or whipping cream, ¼ cup confectioners' sugar and 1 to 2 teaspoons bourbon in small mixer bowl; beat until stiff peaks form.

Chocolate Kiss Tarts

1 package (3 ounces) cream cheese, softened
½ cup butter or margarine, softened

1 cup unsifted all-purpose flour
Filling (below)
24 Hershey's Kisses, unwrapped

Cut 24 three-inch circles of heavy-duty aluminum foil. Combine cream cheese and butter or margarine in small mixer bowl; blend in flour. Shape dough into 24 one-inch balls; press dough down on foil circles, covering each. With thumb and forefinger, turn up edges of dough at five points, forming a star. Place on cookie sheet.

Prepare Filling; spoon 1 teaspoonful into each star. Bake at 350° for 20 to 25 minutes or until lightly browned. Remove from oven; immediately top each tart with an unwrapped Kiss. Cool completely; carefully remove foil.

2 dozen cookies.

Filling

1 egg
¼ cup dark corn syrup
2 tablespoons sugar
1 tablespoon butter or margarine, melted

¼ teaspoon vanilla
¼ cup finely chopped pecans

Beat egg until foamy; add corn syrup, sugar, melted butter or margarine and vanilla. Blend well. Stir in pecans.

Candies

Rich Cocoa Fudge

3 cups sugar	1½ cups milk
⅔ cup unsweetened cocoa	¼ cup butter or margarine
⅛ teaspoon salt	1 teaspoon vanilla

Butter 8- or 9-inch square pan; set aside. Combine sugar, cocoa and salt in heavy 4-quart saucepan; stir in milk. Cook over medium heat, stirring constantly, until mixture comes to full rolling boil. Boil, without stirring, to 234°F (soft-ball stage) or until syrup, when dropped into very cold water, forms a soft ball that flattens when removed from water. (Bulb of candy thermometer should not rest on bottom of saucepan.)

Remove from heat. Add butter or margarine and vanilla; *do not stir*. Cool at room temperature to 110°F (lukewarm). Beat until fudge thickens and loses some of its gloss. Quickly spread in prepared pan; cool. Cut into 1- to 1½-inch squares.

About 3 dozen candies.

Variations

Marshmallow-Nut Cocoa Fudge: Increase cocoa to ¾ cup. Cook fudge as directed. Add 1 cup marshmallow creme with butter or margarine and vanilla; *do not stir*. Cool to 110°F (lukewarm). Beat 10 minutes; stir in 1 cup broken nuts and pour into prepared pan. (Fudge does not set until poured into pan.)

Nutty Rich Cocoa Fudge: Beat cooked fudge as directed. *Immediately* stir in 1 cup broken almonds, pecans or walnuts and quickly spread in prepared pan.

Chocolate-Almond Fudge

4 cups sugar
1¾ cups (7-ounce jar) marshmallow creme
1⅔ cups (13-ounce can) evaporated milk
1 tablespoon butter or margarine
2 cups (12-ounce package) semi-sweet chocolate Mini Chips
1 milk chocolate bar with almonds (8 ounces), chopped
1 teaspoon vanilla
¾ cup chopped slivered almonds

Butter 9-inch square pan; set aside. Combine sugar, marshmallow creme, evaporated milk and butter or margarine in heavy 4-quart saucepan. Cook over medium heat, stirring constantly, until mixture comes to full rolling boil; boil and stir 7 minutes. Remove from heat; *immediately* add Mini Chips and chocolate bar pieces, stirring until completely melted. Blend in vanilla; stir in almonds. Pour into prepared pan; cool completely. Cut into 1-inch squares.

About 6½ dozen candies.

Double-Decker Fudge

1 cup peanut butter chips
1 cup semi-sweet chocolate chips
2¼ cups sugar
1¾ cups (7-ounce jar) marshmallow creme
¾ cup evaporated milk
¼ cup butter or margarine
1 teaspoon vanilla

Measure peanut butter chips into one mixing bowl and chocolate chips into another; set aside. Butter 8-inch square pan; set aside. Combine sugar, marshmallow creme, evaporated milk and butter or margarine in heavy 3-quart saucepan. Cook over medium heat, stirring constantly, until mixture boils; continue cooking and stirring for 5 minutes.

Remove from heat; stir in vanilla. Immediately stir half the hot mixture into peanut butter chips until completely melted. Quickly pour into prepared pan. Stir remaining hot mixture into chocolate chips until completely melted. Quickly spread over top of peanut butter layer; cool. Cut into 1-inch squares.

About 5 dozen candies.

On facing page—Chocolate-Almond Fudge (this page); Nutty Rich Cocoa Fudge (page 201); Double-Decker Fudge (this page)

Chocolate Seafoam

Lighter-than-air confections. Like Cocoa Divinity (facing page), best made on a cool, dry day.

1 block (1 ounce) unsweetened baking chocolate
2 cups packed light brown sugar
¾ cup cold water
½ cup (5.5-ounce can) chocolate-flavored syrup
2 egg whites, at room temperature
1 teaspoon vanilla
½ cup coarsely broken nuts

Melt baking chocolate in top of double boiler over hot, not boiling, water. Set aside over warm water. Combine brown sugar, water and chocolate syrup in heavy 3-quart saucepan. Cook over medium heat, stirring constantly, until sugar dissolves and mixture boils. Continue cooking, without stirring, to 250°F (hard-ball stage) or until syrup mixture, when dropped into very cold water, forms a firm ball that is hard enough to hold its shape, yet plastic. Remove from heat.

Immediately beat egg whites in large mixer bowl until stiff peaks form. Pour hot syrup in a thin stream over beaten egg whites, beating constantly on high speed. Continue beating until mixture forms peaks when dropped from a spoon, about 10 minutes. Quickly stir in vanilla and melted chocolate by hand. Fold in nuts. Drop by teaspoonfuls onto wax-paper-covered cookie sheet; cool. Store in airtight container.

3 to 4 dozen candies.

Chocolate Molasses Caramels

2 cups packed light brown sugar
1 cup light cream
¾ cup dark corn syrup
¼ cup butter or margarine
¼ teaspoon salt
3 blocks (3 ounces) unsweetened baking chocolate, broken into pieces
1 teaspoon vanilla

Generously butter 9-inch square pan; set aside. Combine brown sugar, light cream, corn syrup, butter or margarine and salt in heavy 3-quart saucepan. Cook over medium heat, stirring constantly, until mixture boils. Add baking chocolate pieces; cook, stirring occasionally, to 248°F (firm-ball stage) or until syrup, when dropped into very cold water, forms a firm ball that does not flatten when removed from water. Remove from heat; add vanilla.

Pour into prepared pan; cool. Cut into 1-inch squares with buttered scissors. Wrap individually in plastic wrap or wax paper.

About 7 dozen candies.

Fudge Caramels

2 cups sugar
²⁄₃ cup unsweetened cocoa
⅛ teaspoon salt
1 cup light corn syrup

1 cup evaporated milk
½ cup water
¼ cup butter
1 teaspoon vanilla

Butter 9-inch square pan; set aside. Combine sugar, cocoa, salt and corn syrup in heavy 3-quart saucepan; add evaporated milk and water. Cook over medium heat, stirring constantly, until mixture boils. Cook, stirring frequently, to 245°F (firm-ball stage) or until syrup, when dropped into very cold water, forms a firm ball that does not flatten when removed from water. Remove from heat; stir in butter and vanilla, blending well.

Pour into prepared pan. Cool; cut into 1-inch squares with buttered scissors. Wrap individually in plastic wrap or wax paper.

About 6 dozen candies.

Cocoa Divinity

3 tablespoons shortening
½ cup unsweetened cocoa
2½ cups sugar
¼ teaspoon salt
½ cup light corn syrup
⅓ cup water

2 egg whites, at room
   temperature
1 teaspoon vanilla
¾ cup chopped walnuts
   (optional)

Melt shortening in top of double boiler over hot, not boiling, water; add cocoa and stir until smooth. Set aside over warm water. Combine sugar, salt, corn syrup and water in 2-quart saucepan. Cook over medium heat, stirring constantly, until sugar dissolves and mixture boils. Boil, without stirring, to 246°F; immediately beat egg whites in large mixer bowl until stiff peaks form. Continue cooking syrup mixture, without stirring, to 260°F (hard-ball stage) or until syrup, when dropped into very cold water, forms a firm ball that is hard enough to hold its shape, yet plastic. Remove from heat.

Immediately pour hot syrup in a thin stream over beaten egg whites, beating constantly on high speed. Add vanilla; beat until candy starts to become firm. Quickly blend in reserved cocoa mixture by hand; stir in walnuts. Drop by teaspoonfuls onto wax-paper-covered cookie sheet; cool. Store in airtight container.

About 3½ dozen candies.

Butter Almond Crunch

1½ cups semi-sweet chocolate
     Mini Chips
1¾ cups chopped almonds
1½ cups butter or margarine

1¾ cups sugar
3 tablespoons light corn syrup
3 tablespoons water

Spread 1 cup of the Mini Chips in buttered 13 x 9-inch pan; set aside. Spread almonds in shallow pan; toast at 350° for about 7 minutes or until golden brown. Set aside.

Melt butter or margarine in heavy 3-quart saucepan; blend in sugar, corn syrup and water. Cook over medium heat, stirring constantly, to 300°F (hard-crack stage) or until syrup, when dropped into very cold water, separates into threads that are hard and brittle. Remove from heat; stir in 1½ cups of the toasted almonds.

Immediately spread mixture evenly over Mini Chips in prepared pan, being careful not to disturb chips. Sprinkle with remaining ¼ cup toasted almonds and ½ cup Mini Chips; score into 1½-inch squares. Cool completely; remove from pan. Break into pieces. Store in tightly covered container.

About 2 pounds candy.

Creamy Cocoa Taffy

1¼ cups sugar
¾ cup light corn syrup
⅓ cup unsweetened cocoa
⅛ teaspoon salt

2 teaspoons white vinegar
¼ cup evaporated milk
1 tablespoon butter

Butter 9-inch square pan; set aside. Combine sugar, corn syrup, cocoa, salt and vinegar in heavy 2-quart saucepan. Cook over medium heat, stirring constantly, until mixture boils; add evaporated milk and butter. Continue to cook, stirring occasionally, to 248°F (firm-ball stage) or until syrup, when dropped into very cold water, forms a firm ball that does not flatten when removed from water.

Pour mixture into prepared pan. Cool taffy until comfortable to handle. Butter hands; stretch taffy, folding and pulling until light in color and hard to pull. Place taffy on table; pull into ½-inch-wide strips (twist two strips together, if desired). Cut into 1-inch pieces with buttered scissors. Wrap individually in plastic wrap or wax paper.

About 1¼ pounds candy.

On facing page—top, Chocolate Chip Nougat Log (page 209); bottom, Butter Almond Crunch (this page); in center, assortment includes Cocoa Divinity (page 205) and Creamy Cocoa Taffy (this page)

Easy Chewy Taffy

For taffy lovers who don't have time for the stretch-and-pull. Use the old-fashioned recipe on page 206 for a children's party.

1 bag (14 ounces) light caramels, unwrapped
¾ cup marshmallow creme
½ cup (5.5-ounce can) chocolate-flavored syrup

2 tablespoons butter or margarine

Butter 8-inch square pan; set aside. Combine all ingredients in medium saucepan. Cook over medium heat, stirring constantly, to 234°F (soft-ball stage) or until syrup, when dropped into very cold water, forms a soft ball that flattens when removed from water.

Pour into prepared pan. Cool to room temperature. Cover; chill 1 hour or until firm. Cut into 1-inch squares; wrap individually in plastic wrap or wax paper. Store in cool, dry place.

About 1¼ pounds candy.

English Walnut Toffee

1⅓ cups butter or margarine
1 cup sugar
⅔ cup water
Dash salt
⅔ cup chopped walnuts

½ teaspoon baking soda
1 cup (5.75-ounce package) milk chocolate chips
⅔ cup chopped walnuts

Butter metal cookie sheet; set aside. Combine butter or margarine, sugar, water and salt in heavy 2-quart saucepan. Cook over medium heat, stirring constantly, until mixture boils. Continue cooking, without stirring, to 236°F (soft-ball stage) or until syrup, when dropped into very cold water, forms a soft ball that flattens when removed from water. Stir in ⅔ cup chopped walnuts.

Continue cooking, stirring constantly, until mixture reaches 290°F (soft-crack stage) or until syrup, when dropped into very cold water, separates into threads that are hard but not brittle. Remove from heat; stir in baking soda.

Turn onto prepared cookie sheet; spread to ¼-inch thickness with a greased knife or spatula. Sprinkle milk chocolate chips over top of toffee; allow to soften a few minutes. Spread evenly over surface of candy. Quickly sprinkle with ⅔ cup chopped walnuts. Cool several hours or overnight. Break into pieces. Store well covered.

About 30 candies.

Chocolate Chip Nougat Log

1 cup sugar
⅔ cup light corn syrup
2 tablespoons water
¼ cup egg whites (about 2),
    at room temperature
2 cups sugar
1¼ cups light corn syrup
¼ cup butter or margarine,
    melted

2 teaspoons vanilla
2 cups chopped walnuts
4 or 5 drops red food color
    (optional)
1 cup semi-sweet chocolate
    Mini Chips

Line a 15½ x 10½ x 1-inch jelly roll pan with aluminum foil; butter foil. Set aside. Combine 1 cup sugar, ⅔ cup corn syrup and the water in small heavy saucepan. Cook over medium heat, stirring constantly, until sugar dissolves. Continue cooking without stirring. When syrup reaches 230°F, start beating egg whites in large mixer bowl; beat until stiff, but not dry.

When syrup reaches 238°F (soft-ball stage), or when dropped into very cold water forms a soft ball that flattens when removed from water, remove from heat. Pour hot syrup in a thin stream over beaten egg whites, beating constantly on high speed. Continue beating 4 to 5 minutes or until mixture becomes very thick. Cover and set aside.

Combine 2 cups sugar and 1¼ cups corn syrup in heavy 2-quart saucepan. Cook over medium heat, stirring constantly, until sugar dissolves. Cook, without stirring, to 275°F (soft-crack stage) or until syrup, when dropped into very cold water, separates into threads that are hard but not brittle.

Pour hot syrup all at once over reserved egg white mixture in bowl; blend with a wooden spoon. Stir in melted butter or margarine and vanilla; add walnuts and mix thoroughly. Add red food color. Pour into prepared pan. Sprinkle evenly with Mini Chips. Let cool overnight.

To form into logs, invert pan and remove foil. Cut in half crosswise; roll from cut end, jelly-roll style. Cut into ¼-inch slices. Store, well covered, in cool, dry place.

About 7 dozen candies.

Note: If desired, nougat can be cut into 1-inch squares rather than rolled.

Homemade Chocolate-Coated Candies

Did you ever look at a display of elegant, glossy—and expensive— chocolate-coated candies and wish that you could make them yourself? While that might seem a fantasy best left to the professionals, you need no longer be intimidated. The process is not difficult, but it does take time and patience. And remember, practice makes perfect—coating with chocolate becomes easier each time you do it. Before starting, review pages 211–18. This section contains the important basic information about coating candies as well as recipes for chocolate coatings and several kinds of centers.

Making the centers. Select the recipes for the centers you wish to coat and prepare them at least a day ahead. For variety, try different shapes—balls, cubes, rectangles, triangles, even hearts.

Choosing the right day. Make the coating only on a dry, clear day. Don't even *think* about dipping candies on a humid day! Humidity, steam or wet equipment cause chocolate to thicken, tighten and become grainy. Even a few drops of water can cause problems!

Selecting the coating recipe. We've included recipes for three chocolate coatings; each differs somewhat in preparation. Tempered Chocolate Coating is heated, then cooled to achieve its glossy finish. Easy Semi-Sweet Chocolate Coating relies on the addition of chopped chocolate at the right moment to create the crystals necessary for gloss. "Simply Stirred" Chocolate Coating is easy, but depends on long, patient stirring.

Ingredients. Each coating recipe indicates the kind of chocolate you may use. In addition, you need solid vegetable shortening. *Never* substitute butter, margarine or oil! These contain moisture, which will cause the chocolate to tighten and become grainy.

Assembling the equipment. Before you begin the coating process, assemble the equipment you need:

- Tape and wax paper

- A special candy or laboratory thermometer that registers as low as 80°F (most ordinary candy thermometers do not register below 100°F)

- A rubber scraper

- A glass bowl or glass measuring cup to hold the chocolate and shortening (see recipe for sizes)

- A larger glass bowl or a pan to hold the warm water

- A fondue fork or table fork to dip the center into the coating

What's "bloom"? Two coating recipes refer to "bloom," the term for white or gray spots or streaks that appear when sugar or fat particles separate from chocolate. Bloom does not affect the quality or flavor of chocolate.

In advance, prepare an assortment of centers. Refrigerate until shortly before coating with chocolate.

Assemble all ingredients and utensils before starting procedure. Tape down wax paper on cookie sheet.

Bowl containing chocolate must be completely dry. Don't let even one drop of water into mixture!

Be sure to use a special candy or laboratory thermometer that will register as low as 80°F.

Chocolate-shortening mixture must be stirred and scraped down *constantly* with rubber scraper.

Chocolate mixture should be completely fluid and very smooth before starting to coat centers.

When coating is ready, rest a center on fork; carefully and completely dip into chocolate mixture.

After tapping fork on side of bowl to remove excess coating, invert center onto prepared cookie sheet.

Using tip of fork, immediately decorate top of coated candy with small amount of melted chocolate.

Tempering Chocolate for Dipped Candies

Have you ever wondered why commercially made chocolate-coated candy stays so glossy and firm at room temperature? It's because of a process called *tempering*. Tempering is achieved by heating and cooling chocolate to specific temperatures, causing the formation of cocoa butter crystals. This keeps the chocolate coating firm and glossy without the addition of wax, and refrigeration is unnecessary for storage.

Carefully read the recipe before beginning. Note that the centers you'll coat should be at room temperature, so allow 10 minutes for them to warm up if they've been stored in the refrigerator. Set aside about 2 to 3 hours for the complete tempering procedure. The most important thing to remember is that the process—*temperature changes*—must happen evenly and slowly, with constant stirring. It cannot be rushed.

And don't try to temper chocolate and coat candy on a hot or humid day!

Chocolate Choices for Tempered Coating

Select the type of chocolate for Tempered Chocolate Coating (opposite page) from this chart:

	Amount of Chocolate	Amount of Vegetable Shortening*
Semi-sweet chocolate chips or Mini Chips	12 ounces (2 cups)	2 tablespoons + 2 teaspoons
Milk chocolate chips	11.5 ounces	2 tablespoons
Hershey's Kisses	9 ounces (about 54 Kisses)	2 tablespoons + 1 teaspoon
Milk chocolate bar	8 ounces	2 tablespoons
Special Dark chocolate bar	8 ounces	2 tablespoons + 2 teaspoons
Semi-sweet baking chocolate	8 ounces	2 tablespoons + 2 teaspoons
Unsweetened baking chocolate**	8 ounces	No shortening

*Do not use butter, margarine or oil.
**Best as coating for extra-sweet centers.

Note: For a milder semi-sweet coating, melt 1 Special Dark chocolate bar (8 ounces), 1 milk chocolate bar (8 ounces) and ⅓ cup shortening. Temper chocolate as directed in recipe, but hold chocolate at 88°F while dipping centers.

1. Tempered Chocolate Coating

Carefully review pages 210–12. Remove centers (pages 216–18) from refrigerator about 10 minutes before coating; dipping cold centers may result in cracked coating and/or bloom on the coating. Cover cookie sheet or tray with wax paper; fasten with tape. Set aside.

Step 1: Select type of chocolate from chart (opposite). Place chocolate and shortening in 1½-quart bowl or 4-cup glass measuring cup. Place bowl in larger glass bowl or pan of very warm—not hot—water (120°F) that reaches *halfway* up bowl containing chocolate. *Don't let even one drop of water mix with chocolate!*

Step 2: Stir mixture *constantly* with rubber scraper until chocolate is heated to 108°F and is fluid. Scrape bowl frequently so that chocolate is completely melted and mixture is smooth.

Step 3: When mixture reaches 108°F, remove bowl from water. Stir frequently until mixture cools to 85°F. Continue stirring and scraping constantly until mixture cools to 80°F. Stirring constantly, keep mixture at 80°F for 10 minutes. *This is important because it develops the crystals necessary for gloss.* It may be necessary to set bowl briefly in warm water to maintain temperature.

Step 4: Place bowl in warm water; rewarm mixture to 86°F. Hold coating at that temperature for 5 minutes before dipping centers. *Important: Keep coating at 86°F during entire dipping process.* If temperature drops below 84°F during dipping, the entire tempering process must be repeated from Step 2.

Step 5: Set one center on tines of fondue fork or table fork. Completely dip center into coating. Gently tap fork on side of bowl to remove excess coating. Invert candy onto prepared cookie sheet. Decorate top of coated center with small amount of melted chocolate, using tip of fork. Repeat with remaining centers.

Step 6: Chill candies a maximum of 15 minutes in refrigerator to help harden coating. Remove promptly or bloom may occur. Store candies, well covered, at room temperature (60°–75°F).

Enough coating for about 5 dozen centers.

Note: Chocolate mixture should be fluid at 108°F. If mixture becomes tight or grainy because of humidity, stir in small amount of solid vegetable shortening, 1 teaspoonful at a time, until chocolate is smooth and fluid again. At this point, continue to retemper chocolate, starting with Step 2. *Important: This is an emergency measure only.* Don't try to extend chocolate coatings with extra fat—they will be ruined.

2. Easy Semi-Sweet Chocolate Coating

The Mini Chips that are set aside, then stirred into the melted chocolate have an important task: They "seed" the coating to develop the crystals necessary for a beautiful gloss on the finished candies.

1½ cups semi-sweet chocolate   2 tablespoons shortening*
     Mini Chips

Before starting, review basic information on pages 210–11. Remove centers (pages 216–18) from refrigerator about 10 minutes before coating; dipping cold centers may result in cracked coating and/or bloom on the coating.

Cover cookie sheet or tray with wax paper; fasten with tape. Chop ½ teaspoon Mini Chips into tiny pieces; set aside. Place remaining Mini Chips and the shortening in 2-cup glass measuring cup or 1½-cup wide-mouth jar. Place measuring cup or jar in larger glass bowl or pan of very warm—not hot—water (100°–110°F) that reaches *halfway* up cup or jar. *Don't let even one drop of water mix with chocolate!*

Stir mixture *constantly* with rubber scraper until chocolate is completely melted and mixture is smooth. This process is not difficult, but it does take time. *Don't rush!* If necessary, keep pan over low heat, but do not allow water temperature to exceed 125°F.

Remove cup from water; continue stirring until chocolate is cooled to 88°F. (Cup should feel slightly warm to touch.) Stir reserved chopped Mini Chips into melted chocolate until completely blended.

Keep chocolate mixture between 84°–86°F while dipping (it may be necessary to place cup briefly in warm water). Set one center on tines of fondue fork or table fork. Completely dip center into coating. Gently tap fork on side of cup to remove excess coating. Invert candy onto prepared cookie sheet. Decorate top of coated center with small amount of melted chocolate, using tip of fork. Repeat with remaining centers.

Chill candies a maximum of 15 minutes in refrigerator to help harden coating. Remove promptly or bloom may occur. Store candies, well covered, at room temperature (60°–75°F).

Enough coating for about 4 dozen centers.

*Do not use butter, margarine or oil.

3. "Simply Stirred" Chocolate Coating

The easiest chocolate coating. It must be melted very, very slowly and stirred constantly.

2 milk chocolate bars (8 ounces each), broken into pieces	¼ cup shortening*

OR

2 cups (12-ounce package) semi-sweet chocolate chips	2 tablespoons plus 2 teaspoons shortening*

OR

2 cups (11.5-ounce package) milk chocolate chips	2 tablespoons shortening*

Before starting, review basic information on pages 210–11. Be sure that centers (pages 216–18) are chilled.

Cover cookie sheet or tray with wax paper; fasten with tape. Set aside. Place chocolate and shortening in 4-cup glass measuring cup or 1½-quart glass bowl. Place measuring cup or bowl in larger glass bowl or pan of very warm—not hot—water (100°–110°F) that reaches *halfway* up cup or bowl. *Don't let even one drop of water mix with chocolate!*

Stir mixture *constantly* with rubber scraper until chocolate is completely melted and mixture is smooth. This process is not difficult, but it does take time. *Don't rush!* It will take about 20 minutes to melt the chocolate. If water begins to cool, pour out and add more warm water.

Remove measuring cup or bowl from water. Set one chilled center on tines of fondue fork or table fork. Completely dip center into coating. Gently tap fork on side of cup to remove excess coating. Invert candy onto prepared cookie sheet. Decorate top of coated center with small amount of melted chocolate, using tip of fork. Repeat with remaining centers. Store candies, loosely covered, in a cool, dry place.

Enough coating for about 5 dozen centers.

*Do not use butter, margarine or oil.

Note: If chocolate becomes too thick while coating, return cup or bowl containing chocolate to larger glass bowl or pan with 1 inch of very warm tap water (100°–110°F). Stir mixture constantly until of desired consistency. Be careful not to get any water into mixture. When coating reaches desired consistency, remove from water; continue dipping centers.

Easy Buttercream Centers

| 1 package (3 ounces) cream cheese, softened | 4 cups unsifted confectioners' sugar |
| ½ cup butter or margarine, softened | 1½ teaspoons vanilla |

Beat cream cheese and butter or margarine in large mixer bowl until smooth. Blend in confectioners' sugar and vanilla. (If necessary, chill about 1 hour or until mixture is firm enough to handle.) Shape into 1-inch balls; place on wax-paper-covered tray or cookie sheet. Cover loosely; chill 3 to 4 hours or overnight. Centers should feel dry to touch before coating. Coat centers as directed (pages 210–15).

About 5 dozen centers.

Variations

Chocolate Buttercream Centers: Blend ⅓ cup unsweetened cocoa with confectioners' sugar and vanilla into mixture. Add 1 to 2 teaspoons milk until mixture holds together.

Flavored Buttercream Centers: Use only with "Simply Stirred" Chocolate Coating (page 215). Divide buttercream mixture into three parts. Add any one of the following to each part:

½ teaspoon almond extract	¼ teaspoon orange extract
½ teaspoon brandy extract	¼ teaspoon rum extract
⅔ cup flaked coconut	½ teaspoon strawberry extract
¼ teaspoon mint extract plus 3 drops green food color	plus 3 drops red food color

Chocolate Centers

⅓ cup butter or margarine, softened	1½ teaspoons vanilla
¼ cup heavy or whipping cream	3 cups confectioners' sugar
	½ cup semi-sweet chocolate chips, melted

Combine butter or margarine, cream, vanilla and 1 cup of the confectioners' sugar in small mixer bowl; beat until smooth. Gradually blend in remaining 2 cups confectioners' sugar and chocolate. Chill about 1 hour or until mixture is firm enough to handle.

Shape into 1-inch balls; place on wax-paper-covered tray or cookie sheet. Cover loosely; chill 3 to 4 hours or overnight. Centers should feel dry to touch before coating. Coat centers as directed (pages 210–15).

About 5 dozen centers.

Fondant Cherry Cordial Centers

From your own kitchen: classic chocolate-covered cherries.

Fondant (below)
2 jars (8 ounces each)
  maraschino cherries
  with stems

2 teaspoons water
2 teaspoons light corn syrup

Prepare Fondant; allow to ripen for minimum of 24 hours. Drain cherries, reserving 4 teaspoons juice. Combine Fondant, water, reserved cherry juice and the corn syrup in top of double boiler over hot water. Cook, stirring constantly, to 165°F. Remove from heat; keep top of double boiler over hot water.

Dip cherries in hot fondant mixture. Cool and dry on wax-paper-covered tray. (If mixture begins to harden, stir and reheat over hot water. Do not allow to exceed 165°F.) Dip a second time. Remove stem, if desired, and dry on wax paper. Chill dipped cherries, uncovered, for about 1 hour, or until coating is dry and hardened. Within several hours, coat as directed (pages 210–15). Store, loosely covered, at room temperature. Centers will begin to liquefy in about 24 hours.

About 3 dozen centers.

Fondant

Combine 2 cups sugar, 2 tablespoons corn syrup and ¾ cup boiling water in medium saucepan. Cook over medium heat, stirring constantly, until mixture boils. Cover; continue boiling for 3 minutes without stirring or removing lid. Remove lid; continue cooking *without stirring* to 240°F (soft-ball stage) or until syrup, when dropped into very cold water, forms a soft ball that flattens when removed from water. Immediately pour fondant into small buttered heatproof bowl. Cool to lukewarm (about 110°F).

Stir with spatula just until white and creamy. Remove from bowl onto flat surface; knead with buttered hands until smooth and well blended. Cool; wrap in plastic wrap. Store, tightly covered, in refrigerator for at least 24 hours before using. (May be stored, covered, for several days in refrigerator.)

Easy Cherry Cordial Centers

¼ cup butter	⅛ teaspoon almond extract
2¼ cups confectioners' sugar	About 48 maraschino
1 tablespoon milk	cherries with stems,
½ teaspoon vanilla	drained

Cover cookie sheet or tray with wax paper; set aside. Thoroughly cream butter with confectioners' sugar and milk in small mixer bowl; blend in vanilla and almond extract. (If mixture is too soft, add extra confectioners' sugar.) Mold just enough mixture around each cherry to completely cover cherry. Place on prepared cookie sheet. Cover loosely; chill 3 to 4 hours or overnight.

Remove a third of the centers from refrigerator 10 minutes before dipping; keep remaining centers chilled. (*Do not* remove centers if using "Simply Stirred" Chocolate Coating.) Coat centers as directed (pages 210–15). Store coated cordials, uncovered, at room temperature for about 1 week or until centers liquefy.

About 4 dozen centers.

Below—an assortment of chocolate-coated centers (pages 212–16), cherry cordials (page 217 and this page) and, in cups, leftover chocolate coating on chopped nuts

Peanutty Cocoa Bonbons

2 packages (3 ounces each) cream cheese, softened
1 tablespoon milk
4 cups confectioners' sugar
⅓ cup unsweetened cocoa
1 teaspoon vanilla
1 cup finely chopped nuts (optional)
2 cups (12-ounce package) peanut butter chips
2 tablespoons shortening*

Beat cream cheese and milk in large mixer bowl until fluffy. Blend in confectioners' sugar, cocoa and vanilla. Stir in chopped nuts. Cover; chill several hours or until firm enough to handle. Shape into ¾-inch balls. Place on wax-paper-lined tray or cookie sheet. Chill, uncovered, 3 to 4 hours. (Centers should feel dry to touch before coating.)

To coat, melt peanut butter chips and shortening in top of double boiler over hot, not boiling, water, stirring constantly to blend. With fork, dip chilled centers into peanut butter mixture; remove. (To remove excess coating, slide fork across rim of pan and tap a few times.) Slide from fork onto wax paper, swirling "thread" of peanut butter mixture from fork across top for decoration. (If coating becomes too thick, reheat over hot water.) Chill bonbons, uncovered, 1 hour. Store in cool, dry place.

About 10 dozen candies.

*Do not use butter, margarine or oil.

Chocolate Rum Balls

1 package (12 ounces) vanilla wafer cookies, crushed
¾ cup confectioners' sugar
1½ cups chopped nuts
¼ cup unsweetened cocoa
3 tablespoons light corn syrup
½ cup rum
Confectioners' sugar

Combine crushed vanilla wafers, ¾ cup confectioners' sugar, the nuts and cocoa in large mixing bowl. Blend in corn syrup and rum. Shape into 1-inch balls; roll in confectioners' sugar. Store in airtight container 3 to 4 days to develop flavor. Roll again in confectioners' sugar before serving.

About 4 dozen candies.

Variation
Chocolate Orange Balls: Substitute ½ cup orange juice plus 1 teaspoon grated orange peel for the rum.

Chocolate Truffles

Very easy no-cook version of a favorite creamy confection.

½ cup sweet butter, softened
2½ cups confectioners' sugar
½ cup unsweetened cocoa

1½ teaspoons vanilla
¼ cup heavy or whipping cream
Confectioners' sugar

Cream butter in large mixer bowl. Combine 2½ cups confectioners' sugar and the cocoa; add alternately with vanilla and cream to butter. Blend well. Chill until firm. Shape into 1-inch balls. Roll in confectioners' sugar until well covered. Chill until firm.

About 3 dozen candies.

Variation
Chocolate Rum Truffles: Decrease vanilla to 1 teaspoon and add ½ teaspoon rum extract.

Chocolate Surprises

¼ cup butter or margarine, softened
3 tablespoons light corn syrup
1 teaspoon vanilla

2 cups confectioners' sugar
½ cup unsweetened cocoa
Nuts, candied cherry halves and/or pieces of dried fruits

Cream butter or margarine, corn syrup and vanilla in large mixer bowl until smooth. Gradually beat in part of the confectioners' sugar and cocoa; with hands, mix in remainder to form a firm mixture. Shape a rounded teaspoonful around nut or piece of fruit, covering completely. Roll in additional confectioners' sugar. Store in airtight container. Roll again in confectioners' sugar before serving.

About 3 dozen candies.

Chocolate Chip Bonbons

1 package (3 ounces) cream cheese, softened
2¼ cups confectioners' sugar
1 tablespoon butter or margarine, melted

1 teaspoon vanilla
½ cup semi-sweet chocolate Mini Chips
Finely chopped nuts

Blend cream cheese, confectioners' sugar, butter or margarine and vanilla in small mixer bowl; stir in Mini Chips. Shape into ½-inch balls. (If necessary, chill until firm enough to handle.) Roll in finely chopped nuts. Cover; chill. Store, covered, in refrigerator.

2½ dozen candies.

Cocoa Mints

This makes a generous amount of mints; a good recipe at Christmas or other gift-giving occasions.

9 cups confectioners' sugar
1 cup unsweetened cocoa
½ cup sweet butter, softened
½ cup water
2 teaspoons peppermint extract

Combine all ingredients in large mixing bowl. Mix with hands or spoon until well blended. (If necessary, add more water, ¼ teaspoonful at a time, to hold mixture together.)

Shape mixture into a ball; place on sheet of wax paper and roll out to ¼-inch thickness. Cut into desired shapes with small cutters; chill several hours. Store in airtight container in cool, dry place.

About 3 pounds candies.

Luscious Cocoa-Walnut Balls

3½ cups confectioners' sugar
¾ cup unsweetened cocoa
1⅓ cups (14-ounce can) sweetened condensed milk*
1 teaspoon vanilla
2 cups finely chopped walnuts
Confectioners' sugar

Combine 3½ cups confectioners' sugar and the cocoa in large bowl; add sweetened condensed milk and vanilla. Stir in walnuts. Cover tightly; chill about 30 minutes. Shape into 1-inch balls; roll in confectioners' sugar. Cover tightly; chill at least 2 hours or until firm. Store, covered, in refrigerator.

About 5 dozen candies.

*Do not use evaporated milk.

Chocolate-Pecan Cups

1 cup (6-ounce package) semi-sweet chocolate chips
1 cup peanut butter chips
2 tablespoons vegetable oil
1 cup coarsely chopped pecans

Combine chocolate chips, peanut butter chips and oil in top of double boiler over hot, not boiling, water; stir until chips are melted and mixture is smooth. Remove from heat; stir in chopped pecans. Cool slightly; drop by teaspoonfuls into paper nut cups. Chill until firm. Store in covered container in refrigerator.

About 2 dozen candies.

Chocolate Peanut Clusters

1 cup semi-sweet chocolate chips
1 teaspoon shortening
1 cup unsalted peanuts

Melt chocolate chips with shortening in top of double boiler over hot, not boiling, water. Remove from heat; stir in peanuts. Spoon heaping teaspoonfuls into 1-inch paper candy cups or into paper-lined miniature muffin cups, filling each half full. Cover; chill until firm. (Peel off paper cups, if desired.) Store, covered, in cool, dry place.

About 15 candies.

Rocky Road

2 milk chocolate bars (8 ounces each), broken into pieces
3 cups miniature marshmallows
¾ cup coarsely broken nuts

Line 8-inch square pan with aluminum foil; butter foil. Melt chocolate bar pieces in top of double boiler over hot, not boiling, water; remove from heat. Stir in marshmallows and nuts just until coated. Spread in prepared pan; chill until firm. Cut into pieces.

About 4 dozen candies.

Snacks & Sweet Treats

Cocoa Crunch Energy Squares

½ cup peanut butter
¼ cup unsweetened cocoa
½ cup sugar
½ cup light corn syrup or honey
2 cups bite-size crispy rice
   squares cereal

1 cup granola or natural cereal,
   crumbled
¼ cup unsalted peanuts, raisins
   or chopped pitted dates

Combine peanut butter and cocoa in small bowl; blend well. Set aside. Combine sugar and corn syrup or honey in medium saucepan. Cook over medium heat, stirring constantly, until mixture boils; boil and stir 1 minute. Remove from heat; add peanut butter mixture, stirring until well blended. Stir in cereal, granola or natural cereal and peanuts, raisins or dates. Toss to coat evenly. Spread in buttered 8-inch square pan. Cool. Cut into squares.

About 16 squares.

Cocoa Party Mix

3 cups toasted oat or corn
   cereal rings
3 cups bite-size crispy wheat
   squares cereal
2 cups salted peanuts
2 cups thin pretzel sticks

1 cup raisins
½ cup butter or margarine,
   melted
¼ cup unsweetened cocoa
¼ cup sugar

Combine cereals, peanuts, pretzels and raisins in large mixing bowl. Blend melted butter or margarine, cocoa and sugar in small mixing bowl; stir into cereal mixture. Toss until ingredients are well coated. Pour into 13 x 9-inch pan. Bake at 250° for 1 hour, stirring every 15 minutes. Cool. Store in airtight container.

About 10 cups snack.

Chocolate-Granola Breakfast Bars

Nutritious grab-and-go snacks.

¼ cup butter or margarine, softened
¼ cup shortening
1 cup packed light brown sugar
1 egg
1 teaspoon vanilla
1⅓ cups unsifted all-purpose flour
½ teaspoon baking soda
½ teaspoon salt
½ teaspoon cinnamon
¼ cup milk
1⅔ cups granola or natural cereal, crumbled
1 cup raisins
1 cup flaked coconut
2 cups (12-ounce package) semi-sweet chocolate chips

Cream butter or margarine, shortening, brown sugar, egg and vanilla in large mixer bowl until light and fluffy. Combine flour, baking soda, salt and cinnamon; add alternately with milk to creamed mixture. Stir in granola or cereal, raisins, coconut and chocolate chips.

Spread evenly in aluminum-foil-lined 15½ x 10½ x 1-inch jelly roll pan. Bake at 350° for 20 to 25 minutes or until cake tester comes out clean. Cool completely. Invert pan; peel off foil. Cut into 2 x 1-inch bars.

About 5 dozen bars.

Chocolate Snackin' Corn

½ cup unpopped popcorn
3 tablespoons vegetable oil (if needed)
1½ cups salted peanuts
½ cup packed light brown sugar
½ cup light corn syrup
⅓ cup unsweetened cocoa
¼ cup butter or margarine

Butter a 13 x 9-inch pan; set aside. Pop popcorn in electric popcorn popper or in microwave as directed. (Or heat popcorn and oil in large covered heavy pan over medium-high heat; when corn starts to pop, shake pan constantly until popping stops.) Immediately pour popcorn into prepared pan; add peanuts and stir thoroughly, removing any unpopped corn.

Combine brown sugar, corn syrup, cocoa and butter or margarine in medium saucepan. Cook over medium heat, stirring constantly, until mixture comes to a full boil; boil and stir 1 minute. Drizzle mixture immediately over popcorn and peanuts; quickly stir mixture to blend well. Cool, uncovered, several hours or overnight. Break into pieces; store tightly covered.

About 3 quarts snack.

Chocolate-Peanut Butter Apples

10 to 12 wooden skewers
10 to 12 medium apples, stems
   removed
2 cups (12-ounce package)
   peanut butter chips

⅔ cup unsweetened cocoa
⅔ cup confectioners' sugar
½ cup vegetable oil*

Insert wooden skewer into each washed and thoroughly dried apple. Combine peanut butter chips, cocoa, confectioners' sugar and oil in top of double boiler over hot, not boiling, water; stir constantly until chips are melted and mixture is smooth. Remove from heat.

Dip apples into mixture; twirl to remove excess coating. (If coating becomes too thick, return to low heat or add additional oil, 1 teaspoon at a time.) Allow to cool on wax-paper-covered cookie sheet. Cover; chill, if desired.

10 to 12 apples.

*Do not use butter or margarine.

Chocolatey Trail Mix

Also good off the trail and at a party—or just for snacks anytime.

1 cup semi-sweet chocolate Mini Chips
½ cup salted sunflower kernels
½ cup dry roasted peanuts
½ cup raisins
½ cup chopped dried fruit

Toss ingredients together in small bowl. Store in airtight container.

About 3 cups snack.

Chocolate-Peanut Butter Crispies

1 cup (6-ounce package) semi-sweet chocolate chips
1 cup peanut butter chips
2 tablespoons vegetable oil
1⅓ cups crisp rice cereal
½ cup chopped nuts

Combine chocolate chips, peanut butter chips and oil in top of double boiler over hot, not boiling, water. Stir until chips are completely melted and well blended. Remove from heat; stir in cereal and nuts. Cool slightly; drop by teaspoonfuls into paper nut cups. Chill until firm. Store in covered container in refrigerator.

About 4 dozen snacks.

Chocolate-Marshmallow Turtles

2 cups (12-ounce package) semi-sweet chocolate chips
2 tablespoons shortening
12 large marshmallows
1½ cups pecan halves

Melt chocolate chips and shortening in top of double boiler over hot, not boiling, water; remove from heat. Cool mixture to 85°F.

Meanwhile, cut marshmallows in half horizontally; place on wax paper and flatten slightly. Set aside. On wax-paper-covered tray, form head and hind feet of turtle by arranging 3 pecan halves with ends touching in center; for front feet, place 1 pecan quarter on each side of head. Arrange 24 of these clusters as bases for turtles.

Spoon ½ teaspoon melted mixture into center of each cluster of pecans. To make turtle shell, use a fork to dip each marshmallow half in melted chocolate mixture; place each dipped marshmallow over set of pecan clusters, pressing down slightly. Top with pecan half. Cool completely. Store, covered, in refrigerator.

2 dozen snacks.

Chocolate-Orange Nut Balls

2 cups (11.5-ounce package) milk chocolate chips	3¼ cups vanilla wafer cookie crumbs (12-ounce package wafers)
½ cup orange juice	1 cup finely chopped nuts
3 tablespoons light corn syrup	½ cup confectioners' sugar
½ teaspoon grated orange peel	

Melt milk chocolate chips in top of double boiler over hot, not boiling, water. Remove from heat; add orange juice, corn syrup and orange peel. Combine cookie crumbs, nuts and confectioners' sugar. Blend into chocolate mixture, mixing well. Let stand 30 minutes. Shape into 1-inch balls; roll in additional confectioners' sugar. Store, covered, in refrigerator.

About 4 dozen snacks.

Peanut Butter Drops

1 cup (6-ounce package) semi-sweet chocolate chips	½ cup miniature marshmallows
⅔ cup sweetened condensed milk*	½ cup coarsely chopped peanuts
	¼ cup peanut butter
	1 teaspoon vanilla

Melt chocolate chips in top of double boiler over hot, not boiling, water. Stir in sweetened condensed milk and marshmallows. Cook, stirring constantly, until marshmallows are melted. Remove from heat; stir in chopped peanuts, peanut butter and vanilla. Spoon mixture into small fluted paper candy cups.

About 2½ dozen snacks.

*Do not use evaporated milk.

Coconut-Chocolate Balls

1½ cups vanilla wafer cookie crumbs (about 45 wafers)	⅔ cup confectioners' sugar
⅔ cup flaked coconut	½ cup (5.5-ounce can) chocolate-flavored syrup
	1 teaspoon vanilla

Combine cookie crumbs, coconut and confectioners' sugar in medium bowl. Add syrup and vanilla; mix well. Shape into 1-inch balls; roll in additional confectioners' sugar. Store in airtight container lined with wax paper; roll in additional confectioners' sugar before serving.

About 18 snacks.

Chocolate-Covered Banana Pops

3 large bananas
9 wooden popsicle sticks
2 cups (12-ounce package)
  semi-sweet chocolate chips
2 tablespoons shortening*
1½ cups coarsely chopped
  unsalted peanuts

Peel bananas; cut each into thirds. Insert wooden popsicle stick into each banana piece; place on wax-paper-covered tray. Cover; freeze until firm.

Melt chocolate chips and shortening in top of double boiler over hot, not boiling, water. Remove bananas from freezer just before dipping. Dip each piece into warm chocolate, covering completely; allow excess to drip off. Immediately roll in chopped peanuts. Cover; return to freezer. Serve frozen.

9 pops.

*Do not use butter, margarine or oil.

Peanut Butter-Chocolate Ripple Pops

1 package (3⅛ ounces) vanilla
  pudding and pie filling
  mix*
2 cups milk
1 cup peanut butter chips
½ cup semi-sweet chocolate
  Mini Chips
1 envelope dry whipped
  topping mix (to yield
  2 cups)
½ cup cold milk
½ teaspoon vanilla
10 paper cups (3-ounce size)
10 wooden popsicle sticks

Cook pudding as directed on package, using 2 cups milk. Measure 1 cup cooked pudding into small mixing bowl; immediately add peanut butter chips. Stir until chips are melted and mixture is smooth. Add Mini Chips to remaining hot pudding in saucepan; stir until chips are melted and mixture is smooth. Press plastic wrap directly onto surface of each mixture; chill slightly.

Prepare whipped topping mix as directed on package, using ½ cup cold milk and the vanilla. Add half the whipped topping to peanut butter mixture and half to chocolate mixture; blend each well. Spoon about 1 tablespoon peanut butter mixture into each paper cup; top with 1 tablespoon chocolate mixture. Repeat layers. Insert a popsicle stick into center; freeze 4 hours or until firm. Peel off paper cups to serve.

10 pops.

*Do not use instant mix.

On facing page, clockwise from top—Peanut Butter-Chocolate Ripple Pops (this page); Chocolatey Trail Mix (page 226); Chocolate-Covered Banana Pops (this page); Chocolate-Granola Breakfast Bars (page 224)

Chocolate Pops

Make them, if you must, "for the kids"—then slip them out of the freezer when the kids aren't looking.

1 cup evaporated milk
1 envelope unflavored gelatine
2 tablespoons cold water
¼ cup butter or margarine
1 cup chocolate-flavored syrup, at room temperature
1 teaspoon vanilla
1 cup heavy or whipping cream*

¼ cup confectioners' sugar
10 to 12 paper cups (5-ounce size)
10 to 12 wooden popsicle sticks
¾ cup crushed pretzels, cookie crumbs or chopped nuts

Pour evaporated milk into small mixer bowl; freeze until ice crystals form around edge, about 30 minutes. Combine gelatine and cold water in small custard cup; heat cup in pan of simmering water until gelatine dissolves. Add butter or margarine; blend well. Combine gelatine-butter mixture, syrup and vanilla in large mixing bowl; set aside.

Beat chilled evaporated milk until soft peaks form; fold into chocolate mixture. Beat cream until foamy; gradually add confectioners' sugar. Continue beating until soft peaks form. Fold into chocolate mixture. Spoon into paper cups; insert a popsicle stick in the center of each. Cover; freeze until firm. Peel off paper cups; quickly roll pops in crushed pretzels, cookie crumbs or chopped nuts. Freeze until ready to serve.

10 to 12 pops.

*Or use 2 cups whipped topping and omit confectioners' sugar.

Beverages

Hot Chocolate

1 block (1 ounce) unsweetened
    baking chocolate
2 tablespoons hot water
¼ cup sugar

Dash salt
2 cups warm milk
¼ teaspoon vanilla

Melt baking chocolate in hot water in top of double boiler over hot, not boiling, water; stir until smooth. Add sugar and salt; blend well. Gradually stir in warm milk; heat to serving temperature, stirring occasionally (*do not boil*). Remove from heat; add vanilla. Serve immediately.

3 servings (6 ounces each).

Minty Hot Chocolate

½ cup sugar
6 tablespoons unsweetened
    cocoa
    Dash salt
1 cup water
4 cups milk

4 tablespoons crushed hard
    peppermint candy
½ cup heavy or whipping cream
1 tablespoon confectioners'
    sugar

Combine sugar, cocoa and salt in medium saucepan; stir in water. Cook over medium heat, stirring constantly, until mixture boils; boil and stir 2 minutes. Add milk and 3 tablespoons of the crushed peppermint candy; heat thoroughly (*do not boil*). Remove from heat. Beat with rotary beater until smooth and foamy; pour into cups.

Whip cream and confectioners' sugar until stiff; fold in remaining 1 tablespoon crushed peppermint candy. Top each drink with a heaping spoonful of whipped cream mixture. Serve immediately.

5 servings (8 ounces each).

Favorite Hot Cocoa

Nothing like homemade hot cocoa is as soothingly reminiscent of childhood.

½ cup sugar
¼ cup plus 1 tablespoon
    unsweetened cocoa
Dash salt

⅓ cup hot water
4 cups milk
¾ teaspoon vanilla

Combine sugar, cocoa and salt in medium saucepan; blend in hot water. Cook over medium heat, stirring constantly, until mixture boils; boil and stir 2 minutes. Add milk and heat to serving temperature *(do not boil)*. Remove from heat; add vanilla. Beat with rotary beater until foamy.

About 4 servings (8 ounces each).

Variations

Substitute the following flavors for the vanilla:

Canadian Cocoa: ½ teaspoon maple extract.

Irish Mint Cocoa: ½ teaspoon mint or peppermint extract.

Orange Cocoa Cappuccino: ½ teaspoon orange extract.

Swiss Mocha: 2 teaspoons instant coffee granules.

Viennese Cocoa: ⅛ teaspoon each ground cinnamon and ground nutmeg. Serve with cinnamon stick.

One Serving: Combine 2 tablespoons sugar, 1 tablespoon unsweetened cocoa, dash salt and 1 tablespoon water in small saucepan. Cook over medium heat, stirring constantly, until mixture boils; boil and stir 1 minute. Add 1 cup milk and heat to serving temperature *(do not boil)*. Remove from heat; add ⅛ teaspoon vanilla. Beat with rotary beater until foamy.

Mulled Cocoa

½ cup sugar
¼ cup unsweetened cocoa
⅓ cup water
4 cups milk

¼ cup light or dark rum
    (optional)
Sweetened whipped cream
Cinnamon sticks

Combine sugar and cocoa in medium saucepan; blend in water. Cook over medium heat, stirring constantly, until mixture boils; boil and stir 2 minutes. Add milk; heat to serving temperature, stirring occasionally *(do not boil)*. Remove from heat; add rum. Serve hot garnished with sweetened whipped cream and cinnamon sticks.

6 servings (6 ounces each).

Cocoa for a Crowd

1½ cups sugar
1¼ cups unsweetened cocoa
½ teaspoon salt
¾ cup hot water
4 quarts (1 gallon) milk
1 tablespoon vanilla

Combine sugar, cocoa and salt in 6-quart saucepan; gradually add hot water. Cook over medium heat, stirring constantly, until mixture boils; boil and stir 2 minutes. Add milk; heat to serving temperature, stirring occasionally (*do not boil*). Remove from heat; add vanilla. Serve immediately.

22 servings (6 ounces each).

Homemade Cocoa Mix

2½ cups nonfat dry milk powder
1 cup sugar
½ cup unsweetened cocoa
½ cup non-dairy coffee creamer

Combine all ingredients; blend well. Store in tightly covered container in cool, dry place.

4½ cups mix. (Makes 18 six-ounce servings hot cocoa.)

One serving: Place ¼ cup dry mix in cup; add 6 ounces boiling water. Stir well.

Four servings: Place 1 cup dry mix in pitcher; add 3 cups boiling water. Stir well.

Eighteen servings: Place 4½ cups dry mix in gallon container; add 13½ cups boiling water (3 quarts plus 1½ cups). Stir well.

Mocha Coffee Mix

2 cups confectioners' sugar
1 cup unsweetened cocoa

Combine confectioners' sugar and cocoa; blend well. Store in tightly covered container in cool, dry place.

3 cups mix. (Makes 48 six-ounce servings mocha coffee.)

One serving: Measure 1 tablespoon dry mix in cup; add ¾ cup hot coffee and 1 tablespoon light cream. Stir well. Garnish with a dollop of sweetened whipped cream and sprinkle with cinnamon.

Four servings: Place ¼ cup dry mix in pitcher; add 3 cups hot coffee and ¼ cup light cream. Stir well. Garnish with a dollop of sweetened whipped cream and sprinkle with cinnamon.

Frosty Chocolate Float

2 cups cold milk
1 cup vanilla ice cream, softened
¾ cup chocolate-flavored syrup
3 scoops vanilla ice cream

Measure milk, 1 cup ice cream and the syrup into blender container. Cover; blend on medium speed about 15 seconds or until smooth. Pour into 3 tall glasses; top each with scoop of vanilla ice cream. Serve immediately.

3 servings (10 ounces each).

Variations

Frosty Cherry Float: Add 3 tablespoons maraschino cherry juice before blending.

Frosty Peanut Float: Add 1 tablespoon creamy peanut butter before blending.

Chocolate Soda

¼ cup club soda, chilled
3 tablespoons chocolate-flavored syrup
2 scoops vanilla ice cream
Additional club soda, chilled

Combine ¼ cup club soda and the syrup in tall glass; add vanilla ice cream. Fill glass with additional club soda; stir lightly. Serve immediately.

1 serving (12 ounces).

Variation

Double Chocolate Soda: Substitute chocolate ice cream for the vanilla ice cream.

Peachy Chocolate Shake

⅔ cup peeled fresh peach slices, sweetened, or 1 package (10 ounces) frozen peaches, thawed and drained
2 cups vanilla ice cream, softened
¼ cup chocolate-flavored syrup
¼ cup milk

Puree peaches in blender container; add vanilla ice cream, syrup and milk. Cover; blend on medium speed until smooth. Serve immediately.

3 servings (8 ounces each).

On facing page, left to right—Citrus Twist (page 237); Peachy Chocolate Shake and Chocolate Soda (both this page)

Chocolate Milk Shake

This is the <u>real</u> thing, icy and thick as snow.

3 scoops (about 1 cup) vanilla ice cream, softened
½ cup milk

2 tablespoons chocolate-flavored syrup

Measure all ingredients into blender container. Cover; blend on high speed until smooth. (Or measure all ingredients into medium mixing bowl; beat with rotary beater until thick and smooth.) Serve immediately.

1 serving (8 ounces).

Maple-Chocolate Shake

2 cups milk
2 cups vanilla ice cream, softened

¼ cup chocolate-flavored syrup
1 tablespoon maple syrup

Measure all ingredients into blender container. Cover; blend on medium speed until smooth. Serve immediately.

3 servings (9 ounces each).

Frozen Banana Smoothie

1 cup half-and-half
½ cup mashed ripe banana (about 1 medium)

½ cup crème de banana liqueur
⅓ cup chocolate-flavored syrup
2½ cups ice cubes

Measure all ingredients into blender container. Cover; blend on high speed for 2 minutes. Decrease speed; blend 1 minute longer or until frothy. Serve immediately.

3 servings (9 ounces each).

Mystic Chocolate Mint Meld

2 cups half-and-half
¼ cup chocolate-flavored syrup

¼ cup white crème de menthe

Measure all ingredients into pitcher; stir until well blended. Serve over crushed ice.

2 servings (10 ounces each).

Citrus Twist

2 cups half-and-half
¼ cup chocolate-flavored syrup

3 tablespoons orange-flavored liqueur

Measure all ingredients into pitcher; stir until well blended. Serve over crushed ice.

2 servings (10 ounces each).

Mediterranean Splash

2 cups half-and-half
¼ cup chocolate-flavored syrup

¼ cup anisette

Measure all ingredients into pitcher; stir until well blended. Serve over crushed ice.

2 servings (10 ounces each).

Russian Kiss

2½ cups half-and-half
⅓ cup chocolate-flavored syrup

¼ cup vodka
3 tablespoons coffee-flavored liqueur

Measure all ingredients into pitcher; stir until well blended. Serve over crushed ice.

3 servings (9 ounces each).

Cocoa-Mint Punch

1 cup sugar
½ cup unsweetened cocoa
4 cups milk
1 cup heavy or whipping cream

6 eggs, beaten
½ cup crème de cacao
½ cup white crème de menthe

Combine sugar, cocoa and 1 cup of the milk in medium saucepan. Cook over medium heat, stirring constantly, until sugar is dissolved and mixture is smooth. Remove from heat; add remaining 3 cups milk, the cream, eggs and liqueurs. Chill thoroughly. Beat with rotary beater just before serving. Serve in cups over crushed ice.

12 servings (4 ounces each).

Chocoberry Splash

¾ cup milk
3 tablespoons frozen
   strawberries with syrup,
   thawed
2 tablespoons chocolate-
   flavored syrup

2 tablespoons vanilla ice cream
2 tablespoons club soda
1 scoop vanilla ice cream

Measure all ingredients except club soda and 1 scoop vanilla ice cream into blender container. Cover; blend on medium speed until smooth. Pour into tall glass filled with crushed ice. Add club soda; stir. Top with scoop of vanilla ice cream; garnish with additional fruit, if desired. Serve immediately.

1 serving (12 ounces).

Variations
Substitute the following fruits for the frozen strawberries:

Fresh Strawberry Splash: ¼ cup sweetened fresh strawberries.

Peach Splash: ⅓ cup canned peach slices or pieces, or ½ peeled fresh peach.

Pineapple Splash: 2 slices canned or ¼ cup crushed pineapple.

Raspberry Splash: 3 tablespoons frozen raspberries with syrup, thawed.

Sauces & Toppings

Classic Chocolate Sauce

This rich, bittersweet topping adds excitement to so many desserts— especially ice cream and cake.

2 blocks (2 ounces) unsweetened baking chocolate
2 tablespoons butter or margarine

1 cup sugar
¼ teaspoon salt
¾ cup evaporated milk
½ teaspoon vanilla

Melt baking chocolate and butter or margarine in saucepan over low heat, stirring occasionally. Stir in sugar and salt. Add evaporated milk and blend well. Cook, stirring constantly, until mixture just begins to boil. Remove from heat; add vanilla. Serve warm.

About 2 cups sauce.

Luscious Chocolate Sauce

¼ cup sugar
2 tablespoons flour
½ cup (5.5-ounce can) chocolate-flavored syrup

2 tablespoons milk
1 egg, beaten
¼ cup butter or margarine
½ teaspoon vanilla

Blend sugar and flour in small saucepan. Combine syrup, milk and egg; stir into sugar-flour mixture, blending well. Cook over low heat, stirring constantly with wire whisk or spoon, until mixture boils; boil and stir 1 minute. Remove from heat; blend in butter or margarine and vanilla. Serve warm.

About 1 cup sauce.

Easy Creamy Chocolate Sauce

1 ⅓ cups (14-ounce can) sweetened condensed milk*

¾ cup chocolate-flavored syrup

Combine sweetened condensed milk and syrup in top of double boiler over hot, not boiling, water. Cook, stirring frequently, until thick (about 10 to 15 minutes). Serve warm.

About 2 cups sauce.

*Do not use evaporated milk.

Note: This sauce will thicken as it cools, but may be reheated over hot water to desired consistency.

Hot Fudge Sauce

¾ cup sugar
½ cup unsweetened cocoa
⅔ cup evaporated milk

⅓ cup light corn syrup
⅓ cup butter or margarine
1 teaspoon vanilla

Combine sugar and cocoa in medium saucepan; blend in evaporated milk and corn syrup. Cook over low heat, stirring constantly, until mixture boils; boil and stir 1 minute. Remove from heat; stir in butter or margarine and vanilla. Serve warm.

About 2 cups sauce.

Note: This sauce can be refrigerated for later use. Reheat in saucepan over very low heat, stirring constantly.

Chocolate Nut Sauce

⅓ cup butter
⅔ cup coarsely chopped pecans or almonds
1 ⅓ cups sugar

½ cup unsweetened cocoa
¼ teaspoon salt
1 cup light cream
¾ teaspoon vanilla

Melt butter in medium saucepan over low heat; sauté chopped nuts in melted butter until lightly browned. Remove from heat; stir in sugar, cocoa and salt. Add light cream; blend well. Cook over low heat, stirring constantly, until mixture just begins to boil. Remove from heat; add vanilla. Serve warm.

About 2 cups sauce.

On facing page, clockwise from top— Chocolate Nut Sauce and Hot Fudge Sauce (this page); Chocolate-Peppermint Topping (page 243)

Chocolate Liqueur Sauce

¼ cup butter
1 cup sugar
6 tablespoons unsweetened cocoa

¼ teaspoon salt
¾ cup light cream
1 tablespoon liqueur*

Melt butter in saucepan over low heat; remove from heat. Stir in sugar, cocoa and salt. Add light cream and blend well. Cook over low heat, stirring constantly, until mixture just begins to boil. Remove from heat; stir in liqueur. Serve warm.

About 2 cups sauce.

*Crème de menthe, amaretto, Grand Marnier or other liqueur of your choice.

Chocolate Hard Sauce

Our chocolate interpretation. An excellent companion to fudgey hot puddings.

2 tablespoons butter or margarine, softened
3 tablespoons chocolate-flavored syrup

⅔ cup confectioners' sugar
Dash salt
½ teaspoon vanilla

Cream butter or margarine in small mixer bowl; gradually add syrup. Blend in confectioners' sugar, salt and vanilla; beat until smooth. Cover; chill. Serve on hot desserts.

About ½ cup sauce.

Two-for-One Sauce

½ cup (5.5-ounce can) chocolate-flavored syrup

½ cup chocolate fudge topping

Combine syrup and fudge topping in small saucepan. Cook over low heat, stirring constantly, until mixture is warm and well blended. Serve warm.

About 1 cup sauce.

Cocoa Syrup

Your very own homemade chocolate syrup. This is one of our most requested recipes.

1½ cups sugar
¾ cup unsweetened cocoa
 Dash salt

1 cup hot water
2 teaspoons vanilla

Combine sugar, cocoa and salt in medium saucepan; gradually stir in water, blending until mixture is smooth. Cook over medium heat, stirring constantly, until mixture boils; boil and stir 3 minutes. Remove from heat; add vanilla. Pour into container; cool. Cover; chill.

About 2 cups syrup.

Note: For Chocolate Milk, add 1 to 2 tablespoons Cocoa Syrup to a tall glass of cold milk; stir until blended.

Fudgey Dipping Sauce

½ cup butter or margarine
½ cup unsweetened cocoa
¾ cup sugar
½ cup evaporated milk or light
 cream

1 teaspoon vanilla
 Fruit, marshmallows, pieces
 of cake

Melt butter or margarine in small saucepan over low heat. Remove from heat; immediately stir in cocoa. Add sugar and evaporated milk or light cream; cook over low heat, stirring constantly, until sugar is dissolved and mixture is smooth. Remove from heat; stir in vanilla. Serve while warm. Accompany with a selection of fruit, marshmallows and small pieces of cake for dipping.

About 1½ cups sauce.

Chocolate-Peppermint Topping

1 cup frozen non-dairy whipped
 topping, thawed
3 tablespoons chocolate-flavored
 syrup

4 drops peppermint extract

Combine whipped topping, syrup and peppermint extract in small mixing bowl; blend well. This is a particularly nice topping for angel food cake.

About 1 cup topping.

Chocolate Whipped Cream

1 cup heavy or whipping cream
½ cup (5.5-ounce can) chocolate-flavored syrup
2 tablespoons confectioners' sugar
½ teaspoon vanilla

Combine cream, syrup, confectioners' sugar and vanilla in small mixer bowl; beat until soft peaks form. Especially good on cakes.

About 2¼ cups topping.

Sweetened Whipped Cream

1 cup heavy or whipping cream
1 to 2 tablespoons confectioners' sugar
½ teaspoon vanilla

Combine cream, confectioners' sugar and vanilla in small mixer bowl; beat until stiff peaks form.

About 2 cups topping.

Microwave Specialties

Cocoa Applesauce Muffins

Crunch Topping (below)
¼ cup unsweetened cocoa
¼ cup vegetable oil
¾ cup applesauce
1 egg, beaten
1¼ cups unsifted all-purpose
   flour

¾ cup sugar
¾ teaspoon baking soda
¼ teaspoon salt
¼ teaspoon cinnamon
½ cup chopped nuts

Prepare Crunch Topping; set aside. Combine cocoa and oil in small mixing bowl; stir until smooth. Add applesauce and egg; blend well. Combine flour, sugar, baking soda, salt and cinnamon in medium mixing bowl; stir in applesauce mixture and nuts. Stir just until dry ingredients are moistened.

Fill 6 paper muffin cups (2½ inches in diameter) half full with batter; place in microwave cupcake or muffin maker or in 6-ounce micro-proof custard cups. Sprinkle about 2 teaspoons Crunch Topping on top of each muffin. Microwave on high (full power) for 2½ to 3½ minutes, turning ¼ turn at end of each minute, or until cake tester comes out clean. (Tops may still appear moist.) Let stand several minutes. (Moist spots will disappear upon standing.) Repeat cooking procedure with remaining batter. Serve warm.

12 to 14 muffins.

Crunch Topping
Microwave 1 tablespoon butter or margarine in small micro-proof bowl on high for 15 seconds or until melted; add 2 tablespoons unsweetened cocoa and blend until smooth. Stir in ¼ cup packed light brown sugar, ¼ cup chopped nuts, 2 tablespoons flour and ¼ teaspoon cinnamon.

Chocolate Chip Bran Muffins

Wholesome homemade muffins every morning! Prepare the batter up to several days in advance. Keep in the 'fridge, use a little each time.

1½ cups bran flakes cereal
½ cup boiling water
1 cup buttermilk
¼ cup vegetable oil
1 egg, beaten
1¼ cups unsifted all-purpose flour
½ cup sugar

1 teaspoon baking soda
¼ teaspoon salt
½ cup semi-sweet chocolate Mini Chips
¼ cup finely chopped dried apricots
Bran flakes cereal

Combine 1½ cups bran flakes cereal and boiling water in medium mixing bowl; blend well. Cool. Add buttermilk, oil and egg; blend well. Combine flour, sugar, baking soda and salt in medium mixing bowl; stir in cereal mixture, Mini Chips and apricots. Stir just until dry ingredients are moistened.

Fill 6 paper muffin cups (2½ inches in diameter) half full with batter; place in microwave cupcake or muffin maker or in 6-ounce micro-proof custard cups. Sprinkle 2 teaspoons bran flakes cereal on top of each muffin. Microwave on high (full power) for 2½ to 3½ minutes, turning ¼ turn at end of each minute, or until cake tester comes out clean. (Tops may still appear moist.) Let stand several minutes. (Moist spots will disappear upon standing.) Repeat cooking procedure with remaining batter. Serve warm.

About 1½ dozen muffins.

Below—in center, Cocoa Applesauce Muffin (page 245); Chocolate Chip Bran Muffin (this page)

Chocolate Chip Oatmeal Coffee Cake

½ cup quick-cooking oats
¾ cup boiling water
  Graham cracker crumbs
¾ cup unsifted all-purpose flour
¾ cup packed light brown sugar
½ teaspoon baking soda
½ teaspoon cinnamon
¼ teaspoon baking powder

⅓ cup shortening
2 eggs
1 cup semi-sweet chocolate
  Mini Chips
⅓ cup chopped nuts
  Browned Butter Glaze
  (below)

Combine oats and boiling water in small mixing bowl; set aside to cool. Grease 1½-quart micro-proof tube pan; line bottom with wax paper. Grease wax paper; dust with graham cracker crumbs. Combine remaining ingredients except Mini Chips, nuts and Browned Butter Glaze in small mixer bowl. Beat on low speed until blended; blend in cooled oat mixture, ¾ cup of the Mini Chips and the nuts. Spread batter in prepared pan; cover pan with sheet of wax paper.

Microwave on inverted saucer or microwave rack on medium (½ power) for 5 minutes, rotating ¼ turn after 3 minutes. Microwave on high (full power) for 2 to 5 minutes or until top no longer appears moist. Cover with aluminum foil and let stand 10 minutes. (While standing, cake should pull away from side of pan and cake tester should come out clean.) Immediately invert onto serving plate; cool. Glaze with Browned Butter Glaze; sprinkle with remaining ¼ cup Mini Chips.

6 to 8 servings.

Browned Butter Glaze

Microwave 1½ tablespoons butter in small micro-proof bowl on high (full power) for 2 to 3 minutes or until browned but not burned. Stir in 1½ cups confectioners' sugar and 1 to 3 tablespoons milk; beat until smooth and of glaze consistency.

Peach-Chip Coffee Cake

⅓ cup peach preserves
2 cups (16-ounce can) peach slices, well drained
¼ cup maraschino cherries, drained
1½ cups unsifted all-purpose flour
½ cup sugar
1½ teaspoons baking powder
½ teaspoon salt
½ teaspoon cinnamon
½ cup butter or margarine
½ cup milk
1 egg, slightly beaten
½ teaspoon vanilla
½ cup semi-sweet chocolate Mini Chips

Cut wax paper to fit bottom of 1½-quart micro-proof tube pan; place in pan. Spread peach preserves evenly over bottom of prepared pan; arrange peach slices and cherries in decorative design over preserves.

Combine flour, sugar, baking powder, salt and cinnamon in large mixing bowl. Cut in butter or margarine until mixture resembles fine crumbs. Combine milk, egg and vanilla; add to dry ingredients, stirring until blended. (Batter will be slightly lumpy.) Add Mini Chips. Spread batter carefully over fruit; cover pan loosely with sheet of wax paper.

Microwave on inverted saucer or microwave rack on high (full power) for 7 to 9 minutes, rotating ¼ turn every 3 minutes of cooking time, or until cake tester comes out clean. Let stand 10 minutes. Loosen cake from side of pan. Invert onto serving plate; remove wax paper. Serve warm.

8 to 10 servings.

Microwave Hints

● Because microwaves bounce around the microwave oven in a random pattern, food often cooks faster in one area of the oven than in others, or even in different parts of the same dish. This is why it is very important to rotate dishes or to stir food (from outside edges, which are hotter, toward the center) when microwaving.

● The "standing time" allows the heat in the food to be evenly distributed. It is important not to overheat food during microwaving because the food continues to cook (and chocolate continues to melt) while standing.

● When greased pans are called for, be sure to use solid vegetable shortening.

Cocoa Streusel Coffee Cake

A beautiful orange-flavored coffee cake with a crunchy cocoa-nut streusel.

1½ cups unsifted all-purpose flour
¾ cup packed light brown sugar
2 teaspoons baking powder
½ teaspoon salt
¼ cup shortening
2 eggs, slightly beaten

⅔ cup orange juice
½ teaspoon grated orange peel
3 tablespoons butter or margarine
¾ cup confectioners' sugar
½ cup chopped nuts
¼ cup unsweetened cocoa
Cocoa Glaze (below)

Combine flour, brown sugar, baking powder and salt in medium mixing bowl; cut in shortening with pastry blender or knives until mixture resembles coarse crumbs. Add eggs, orange juice and orange peel; stir just until blended. (Batter will be lumpy.) Set aside.

Microwave butter or margarine in small micro-proof bowl on high (full power) for 30 seconds or until melted. Stir in confectioners' sugar, nuts and cocoa to form crumb mixture; set aside.

Cut wax paper to fit bottom of 1½-quart micro-proof tube pan; place in pan. Grease bottom and side of pan. Spread half the batter evenly in bottom of prepared pan. Sprinkle half the crumb mixture over batter. Spread with remaining batter and sprinkle with remaining crumb mixture; cover pan loosely with sheet of wax paper.

Microwave on inverted saucer or microwave rack on high for 5 to 7 minutes or until cake tester comes out clean. Cover with aluminum foil and let stand 10 minutes. Invert onto serving plate; remove wax paper. Cool slightly; glaze with Cocoa Glaze.

9 to 12 servings.

Cocoa Glaze

1 tablespoon butter or margarine
2 tablespoons unsweetened cocoa

1½ tablespoons water
¾ cup confectioners' sugar
½ teaspoon vanilla

Microwave butter or margarine in small micro-proof bowl on high for 10 to 15 seconds or until melted; stir in cocoa and water. Microwave on high for 10 to 20 seconds or until mixture is thick and smooth when stirred. Blend in confectioners' sugar and vanilla; beat until smooth. (If glaze is too thick, add water, a few drops at a time, until of desired consistency.) Pour over coffee cake.

Chocolate Upside-Down Cake

3 tablespoons butter or margarine
⅓ cup packed light brown sugar
1 can (16 ounces) pineapple slices, drained
⅓ cup maraschino cherries, drained
¼ cup pecan pieces
1 cup unsifted all-purpose flour

1 cup sugar
⅓ cup unsweetened cocoa
¾ teaspoon baking soda
¼ teaspoon salt
¾ cup sour cream
¼ cup butter or margarine, softened
2 eggs
1 teaspoon vanilla

Microwave 3 tablespoons butter or margarine in 2-quart micro-proof tube pan on high (full power) for 30 to 60 seconds or until melted. Stir in brown sugar; spread evenly in pan. Arrange fruits and nuts in design in pan.

Combine flour, sugar, cocoa, baking soda and salt in large mixer bowl. Blend in sour cream, ¼ cup butter or margarine, the eggs and vanilla; beat 2 minutes on medium speed. Carefully pour over fruit and nuts in pan; cover pan with sheet of wax paper. Microwave on inverted saucer or microwave rack on high for 8 to 10 minutes, rotating ¼ turn every 3 minutes, or until top no longer appears moist. Cover with foil; let stand 15 minutes. (While standing, cake should pull away from pan and cake tester should come out clean.) Immediately invert onto serving plate; cool.

9 to 12 servings.

Microwave Power Levels

Most microwave ovens manufactured today have a fairly uniform "high" setting, which uses full power. At lower settings, however, power levels vary considerably from brand to brand and model to model. Therefore, to help you achieve best results, settings for the recipes in this chapter are stated as percentages of power:

High	full power	600-700 watts
Medium-high	⅔ power	425-475 watts
Medium	½ power	175-225 watts
Warm		75-125 watts

Because individual ovens vary so, it's best to rely on the desired result ("until mixture boils," for example) as well as the recommended cooking time to determine doneness.

Cocoa Fudge Frosting

Chocolate frostings and glazes are a snap to make when you use the microwave for melting.

½ cup butter or margarine
½ cup unsweetened cocoa
3⅔ cups (1-pound box)
   confectioners' sugar
⅓ cup milk
1 teaspoon vanilla

Microwave butter or margarine in small micro-proof mixer bowl on high (full power) about 1 minute or until melted. Stir in cocoa until smooth; microwave on high 30 to 60 seconds or until mixture boils. Add confectioners' sugar, milk and vanilla; beat with mixer until smooth and of desired consistency. Spread while warm.

About 2 cups frosting.

Fudgey Cream Cheese Frosting

2½ blocks (2½ ounces)
   unsweetened baking
   chocolate
1 package (3 ounces) cream
   cheese
¼ cup milk
3⅔ cups (1-pound box)
   confectioners' sugar

Microwave baking chocolate in small micro-proof bowl on high (full power) for 1 to 1½ minutes or until chocolate is softened and smooth when stirred. Combine cream cheese and milk in small micro-proof bowl; microwave on high for 30 to 45 seconds or just until softened. Add melted chocolate and confectioners' sugar; beat until smooth.

About 2 cups frosting.

Chocolate-Marshmallow Glaze

⅓ cup sugar
3 tablespoons water
1 cup semi-sweet chocolate
   Mini Chips
3 tablespoons marshmallow
   creme
Hot water

Combine sugar and 3 tablespoons water in small micro-proof bowl. Microwave on high (full power) about 45 to 60 seconds or until boiling; stir until sugar is dissolved. Immediately add Mini Chips; stir until melted. Blend in marshmallow creme. If a thinner glaze is desired, add hot water, a teaspoonful at at time.

About 1 cup glaze.

Crème de Cacao Pie

9-inch baked pastry shell
1 envelope unflavored gelatine
½ cup cold milk
¼ cup butter or margarine
⅓ cup sugar
6 tablespoons unsweetened cocoa

3 egg yolks, slightly beaten
¼ cup crème de cacao
3 egg whites
⅓ cup sugar

Bake pastry shell; set aside. Sprinkle gelatine onto cold milk in small bowl; let stand 5 minutes to soften. Microwave butter or margarine in micro-proof bowl on high (full power) for 30 to 60 seconds or until melted; stir in ⅓ cup sugar and the cocoa. Add gelatine mixture; blend well. Stir in beaten egg yolks; blend well. Microwave on medium (½ power) for 2½ to 3½ minutes, stirring frequently, or until mixture is hot; *do not boil.* Stir in crème de cacao; cool.

Beat egg whites in large mixer bowl until foamy; gradually add ⅓ cup sugar, beating until stiff peaks form. Fold into chocolate mixture; pour into cooled shell. Cover; chill until firm.

8 servings.

Microwave Hershey Bar Pie

9-inch baked crumb crust
1 milk chocolate bar (8 ounces), broken into pieces
⅓ cup milk
1½ cups miniature marshmallows

1 cup heavy or whipping cream
Sweetened whipped cream
Chilled cherry pie filling (optional)

Bake crumb crust; set aside. Combine chocolate bar pieces, milk and miniature marshmallows in medium micro-proof bowl. Microwave on high (full power) about 1½ to 2½ minutes or until chocolate is softened and mixture is melted and smooth when stirred. Cool completely.

Whip cream until stiff; fold into chocolate mixture. Spoon into crust. Cover; chill several hours or until firm. Garnish with sweetened whipped cream; serve with chilled cherry pie filling.

8 servings.

On facing page, from top—Microwave Hershey Bar Pie and Crème de Cacao Pie

Cool Chocolate Cream Pie

8-inch baked pastry shell
  or crumb crust
⅓ cup cornstarch
¼ teaspoon salt
1¾ cups milk

1 cup chocolate-flavored syrup
2 eggs yolks, beaten
1 teaspoon vanilla
  Sweetened whipped cream
  (optional)

Bake pastry shell or crumb crust; set aside. Combine cornstarch, salt, milk, syrup and egg yolks in medium micro-proof bowl. Microwave on medium-high (⅔ power) for 6 to 8 minutes, stirring every 2 minutes with wire whisk, until mixture is smooth and thickened. Stir in vanilla.

Pour into cooled shell or crust; press plastic wrap onto surface. Chill several hours or overnight. Garnish with sweetened whipped cream.

6 servings.

Melting Chocolate in a Microwave Oven

It's neat, easy and quicker than quick. For best results, follow these procedures:

Unsweetened Baking Chocolate and Semi-Sweet Chocolate: Unwrap, break blocks in half and place desired amount in micro-proof measuring cup or bowl. Microwave on high (full power) for minimum time listed below or until chocolate is softened; stir. Allow to stand several minutes to finish melting; stir again. (If unmelted chocolate still remains, return to microwave for an additional 30 seconds; stir until fluid.)

1 block (1 ounce)	1 to 1½ minutes
2 blocks (2 ounces)	1½ to 2 minutes
3 blocks (3 ounces)	2 to 2½ minutes
4 blocks (4 ounces)	2½ to 3 minutes

Chips (Semi-Sweet, Milk, Mini Chips or Peanut Butter): Place 1 cup (about 6 ounces) chips in 2-cup micro-proof measuring cup or bowl. Microwave on high (full power) for 1 to 1½ minutes or until softened; stir. Allow to stand for several minutes to finish melting; stir.

Chocolate Cheesecake

Cocoa Crumb Crust (below)
1 envelope unflavored gelatine
½ cup cold water
¼ cup sugar
2 packages (8 ounces each)
  cream cheese, softened
½ cup unsweetened cocoa
1⅓ cups (14-ounce can)
  sweetened condensed
  milk*
Cheesecake Topping
  (optional, below)

Prepare Cocoa Crumb Crust; set aside. Sprinkle gelatine onto cold water in small micro-proof bowl; let stand 5 minutes to soften. Microwave on high (full power) for 1 to 1½ minutes or until gelatine is dissolved. Add sugar; stir until dissolved.

Combine cream cheese and cocoa in large mixer bowl; beat until smooth and well blended. Add sweetened condensed milk; blend well. Add gelatine mixture; mix thoroughly. Pour onto crust; chill several hours or until firm. Spread with Cheesecake Topping.

9 servings.

*Do not use evaporated milk.

Cocoa Crumb Crust
Combine 1¼ cups graham cracker crumbs, ¼ cup sugar and 2 table-spoons unsweetened cocoa in 8- or 9-inch square micro-proof dish. Place ⅓ cup butter or margarine in dish with crumb mixture; microwave on high for 1 to 1½ minutes or until butter or margarine is melted. Blend well; press onto bottom of pan.

Cheesecake Topping
Blend 1 cup sour cream, ¼ cup sugar and 2 teaspoons vanilla.

Microwave Hershey Bar Mousse

1 milk chocolate bar (8 ounces),
  broken into pieces
¼ cup water
2 eggs, beaten
1 cup heavy or whipping cream

Combine chocolate bar pieces and water in medium micro-proof bowl. Microwave on high (full power) for 1½ to 2 minutes or until mixture is melted and smooth when stirred. Stir in beaten eggs. Microwave on medium (½ power) for 1½ to 2½ minutes or until mixture is hot but not boiling. Cool slightly. Whip cream until stiff; fold into cooled chocolate mixture. Pour into 8-inch square pan. Cover; freeze until firm. Cut into squares.

4 servings.

Chocolate Mousse

Our microwave version of a classic chocolate dessert.

6 tablespoons unsweetened cocoa
2 tablespoons vegetable oil
1 envelope unflavored gelatine
1 cup cold milk
⅓ cup sugar
⅛ teaspoon salt
3 egg yolks, beaten
1 teaspoon vanilla

3 egg whites, at room temperature
⅓ cup sugar
1 cup heavy or whipping cream, whipped, or 2 cups frozen non-dairy whipped topping, thawed
Sweetened whipped cream or whipped topping (optional)

Blend cocoa and oil in large micro-proof bowl until smooth; set aside. Sprinkle gelatine onto cold milk in micro-proof measuring cup; let stand 5 minutes to soften. Microwave on high (full power) for 1 to 1½ minutes or until mixture is warm and gelatine is dissolved. Add gelatine-milk mixture, ⅓ cup sugar, the salt and egg yolks to cocoa mixture. Microwave on medium (½ power) for 5 minutes; stir well. Microwave on medium for 2 to 3 minutes or until mixture is hot and slightly thickened; stir in vanilla. Press plastic wrap onto surface; chill until mixture mounds when dropped from spoon.

Beat egg whites in small mixer bowl until foamy; gradually add ⅓ cup sugar, beating until stiff peaks form. Gently fold egg whites and whipped cream or whipped topping into chocolate mixture. Spoon mixture into dessert dishes; chill until firm. Garnish with sweetened whipped cream or whipped topping.

About 8 servings.

Chocolate Pudding

⅔ cup sugar
¼ cup unsweetened cocoa
3 tablespoons cornstarch
¼ teaspoon salt

2¼ cups milk
2 tablespoons butter or margarine
1 teaspoon vanilla

Combine sugar, cocoa, cornstarch and salt in medium micro-proof bowl; gradually stir in milk. Microwave on high (full power) for 5 minutes, stirring twice during cooking time. Microwave on high 2 to 3 minutes or until mixture is cooked and thickened. Stir in butter or margarine and vanilla. Pour into dessert dishes; press plastic wrap onto surface. Cool; chill thoroughly.

4 or 5 servings.

Chocolate Pudding in a Cloud

1 package (3⅛ ounces) vanilla pudding and pie filling mix*	2 cups milk
¼ cup unsweetened cocoa	1¾ cups (4-ounce container) frozen non-dairy whipped topping, thawed
¼ cup sugar	

Combine pudding and pie filling mix, cocoa and sugar in 2-quart micro-proof bowl. Add milk; stir to blend. Microwave on high (full power) for 3 minutes; stir with wire whisk. Microwave on high for 1½ to 3 additional minutes, stirring occasionally, until mixture boils. Press plastic wrap onto surface; cool. Chill thoroughly.

Spoon whipped topping into 6 dessert dishes. With back of spoon, make depression in center of topping and spread up side of dish. Spoon chilled chocolate pudding into center of each dish. Serve immediately or chill until ready to serve.

6 servings.

*Do not use instant mix.

Cherry-Chocolate Chip Bread Pudding

Contemporary microwave treatment of a homey old-fashioned dessert.

2 cups (21-ounce can) cherry pie filling	½ cup sugar
3 cups bread cubes (about 4 slices)	1 cup milk
¼ cup butter or margarine	3 eggs
1 tablespoon lemon juice	½ teaspoon vanilla or almond extract
¾ cup semi-sweet chocolate Mini Chips	Cinnamon

Spread pie filling in shallow 1½-quart micro-proof tube pan. Sprinkle bread cubes evenly over pie filling. Microwave butter or margarine in micro-proof cup or bowl on high (full power) for 45 to 60 seconds or until melted; drizzle evenly over bread. Sprinkle with lemon juice; spread Mini Chips evenly over top.

Combine sugar, milk, eggs and vanilla or almond extract in small mixing bowl; beat well. Pour slowly over bread cube mixture; press cubes gently into milk mixture. Sprinkle with cinnamon; cover pan with sheet of wax paper. Microwave on medium (½ power) for 17 to 19 minutes or until bread mixture is almost set, rotating ¼ turn every 5 minutes. Let stand, covered with wax paper, for 30 minutes. Serve warm; scoop onto serving plates with cherries on top.

6 to 8 servings.

Chocolate-Rum Fudge Pudding Cake

1 cup unsifted all-purpose flour
¾ cup sugar
3 tablespoons unsweetened cocoa
2 teaspoons baking powder
½ teaspoon salt
½ cup milk
2 tablespoons vegetable oil

1 teaspoon vanilla
⅔ cup chopped nuts
¾ cup packed light brown sugar
¼ cup unsweetened cocoa
1 cup boiling water
¼ cup light or dark rum
Rum Whipped Cream (below) or ice cream

Combine flour, ¾ cup sugar, 3 tablespoons cocoa, the baking powder and salt in large mixing bowl. Stir in milk, oil, vanilla and half the nuts. Spread batter in 2- or 2½-quart micro-proof casserole or baking dish. Combine brown sugar, ¼ cup cocoa, remaining nuts, the boiling water and rum in small bowl. Pour over batter in dish; *do not mix.* Cover with sheet of wax paper.

Microwave on high (full power) for 7 to 9 minutes, rotating ¼ turn halfway through cooking time, or until cake rises to surface and sauce forms on bottom. Let stand 10 minutes before serving. Serve warm or cold topped with Rum Whipped Cream or ice cream.

6 to 8 servings.

Rum Whipped Cream
Combine 1 cup heavy or whipping cream, 2 tablespoons confectioners' sugar and 1 tablespoon rum in small bowl; beat until stiff peaks form.

Easy Chocolate Mint Dessert

1 milk chocolate bar (8 ounces), broken into pieces
3 tablespoons coarsely chopped walnuts

2 cups heavy or whipping cream
2 tablespoons white crème de menthe
Chocolate curls (optional)

Microwave chocolate bar pieces in small micro-proof bowl on high (full power) for 1 to 2 minutes or until softened; stir until melted and smooth. Stir in walnuts; cool slightly. Beat cream and crème de menthe until stiff; fold cooled chocolate mixture into cream mixture. Spoon into dessert dishes. Cover; chill until firm. Garnish with chocolate curls.

8 servings.

Chocolate-Peanut No-Bake Cookies

5 cups corn flakes
1 cup semi-sweet chocolate
   chips
1 cup peanut butter chips
1 tablespoon shortening
½ cup raisins (optional)

Crush corn flakes (about 2⅓ cups crushed flakes); set aside. Place chocolate chips, peanut butter chips and shortening in medium micro-proof mixing bowl. Microwave on high (full power) for 1 to 2 minutes or until chips are softened and mixture is melted and smooth when stirred. Add crushed corn flakes and raisins; stir until well coated. Drop by teaspoonfuls onto wax-paper-covered tray. Cover; chill until firm. Store at room temperature in tightly covered container.

About 3½ dozen cookies.

Cocoa Brownies

⅓ cup butter or margarine
2 tablespoons shortening
6 tablespoons unsweetened
   cocoa
1 cup sugar
2 eggs
½ teaspoon vanilla
1 cup unsifted all-purpose flour
¼ teaspoon baking powder
¼ teaspoon salt
½ cup chopped nuts
   Vanilla ice cream (optional)
   Chocolate-flavored syrup
   (optional)

Place butter or margarine and shortening in medium micro-proof mixing bowl; microwave on high (full power) about 1 minute or until melted. Stir in cocoa, blending until smooth; blend in sugar. Add eggs and vanilla; beat well. Stir in flour, baking powder, salt and nuts.

Spread in lightly greased 8-inch round micro-proof baking dish. Microwave on medium (½ power) for 7 minutes, turning ¼ turn every 3 minutes. Microwave on high for 2 to 3 minutes or until brownies begin to puff on top. (Do not microwave until completely dry on top; a 1-inch wet spot should remain in center.) Cover with aluminum foil and let stand for 20 minutes or until set. Cut into wedges; serve topped with ice cream and syrup.

6 servings.

Chocolate Crackles

10 tablespoons butter or
   margarine
6 tablespoons unsweetened
   cocoa
2 cups unsifted all-purpose
   flour
1 cup sugar

2 teaspoons baking powder
½ teaspoon salt
2 eggs
1 teaspoon vanilla
½ cup chopped nuts
   Confectioners' sugar

Microwave butter or margarine in medium micro-proof bowl on high (full power) for 45 to 60 seconds or until melted. Add cocoa; blend well. Beat in flour, sugar, baking powder, salt, eggs and vanilla. Stir in nuts. Refrigerate at least 8 hours or until firm.

Shape dough into 1-inch balls; roll in confectioners' sugar. Place 8 balls 2 inches apart in circular shape on wax paper in microwave oven. Microwave on medium (½ power) for 1 to 2 minutes or until surface is dry but cookies are soft when touched. Cool on wax paper.

About 4 dozen cookies.

Below, left to right—Chocolate Crackles (this page); Easy Rocky Road (page 261); Fast Chocolate-Pecan Fudge (page 262)

Easy Rocky Road

2 cups (12-ounce package) semi-sweet chocolate chips
¼ cup butter or margarine
2 tablespoons shortening

5 cups (10½-ounce bag) miniature marshmallows
½ cup chopped nuts

Place chocolate chips, butter or margarine and shortening in large micro-proof bowl. Microwave on medium (½ power) for 5 to 7 minutes or until chips are softened and mixture is melted and smooth when stirred. Add marshmallows and nuts; blend well. Spread evenly in buttered 8-inch square pan. Cover; chill until firm. Cut into 2-inch squares.

16 squares.

Peanutty Chocolate Snack Squares

5 graham crackers, broken into squares
½ cup sugar
1 cup light corn syrup

1 cup (6-ounce package) semi-sweet chocolate chips
1 cup peanut butter
1 cup dry roasted peanuts

Line bottom of 8-inch square pan with graham cracker squares, cutting to fit as necessary. Combine sugar and corn syrup in 2-quart micro-proof bowl. Microwave on high (full power), stirring every 2 minutes, until mixture boils; boil 3 minutes. Stir in chocolate chips, peanut butter and peanuts. Pour over crackers; spread carefully. Cover; refrigerate until firm. Cut into 2-inch squares.

16 squares.

Easiest-Ever Cocoa Fudge

3⅔ cups (1-pound box) confectioners' sugar, sifted
½ cup unsweetened cocoa
½ cup butter or margarine, cut into pieces

¼ cup milk
½ cup chopped nuts (optional)
1 tablespoon vanilla

Combine confectioners' sugar, cocoa, butter or margarine and milk in medium micro-proof bowl. Microwave on high (full power) for 2 to 3 minutes or until butter or margarine is melted. Stir until mixture is smooth. Stir in nuts and vanilla; blend well. Spread evenly in buttered 8-inch square pan; cool. Cut into 1-inch squares.

About 5 dozen candies.

Fast Chocolate-Pecan Fudge

When you want a rich candy— fast. Fudges are perfect for the microwave and vice versa.

½ cup butter or margarine
¾ cup unsweetened cocoa
4 cups confectioners' sugar
1 teaspoon vanilla

½ cup evaporated milk
1½ cups coarsely chopped
pecans
Pecan halves (optional)

Microwave butter or margarine in 2-quart micro-proof bowl on high (full power) for 1 to 1½ minutes or until melted. Add cocoa; stir until smooth. Stir in confectioners' sugar and vanilla; blend well (mixture will be dry and crumbly). Stir in evaporated milk. Microwave on high for 30 to 60 seconds or until mixture is hot. Stir mixture until smooth; add chopped pecans.

Pour into aluminum-foil-lined 9-inch square pan. Garnish with pecan halves. Cover; chill until firm, about 2 hours. Cut into 1-inch squares. Store, covered, in refrigerator.

About 6½ dozen candies.

Chocolate Chip Fudge

1⅓ cups (14-ounce can)
sweetened condensed
milk*
2 cups (12-ounce package)
semi-sweet chocolate
chips

½ cup chopped nuts (optional)
1 teaspoon vanilla

Combine sweetened condensed milk and chocolate chips in medium micro-proof bowl. Microwave on high (full power) for 1 to 1½ minutes or until chips are softened and mixture is melted and smooth when stirred. Stir in nuts and vanilla. Spread evenly in buttered 8-inch square pan. Cover; chill until firm. Cut into 1-inch squares.

About 5 dozen candies.

*Do not use evaporated milk.

Chocolate Toffee Grahams

1 tablespoon butter or margarine
5 graham crackers, broken into squares
½ cup butter or margarine
½ cup packed light brown sugar
½ cup sliced almonds
5 milk chocolate bars (1.45 ounces each)

Microwave 1 tablespoon butter or margarine in 8-inch square micro-proof pan on high (full power) for 30 to 60 seconds or until melted; spread over bottom and ¼ inch up sides. Line bottom of pan with graham cracker squares, cutting to fit as necessary; set aside.

Combine ½ cup butter or margarine and the brown sugar in small micro-proof bowl. Microwave on high for 1 minute; beat until smooth. Microwave for 2 minutes on high; carefully spread over graham crackers. Sprinkle almonds on top. Microwave on high until mixture boils, rotating ¼ turn several times during cooking; boil 1 minute.

Cool 2 minutes; place chocolate bars on top. When soft, spread chocolate evenly over top. Loosen edges; cut into quarters, then into small pieces. For crisp toffee, store, covered, in refrigerator.

About 4 dozen pieces.

Microwave Hot Cocoa

5 tablespoons sugar
3 tablespoons unsweetened cocoa
Dash salt
3 tablespoons hot water
2 cups milk
¼ teaspoon vanilla

Combine sugar, cocoa, salt and hot water in 1-quart micro-proof measuring cup. Microwave on high (full power) for 1 to 1½ minutes or until boiling. Add milk; microwave on high for 1½ to 2 minutes or until hot. Stir in vanilla; blend well.

4 servings.

One serving: Place 2 heaping teaspoons sugar, 1 heaping teaspoon unsweetened cocoa and dash salt in micro-proof cup. Add 2 teaspoons cold milk; stir until smooth. Fill cup with milk; microwave on high for 1 to 1½ minutes or until hot. Stir to blend.

Easy Hot Fudge Sauce

This hot fudge sauce is so fast you can cook it even after the ice cream's on the table.

½ cup unsweetened cocoa
1⅓ cups (14-ounce can) sweetened condensed milk*

3 tablespoons milk
1 tablespoon butter or margarine
1 teaspoon vanilla

Combine cocoa, sweetened condensed milk and milk in medium micro-proof bowl. Microwave on high (full power) for 1 minute; stir. Microwave on high for 1 to 1½ minutes, stirring with wire whisk after each minute, or until mixture is smooth and hot. Stir in butter or margarine and vanilla. Serve warm.

About 1½ cups sauce.

*Do not use evaporated milk.

Microwave Classic Chocolate Sauce

2 blocks (2 ounces) unsweetened baking chocolate
2 tablespoons butter

1 cup sugar
¼ teaspoon salt
¾ cup evaporated milk
½ teaspoon vanilla

Place baking chocolate and butter in small micro-proof bowl. Microwave on high (full power) for 1 minute or until chocolate is softened and mixture is melted and smooth when stirred. Add sugar, salt and evaporated milk; blend well. Microwave on high for 2 to 3 minutes, stirring with wire whisk after each minute, or until mixture is smooth and hot. Stir in vanilla. Serve warm.

About 1½ cups sauce.

Fun & Frills

Chocolate and fun go hand in hand—and this chapter proves the point. On the following pages you will find fun-to-make chocolate decorations and trims. They look impressive, but they're actually easy. Here, too, are some unusual treats—Chocolate Teddy Bears, Homemade Chocolate Liqueur and Chocolate-Dipped Strawberries among them. They're perfect for gift-giving too!

Share the fun with friends and have a chocolate party. If chocolate "anything" brings a smile to just about every face, imagine what chocolate "everything" will do. Here are some ideas to get your own imagination going:

- Celebrate a new baby, a new house or a bride-to-be with a Chocolate Shower. A chocolate cake with an appropriate decoration piped on, a crowd-size mousse and a chocolate ice cream dessert will provide plenty of variety and tastes for all.
- Have a happy Chocolate Anniversary Party. Everybody knows about wood and paper and silver, of course, but who's to say you can't break tradition? Let our Heavenly Heart Cake (redecorated for the occasion) take center stage, then add a chocolate cheesecake and a pie or two.
- Who could resist a Chocolate Birthday Party? Set the table with Chocolate Place Cards and Chocolate Party Cups (both recipes are in this chapter). Light the candles on a favorite chocolate cake and set out the fixings for make-your-own sundaes, with a selection of ice creams and toppings. And think about a new-fashioned chocolate taffy pull for one of the games.
- Spark up summer with a Chocolate Pool Party. "Come for a dip, and have a dip." All you need is one of our fondues or Chocolate Dipping Sauce and a host of dippers. It's elegant but easy.
- Start a lazy weekend off right with a Chocolate Brunch. Spread the buffet table with plenty of options—Chocolate Waffles or Chocolate Chip Pancakes and chocolatey muffins, nut breads and coffee cakes. And don't forget the cocoa drinks, both hot and cold.
- A Chocolate Dessert Buffet is a great idea for after theater, after golf, after anything. Choose chocolate desserts that can be made well in advance: a frosty bombe, a handsome Bavarian and something spectacular from our "Showstoppers" chapter.

Frills from Decorator's Tips

With just a little practice, all your desserts can have that professional-looking finish.

Start with a pastry bag and a selection of tips. Choose a reusable nylon or plastic bag or a disposable parchment bag in the size best suited to your needs. (Parchment and plastic bags are the most practical for handling melted chocolate.) The standard bag is 12 to 14 inches, but a smaller size is often more useful for decorative pipings. Tips are also available in various sizes and shapes — star, petal, leaf, writing. Most bags can be fitted with a coupler, which allows you to change tips easily.

Fit the tip into the bag, making sure that it protrudes evenly. (Or fit the coupler into the bag and attach the tip.) Fold down about a third of the bag to form a cuff. Slip one hand under the cuff to hold the bag open. Spoon in the frosting (filling, whipped cream, what have you), keeping the bag less than half full. Unfold the top, then twist or make roll-over folds to close the bag. Use one hand to hold the bag and squeeze out the frosting; use the other to guide the tip. Continue to twist or fold down the end of the bag as you work.

Whether you're an experienced or a beginning decorator, always make a few practice borders or scrolls on wax paper before decorating the dessert.

Different frostings and tips can create a variety of borders and special effects.

Allegretti Icing

Sometimes referred to as Shadow Icing.

This is an easy way to add a special touch to any cake frosted with a light chocolate or other contrasting color frosting.

Combine 1 block (1 ounce) unsweetened baking chocolate and ½ teaspoon shortening in small saucepan. Heat over low heat, stirring constantly, until chocolate is melted and mixture is smooth. Remove from heat; cool slightly. Drizzle melted chocolate from tip of teaspoon around edge of cake, allowing chocolate to drizzle down side to form "icicles."

Grated Chocolate

The easiest of all chocolate garnishes — all you need is a grater and a firm bar or block of chocolate. Simply rub the chocolate across the grater, letting the shreds fall onto a piece of wax paper. Most hand graters offer a choice of grating surfaces, one larger than the other — the choice is yours! A mouli grater will also do the job quickly and neatly.

If your dessert offers a fairly large surface — a pie, cake or cold soufflé, for example — you can use the grated chocolate to form a design. (See the photograph of Black Bottom Pie on page 86.)

Chocolate Triangles and Wedges

Set a single wedge or triangle, point down, into an individual mousse, or circle a series of triangles or wedges atop a frosted cake. (See the cover photograph.)

Melt semi-sweet chocolate in top of double boiler over hot, not boiling, water; stir until completely melted. (Or melt in microwave oven; see page 254.) With spatula, spread melted chocolate into square or circle on wax-paper-covered cookie sheet. (Use 4 ounces chocolate for a 7-inch circle or square.) Chill 5 to 8 minutes or just until chocolate begins to set.

With sharp knife, cut chocolate square into smaller squares; cut each small square diagonally in half to make triangles. Cut chocolate circle into wedges, as if cutting a pie. Do not try to separate at this time. Chill several hours or until very firm. Carefully peel wax paper away from chocolate; separate triangles or wedges. Place on tray; cover and refrigerate until ready to use.

Chocolate Curls

Chocolate curls can be tiny and delicate or extravagantly wide. Choose the size that's appropriate for the dessert. The secret to successful curls is to have the chocolate at the proper temperature. It should feel slightly warm but still firm. In fact, on a warm day, room temperature might be fine.

To warm, place unwrapped chocolate on a cookie sheet. Place in cool oven; watch carefully! (Or place in microwave oven on high power for about 30 seconds or just until chocolate feels warm.) With even pressure, draw a vegetable peeler along the *underside* of the chocolate; a curl will form naturally. Use a toothpick to lift the curl onto wax-paper-covered tray. Continue making curls in this manner until you have the desired number. Refrigerate until firm.

For narrow curls, you can use the side of a candy bar. For short, medium-size curls, use one or two blocks. For large curls, use the entire width of the bar.

Note: When firm, chocolate curls can be refrigerated in a covered container and stored almost indefinitely.

Chocolate Leaves

You can use any size or shape that's appropriate...or that suits your fancy. Just make sure the leaves are thoroughly washed and dried.

Melt semi-sweet or milk chocolate in top of double boiler over hot, not boiling, water; stir until completely melted. (Or melt in microwave oven; see page 254.) With small soft-bristled pastry brush, brush melted chocolate on *underside* of each leaf. (The underside provides the attractive vein markings.) Avoid getting chocolate on the front of the leaf; it will make removal difficult. Place on wax-paper-covered cookie sheet; chill until firm.

Carefully peel the leaves away from the chocolate; do not try to peel the chocolate from the leaves. Cover and refrigerate until ready to use.

Note: Most leaves are safe to use providing they have been thoroughly washed to remove all traces of insecticides or sprays. If in doubt, check with your florist. Rose leaves and lemon leaves are particularly attractive.

Chocolate Silhouettes and Designs

Add a boutique touch to your homemade candies by decorating the tops with a contrasting shade of chocolate: a milk chocolate swirl on a semi-sweet coating, for example. See the photograph on page 218.

Here's an opportunity to let your creativity shine. You can easily form any outline or design — hearts, butterflies, Christmas trees, scrolls, names, even lacy patterns. Or you can place a drawing or pattern under the wax paper and trace the melted chocolate directly over it.

Melt semi-sweet or milk chocolate in top of double boiler over hot, not boiling, water; stir until completely melted. (Or melt in microwave oven; see page 254.) Cool slightly. Spoon melted chocolate into small pastry bag fitted with a small writing tip (see note). Pipe chocolate in a steady flow into desired design on wax-paper-covered tray. Place tray in refrigerator until shapes are firm. Carefully peel wax paper away from chocolate. Cover and refrigerate until ready to use.

Note: When handling small amounts of melted chocolate, a parchment tube or heavy envelope with a tiny portion of the corner snipped off works well. Remember, too, melted chocolate tends to run freely, so keep the tip pointed upward between designs.

Chocolate Butterflies

Melt semi-sweet chocolate in top of double boiler over hot, not boiling, water; stir until completely melted. (Or melt in microwave oven; see page 254.) Cool slightly. Spoon melted chocolate into small pastry bag fitted with a writing tip or into parchment bag (see note on page 269). On wax-paper-covered tray, pipe chocolate in a steady flow into shape of 2 butterfly wings. (Make 2 separate wings for each butterfly.) Fill wings with designs if desired. Place tray in refrigerator just until shapes are firm.

Meanwhile, fold a small, narrow strip of double-thickness aluminum foil into an "M" shape. Pipe a strip of melted chocolate into the center of the "M" to form the body of the butterfly. Remove wings from refrigerator and carefully peel wax paper away from chocolate. Tuck the chocolate wings into the melted chocolate, allowing the wings to rest against the sloped sides of the "M" (see diagram). Return to the refrigerator until set. Just before using, peel the foil away from the chocolate.

Chocolate Cutouts

Use your favorite cookie cutters or even canapé cutters for these sprightly garnishes.

Melt ⅔ cup semi-sweet chocolate Mini Chips or 4 ounces milk chocolate in top of double boiler over hot, not boiling, water; stir until completely melted. (Or melt in microwave oven; see page 254.) With spatula, spread melted chocolate into 7-inch square, about ⅛ inch thick, on wax-paper-covered cookie sheet. Chill 5 to 8 minutes or just until chocolate begins to set.

Press small cookie cutters into chocolate, pressing down to cookie sheet. Do not try to remove or separate cutouts at this time. Chill several hours or until very firm. Carefully peel wax paper away from chocolate, removing cutout shapes. Place cutouts on tray; cover and refrigerate until ready to use.

Note: For larger cutouts, it may be necessary to make several squares.

Chocolate Party Cups

These attractive "dishes" are perfect for ice cream. Or for an elegant dessert, fill with your favorite mousse and top with grated chocolate.

2 cups (12-ounce package) semi-sweet chocolate chips

2 teaspoons shortening (not butter, margarine or oil)

Melt chocolate chips and shortening in top of double boiler over hot, not boiling, water; remove from heat. Cool slightly.

Place twelve paper baking cups (2¾ inches in diameter) in muffin pans. Using a narrow, soft-bristled pastry brush, thickly and evenly coat inside pleated surface and bottom of each cup. Chill coated cups 10 minutes or until set; coat any thin spots again. (If necessary, chocolate mixture may be reheated over hot water.) Cover tightly; chill until very firm, about 1 hour. Carefully peel paper from each cup. Cover and chill at least 1 hour. Fill chilled cups as desired.

About 12 cups.

Variation

Chocolate Liqueur Cups: Use paper candy cups in miniature muffin pans. Follow coating directions above using 1 cup semi-sweet chocolate chips and 1 teaspoon shortening. To serve, fill each chilled cup with about 1½ teaspoons of your favorite liqueur.

18 to 22 cups.

Chocolate Teddy Bears

2/3 cup butter or margarine, softened
1 cup sugar
2 teaspoons vanilla
2 eggs
2½ cups unsifted all-purpose flour

½ cup unsweetened cocoa
½ teaspoon baking soda
¼ teaspoon salt
Decorator's Frosting (optional, below)

Cream butter or margarine, sugar and vanilla in large mixer bowl until light and fluffy. Add eggs; blend well. Combine flour, cocoa, baking soda and salt; gradually add to creamed mixture, blending thoroughly. Chill until dough is firm enough to handle.

For each bear, form a portion of the dough into 1 large ball (1 to 1½ inches) for body, 1 medium-size ball (¾ to 1 inch) for head, 4 small balls (½ inch) for arms and legs, 2 smaller balls for ears, 1 tiny ball for nose and, if desired, 4 tiny balls for paws.

On ungreased cookie sheet, slightly flatten the large ball. Attach medium-size ball for head by overlapping slightly onto the body. Place balls for arms and legs against the body; place ears against the head. Add a tiny ball to the head for nose. If using tiny balls for paws, place them on arms and legs. With a wooden pick, draw eyes and mouth. (Pierce small hole with wooden pick through top of cookie if using as Christmas tree ornament.)

Bake at 350° for 6 to 8 minutes or until set. Cool 1 minute. Remove from cookie sheet; cool completely on wire rack. Prepare Decorator's Frosting; decorate bears as desired. Store in covered container. (If using as ornaments, allow cookies to dry several hours or overnight before hanging; pull ribbon through hole. Do not decorate with frosting.)

About 14 cookies.

Decorator's Frosting

1½ to 1¾ cups confectioners' sugar
2 tablespoons shortening

1 to 2 tablespoons milk
½ teaspoon vanilla
Food color (optional)

Combine all ingredients except food color in small mixer bowl; beat until smooth and of desired consistency. Tint with several drops of food color, blending well.

Chocolate Greeting Cards or Place Cards

These greeting-eating cards are sure to make every day special. And the place cards will make kids of all ages sit up and take notice.

2 cups semi-sweet chocolate Mini Chips

Decorator's Frosting (page 272)

Melt Mini Chips in top of double boiler over hot, not boiling, water; stir until completely melted. Spread into rectangle, about 9 x 12 inches, on wax-paper-covered cookie sheet or shallow pan. The chocolate should be about ⅛ inch thick. Chill for 5 to 8 minutes or just until chocolate begins to set. With sharp knife, cut chocolate into 4 large cards or twenty 1½ x 3-inch place cards. Do not try to separate cards at this time. Cover; chill several hours or until very firm.

Carefully peel wax paper away from cards. Gently break cards apart at score marks. Place on tray; cover and refrigerate until ready to use.

Remove cards from refrigerator about 10 minutes before decorating. Prepare Decorator's Frosting. Using writing or other decorator's tip, decorate cards with names, messages and/or designs.

4 large or 20 small cards.

Meringue Mushrooms

These add just the right touch to our Bûche de Noël. See the photograph on page 159.

2 egg whites, at room temperature
⅛ teaspoon cream of tartar
6 tablespoons sugar
¼ teaspoon vanilla
⅓ cup semi-sweet chocolate chips
¼ teaspoon shortening
Unsweetened cocoa

Lightly grease large cookie sheet; dust with flour. Set aside. Beat egg whites and cream of tartar in small mixer bowl until foamy. Gradually add sugar, 1 tablespoon at a time, beating well after each addition. Add vanilla; beat until stiff peaks form.

Spoon meringue into large pastry bag with large plain tip. Pipe 15 mounds onto prepared cookie sheet, making each mound about 1½ inches in diameter to resemble a mushroom cap. Dip finger into cold water and smooth top of each cap. Pipe remaining meringue into 15 upright 1¼-inch lengths to resemble mushroom stems. Bake in preheated 200° oven for 1¾ hours. Without opening door, turn off oven; let meringues remain in oven for 30 minutes. Cool completely on cookie sheet on wire rack.

With tip of small knife, cut small hole in center of underside of each mushroom cap. Melt chocolate chips and shortening in top of double boiler over hot, not boiling, water. Place small amount of melted chocolate in hole; spread underside of cap with chocolate. Attach stem to cap by inserting pointed end into chocolate-filled hole. Repeat with remaining caps and stems. Let dry, upside down, until chocolate is set, about 1 to 2 hours. Store in tightly covered container.

Just before serving, lightly sift cocoa through small strainer over tops of mushroom caps. Serve with after-dinner coffee or use to decorate "log" cakes or other desserts. Piled into a pretty basket or decorative container, Meringue Mushrooms make a handsome edible centerpiece.

About 15 meringue mushrooms.

Note: Meringue Mushrooms can be made smaller if desired. If mixing sizes, however, it's best to bake in batches of uniform size.

Homemade Chocolate Liqueur

1½ cups sugar
¾ cup water
3 cups vodka

5 tablespoons unsweetened cocoa
1 vanilla bean, split

Combine sugar and water in small saucepan; cook over medium heat, stirring occasionally, until mixture boils. Reduce heat to low; simmer, stirring occasionally, until sugar has completely dissolved. Remove from heat; cool to room temperature. Measure 1 cup of the mixture; combine with vodka, cocoa and vanilla bean in clean 2-quart glass container. Cover tightly; keep in cool, dark place for 14 days, shaking thoroughly every 2 days.

Strain liqueur through dampened coffee filter paper into clean glass container. (Change filter paper in mid-process or, if necessary, let drip overnight as cocoa residue is very thick.) Repeat straining process if residue remains. Remove vanilla bean. Cover tightly; let liqueur age in cool, dark place for at least 1 month.

About 1 quart liqueur.

Chocolate-Dipped Strawberries

1 cup semi-sweet chocolate chips
1 tablespoon shortening

1 pint large strawberries, with stems, washed and chilled

Melt chocolate chips and shortening in top of double boiler over hot, not boiling, water; stir until smooth. Holding each berry by stem or hull, dip berry about ⅔ of the way into chocolate mixture. Shake gently to remove excess chocolate. Place dipped berries on wax-paper-covered plate or tray; allow chocolate to harden slightly, about 30 minutes.

About 12 large berries.

Index